OECD Reviews of Regulatory Reform

Regulatory Policy in Lithuania

FOCUSING ON THE DELIVERY SIDE

OECD
BETTER POLICIES FOR BETTER LIVES

Please cite this publication as:
OECD (2015), *Regulatory Policy in Lithuania: Focusing on the Delivery Side*, OECD Reviews of Regulatory Reform, OECD Publishing, Paris.
http://dx.doi.org/10.1787/9789264239340-en

ISBN 978-92-64-23706-3 (print)
ISBN 978-92-64-23934-0 (PDF)

Serie: OECD Reviews of Regulatory Reform
ISSN 1563-4973 (print)
ISSN 1990-0481 (online)

Photo credits: Cover © Wesley Hitt/Getty Images

Corrigenda to OECD publications may be found on line at: *www.oecd.org/about/publishing/corrigenda.htm*.

Foreword

Lithuania has embarked upon an ambitious reform programme that addresses not only the development of new regulations but also inspection and enforcement. The goal is to effectively implement regulations while placing the lightest possible administrative burden on citizens and businesses.

The *OECD Review of Regulatory Policy in Lithuania* takes stock of the development and implementation of these reforms, with a special focus on inspections and enforcement and on territorial planning and construction permits, which form a crucial part of Lithuania's reform efforts. The review assesses the capacity to manage and implement these reforms and identifies practical recommendations for enhancing trust in regulatory insititutions, strengthening regulatory effectiveness and supporting growth and competitiveness. The review finds that the reforms have successfully established some of the essential tools for improving regulation. For example, requirements for better regulation are largely in place, consultation is a common practice, business licences are being simplified and some highly innovative solutions such as requirements for assistance and advice to businesses have been introduced in the field of inspection and enforcement. However, challenges remain to effectively implement these tools and maximise their impact. The review makes specific recommendations to address these challenges, highlighting, for example, the need for stronger steering and oversight of reform implementation, clear guidance, better use of evidence and analysis in decision making and proactive communication within and outside government on key better regulation objectives. The review complements the *OECD Public Governance Review of Lithuania*, which looks at open and inclusive policy making. Taken together, the recommendations presented in these reviews can help improve economic performance, social welfare, open and inclusive policy making, government-citizen relations and trust in public institutions.

The review methodology draws on two decades of peer learning reflected in the *2012 Recommendation of the OECD Council on Regulatory Policy and Governance*, the first international instrument to address regulatory policy, management and governance as a whole-of-government activity. The Recommendation identifies the measures that governments can and should take to support the implementation of systemic regulatory reform. These measures are used as a baseline for assessing regulatory management capacity in Lithuania. The review also draws on the *2014 OECD Best Practice Principles for Regulatory Policy: Regulatory Enforcement and Inspections*, which address the design of the policies, institutions and tools to promote effective compliance and the process of reforming inspection services to achieve results.

Data and information for the review were collected through detailed questionnaires completed by the Lithuanian government in October 2014 (overall regulatory policy and governance) and January 2015 (construction permits and territorial planning). The review team also held discussions in Vilnius with Lithuanian officials and external stakeholders in November 2014 and January 2015, and received detailed comments from the Lithuanian authorities on early drafts of the review. Information presented in the review reflects the situation up until June 2015.

Country reviews of regulatory policy reform contribute to the programme on regulatory governance led by the OECD Regulatory Policy Committee with the support of the Regulatory Policy Division of the OECD Public Governance and Territorial Development Directorate. The Directorate's mission is to help government at all levels design and implement strategic, evidence-based and innovative policies to strengthen public governance, respond effectively to diverse and disruptive economic, social and environmental challenges and deliver on government's commitments to citizens. The goal is to support countries in building better government systems and implementing policies at both national and regional level that lead to sustainable economic and social development.

Acknowledgements

The review was prepared by a multidisciplinary team, led by Daniel Trnka, Senior Policy Analyst, with the encouragement and support of Rolf Alter, Director, Public Governance and Territorial Development Directorate, and Nick Malyshev, Head, Regulatory Policy Division, Public Governance and Territorial Development Directorate. The following team members took primary responsibility for different sections of the review: Lorenzo Allio (external expert) for territorial planning and construction permits; Sophie Bismut (external expert) for regulatory reform and policies, the institutional framework and capacity for regulatory policy, transparency, consultation and communication; Florentin Blanc (external expert) for compliance, enforcement and inspections; Filippo Cavassini for public governance and socio-economic challenges, the development of new regulation and the interface between national and sub-national levels of government; and Daniel Trnka for the management and rationalization of existing regulation, *ex post* evaluation and the interface between the EU and the national government. Cornelia Hoffmann provided initial research assistance. Deborah Barry-Roe lent administrative and organisation support. Jennifer Stein co-ordinated the editorial process.

The team included two peers from the members of the OECD Regulatory Policy Committee, who actively participated in the first fact-finding mission to Lithuania and provided key inputs throughout the development of the review: Helena Braun, Advisor, Better Regulation, Legislative Policy Department, Ministry of Justice, Estonia; Zoe Dayan, Deputy Director, Better Regulation Delivery Office, Department for Business, Innovation and Skills, United Kingdom.

The review would have not been possible without the support of the government of Lithuania. The team would like to thank in particular Jolita van Otterlo, Director, Monika Beniulytė, Advisor, and Laura Kinkaite, Advisor, Business Environment Improvement Department of the Ministry of Economy for the unique assistance in collecting data and information, organising the team's fact-finding missions to Lithuania and providing feedback throughout the development of the review.

Table of contents

Acronyms and abbreviations 11

Country profile: Lithuania 13

Executive summary 15

Assessment and recommendations 19

Chapter 1. Governance and well-being in Lithuania: The context of regulatory policy reform ... 43

Public governance: From communism to EU accession 44
Growth and well-being: Economic performance, public finances and social challenges 47
Fit-for-purpose public policies and institutions? 52
Bibliography 56

Chapter 2. Regulatory reform and policies in Lithuania 57

Drivers of the agenda for Better Regulation in Lithuania 58
Key measures for Better Regulation in Lithuania 58
Communication on Better Regulation policy 61
E-government and Better Regulation 61
Ex post evaluation of regulatory policies 61
Bibliography 64

Chapter 3. Institutional framework and capacities for regulatory policy in Lithuania 65

Key players for regulatory management in the executive 66
Other players 67
Resources and training 68
Bibliography 71

Chapter 4. Transparency, consultation and communication in Lithuania 73

Public consultation on regulations 74
Public communication on regulations 77
Bibliography 79

Chapter 5. The development of new regulations in Lithuania 81

The structure of regulations in Lithuania 82
Trends in the production of new regulation 82
Procedures for making new regulation 84
Ex ante impact assessment of new regulation 87
Alternatives to regulation 93
Risk-based approaches 93
Bibliography 94

Chapter 6. **The management and rationalisation of existing regulations in Lithuania** 95

Reducing administrative burdens 96
Bibliography 109

Chapter 7. **Compliance, inspections and enforcement in Lithuania** 111

The baseline for reviewing inspection and enforcement reform 112
History and overview of inspection reform in Lithuania 113
Bibliography 139

Chapter 8. **The interface between supra-national, sub-national and national levels of government in Lithuania** 141

Structures, responsibilities and funding of local governments 142
Better Regulation policies deployed at the local level 145
Co-ordination mechanisms 147
The interface between the national level and the EU 148
Bibliography 152

Chapter 9. **Territorial planning and construction permits in Lithuania** 153

The importance of efficient territorial planning, urban zoning and construction permits 154
Modernising construction permit and territorial planning procedures in Lithuania 161
Putting the reform in context: Reaping the spill-over potentials 176
Bibliography 185

Annex A. **The importance of inspections and compliance** 187

Annex B. **Organisations met during the fact-finding missions** 197

Tables

1. Structure and functions of the recommended Better Regulation institutions 22
2.1. Countries publishing performance reports by policy tool/programme 62
7.1. Inspections and enforcement reform and system performance checklist 135
8.1. Municipalities' functions 143
9.1. Key criteria for building new manufacturing facilities in the CEE region 162
9.2. Motives for investing in CEE countries (2010-14) 162
9.3. Lithuania's Doing Business construction permit index (2006-2013) 163
9.4. Doing Business construction permit index 2012 (Lithuania and 13 neighbouring countries) .. 164
9.5. Doing Business construction permit index 2015 174
9.6. Illustrative direct consequences of barriers on costs, delays, volume and risk 180

Figures

1. Impact assessment process: State of play and proposed reforms 25
1.1. Gap in GDP per capita with EU average 47
1.2. GDP, percentage change over previous year 48
1.3. FDI inward stocks 48
1.4. Unemployment rate 49
1.5. Fiscal balance and public debt 50
1.6. Public expenditure consolidation 50

1.7. General government expenditures 51
1.8. People at risk of poverty and social exclusion 52
1.9. Emigration and GDP growth 52
1.10. Satisfaction and confidence with public institutions and services 53
1.11. VAT Gap (2012) 54
1.12. Product Market Regulation indicator (2013) 54
1.13. Lithuania's ranking in the Doing Business data 55
4.1. Minimum periods for consultations with the public 76
5.1. Presented and adopted laws in Lithuania 83
5.2. Adopted laws in Lithuania and Estonia 83
5.3. Government legal checks on draft legislation 86
7.1. Percentage of all businesses inspected in a given year 122
7.2. Percentage of businesses inspected in a given year, by agency 123
7.3. Average number of inspection visits per inspected business, per year 123
7.4. Changes in burden from time lost during inspections 124
8.1. Central and local government expenditures, 2013 143
8.2. Central and local government revenues 144
8.3. Municipalities' main revenue sources 145
8.4. The process of transposition of EU legislation in Lithuania 150
9.1. Share of direct public investment by economic function undertaken by sub-national governments, 2011 155
9.2. Change in sub-national government expenditure in the EU (2000-2013) 155
9.3. The simplified construction permit procedure in Lithuania 166
9.4. Frequency of obstacles to daily operations 174
9.5. Enhancing the synergies between construction permit procedures and zoning 177

Acronyms and abbreviations

ALA	Association of Local Authorities
AMB	Administrative Management Bureau
CBA	Cost-Benefit Analysis
CEA	Cost-Effectiveness Analysis
CEE	Central and Eastern European
CTIF	International Association of Fire and Rescue Services
DTF	"distance to frontier"
EU FVO	EU Food and Veterinary Office
EFSA	European Food Safety Agency
EIA	Environmental Impact Assessment
EPA	Environmental Protection Agency
GPSD	EU General Product Safety Directive
IPAC	Institute of Public Administration of Canada
LTL	Lithuanian Litas
OPS	Ontario Public Service
OSH	Occupational Safety and Health
PIR	Post Implementation Reviews
PSC	Point of Single Contact
RAPEX	Rapid Alert System for dangerous non-food products
REFIT	Regulatory Fitness and Performance programme
RIA	Regulatory Impact Assessment
SEA	Strategic Environmental Assessment
SFVS	State Food and Veterinary Service
SHCAA	State Health Care Accreditation Agency
SIRIP	State Information Resources Interoperability Platform
SLI	State Labour Inspectorate
SNFPI	State Non-Food Products Inspectorate
STI	State Tax Inspectorate
STPCI	State Territorial Planning and Construction Inspectorate
VTTL	VAT Total Tax Liability

Country profile: Lithuania

Geography, population and living standards	
Area (sq. km)	65 300
Population	2 971 905
Population density (sq. km)	45.5
Urban population	67.1% of total population
Population growth rate	-0.29% (2014 est.)
Total fertility rate	1.29 children born/woman (2014 est.)
Life expectancy	75.98 years
Ethnic groups	Lithuanian 84.1%, Polish 6.6%, Russian 5.8%, Belarusian 1.2%, other 1.1%, unspecified 1.2% (2011 est.)
Government	
State structure	Unitary state
Executive	President elected by popular vote for a five-year term (eligible for a second term) Prime Minister appointed by the President on the approval of the Parliament
Legislative	Unicameral parliament (*Seimas*) 141 seats 71 members elected in single-member districts, 70 elected by proportional representation Members to serve four-year terms
Elections	Last presidential elections held on 11 and 25 May 2014 (next to be held in May 2019) Last parliamentary elections held on 14 and 28 October 2012 (next to be held in October 2016)
Political situation	The government is headed by Algirdas Butkevicius of the Social Democratic Party (LSDP). It includes the Labour Party and the right-wing Order and Justice. The coalition has 80 seats out of 141 in the *Seimas.*
Legal system	Civil law system; legislative acts can be appealed to the Constitutional Court
Administrative-territorial structure	60 municipalities The **local council** is the municipality's legislative and decision-making body and is made up of members elected by direct universal suffrage for four years. It adopts the budget, enacts local legislation, and has the power to establish smaller territorial units. The mayor is directly elected and is a member of the local council.

Source: Eurostat database; the World Bank database; Economist Intelligence Unit.

Executive summary

The government of Lithuania has taken action to strengthen regulatory policy. Recently, it has focused on the implementation of regulatory policies, with new measures for inspections and construction permits. Improving the entire policy cycle, from law-making to implementation, is crucial for creating a regulatory environment that attracts investment, supports growth and contributes to society's well-being.

The *OECD Review of Regulatory Policy in Lithuania* assesses the pace, depth and progress in developing and implementing these reforms. It is clear that efforts have been made to develop tools and policies for effective regulatory management, including through innovative practices. The challenge is to ensure that these efforts are better linked and co-ordinated across government and effectively implemented so that they have a real impact for citizens and businesses.

Key findings

- A number of laws and resolutions have set requirements for better regulation. However, measures were taken largely independently from one another, with limited communication on the overall objectives and results. There is no dedicated unit promoting and ensuring the implementation of better regulation.
- Consultation is a common practice. There are, however, areas for improvement, including on the time allowed for consultation and, more generally, the methodology and guidance for public consultation.
- The requirements for a proportionate regulatory impact assessment (RIA) are largely in place, but the RIA is mostly used to justify choices already made, and quality controls are diffuse. There are no clear guidelines on the laws and regulations which should undergo a more in-depth RIA.
- A programme to screen all licences and permits needed to start a business has led to the review of about 423 types of licenses. There is an obligation for individual ministries not to increase the overall administrative burden (a form of "one-in one-out" approach). However, the implementation and enforcement of the "one-in one-out" obligation is rather weak.
- Ministries should conduct reviews of existing regulation. However, there is little pressure put on ministries to appropriately review regulations. The results of these reviews are not analysed.
- Better regulation reforms have introduced requirements for impact assessment, stakeholder engagement and administrative burden reduction at the municipal level. However, there is little control on the implementation of these requirements.

- In its interactions with the European Union (EU), Lithuania has developed some relatively rare approaches. For example, it has created a special information system that enables online co-operation among state institutions and external stakeholders in the negotiation of EU legislation. An impact assessment of the EU legislative drafts is also prepared. Special attention is paid to avoid unnecessary administrative burden in the transposition of EU law (gold-plating).
- The reform of inspections has introduced some highly innovative solutions, including a requirement for inspection institutions to provide methodological assistance to economic entities. Areas for improvement include a better definition of the foundations and principles for inspection planning. The reform has also suffered from some implementation gaps and a relatively informal steering and co-ordination mechanism.
- The pace of reform implementation appears to have slowed down. Sustained implementation efforts and further action are needed, especially for those areas that are still missing, such as the governance of inspectorates, professionalism and training.
- Lithuania is among the top 15 economies in the world in terms of ease of obtaining construction permits. This result reflects an ambitious reform that has simplified the legal framework, reducing the overall number of days, procedures and institutional actors involved.
- However, the reform was not based on a robust assessment of the administrative burden and compliance costs actually imposed on developers. Also, the reform has not taken sufficient account of the likely difficulties that the municipalities would face in implementing the new deadlines and procedural requirements.

Key recommendations

- Bring the different elements of better regulation policy together in an integrated strategic plan for better regulation, with clear objectives, a communication strategy and a systemic framework for performance evaluation.
- Establish a high-level co-ordination body to steer and oversee the implementation of the strategic plan for better regulation as well as a better regulation unit within the Centre of Government to provide operational support for the work of this high-level co-ordination body.
- Develop guidelines for public consultation and allow more time for consultation, make use of digital tools and use the preparation of RIA to collect feedback from stakeholders.
- Start the preparation of RIA early in the decision-making process, consider the introduction of some threshold test to determine more systematically the legislative proposals that require an in-depth RIA, and strengthen and consolidate controls on the quality of impact assessment within the recommended better regulation unit.
- Introduce a more systemic programme of *ex post* reviews of regulations, including a timeline for the planned reviews, and guidance and methodologies for these evaluations.

- Ensure that the cap on administrative burdens on businesses, together with the simplification measures for 2014-15, are properly implemented and enforced, and ensure better co-ordination of e-government projects and the linking of these projects with administrative simplification efforts.
- Explore mechanisms to communicate more actively with municipalities on the benefits of better regulation and involve municipalities in the implementation of the Better Regulation agenda.
- Make sure that a proportionate analysis of impacts is carried out when preparing relevant positions to draft EU legislation. Implement the recommendations and methodology for preventing unnecessary administrative burdens in the process of EU law implementation.
- Review goals and missions of inspectorates; consolidate inspectorates on the basis of new missions and a newly defined governance model; build a framework for inspectors' professionalism.
- Strengthen the co-ordination framework (including guidelines) for the reform of inspectorates and further develop and strengthen performance management and impact data collection.
- Continue the development and implementation of risk-based approaches in conducting inspections, allocate resources based on data and risk analysis, introduce a system for shared information management.
- Streamline and strengthen the governance of the various institutions responsible for strategic planning and territorial planning, scale up support to administrations implementing the construction permit reforms, and ensure effective implementation of the simplification and digitalisation measures.

Assessment and recommendations

1. Socio-economic challenges

Lithuania has been successful in transitioning from a pervasive and underperforming state apparatus to a modern public administration, but institutional challenges remain. Since regaining independence in March 1990, Lithuania has undergone a series of institutional reforms that paved the way for EU accession and NATO membership in 2004 and the adoption of the euro in January 2015. Lithuania has reformed the civil service, introducing a clear separation between political and professional functions, and streamlined central and local administrative and institutional structures. However, as for a number of former communist countries, ministries tend to work in silos, with limited horizontal co-ordination. Some of the reforms introduced to meet EU accession requirements, including evidence-based policy making and strategic planning, have not yet been fully mainstreamed.

Lithuania has recovered rapidly from the economic crisis. Nevertheless, significant challenges remain in terms of closing the welfare gap with other EU countries and making the economy more competitive in attracting jobs and investment as well as supporting inclusive growth. As a small, open economy, Lithuania is confronted with the need to improve the country's overall competitiveness and attractiveness for national and international investors. In an environment in which trust in government is relatively low, ensuring the efficiency and effectiveness of public institutions in developing and implementing public policies becomes even more important. A regulatory environment that supports business can attract investment and support growth. Regulatory policy has a role to play.

2. Regulatory reform and policies

Lithuania has introduced a set of useful and important reforms to strengthen regulatory policy. The initial focus was on reducing administrative burden, largely in response to EU initiatives, and building the foundation of a high-quality rule-making process. In recent years the agenda has given a stronger focus to the implementation of *ex ante* impact analysis and has broadened to the implementation of regulation, with new measures in the area of enforcement. Reforms have included the introduction of requirements for impact assessment, requirements for stakeholder consultation, Common Commencement Dates for new legislation, administrative burden reduction measures, improvement of EU negotiation and transposition and consolidation and streamlining of inspection and enforcement institutions.

While a number of pieces of legislation and government resolutions have been adopted, this significant effort still falls short of an overall policy for better regulation. The 2008 programme for better regulation set some principles and objectives, but the government has developed limited strategic thinking on the system-wide benefits of better regulation. A number of requirements (for example regarding impact assessment and administrative burden reduction) have been set out in different legal documents, but the government has not issued a comprehensive policy action plan covering the various aspects of Better Regulation and measures have been taken largely independently from each other. Two main issues need to be addressed more particularly. First, the improvement of the regulatory framework requires making fewer and better laws, but the measures for better regulation have not directly addressed this issue. Second, the efforts to reduce administrative burden on business and citizens need to be supported by a more effective implementation of impact assessment when making new legal acts, so as to avoid the creation of new burdens (see Chapter 5).

There have been limited efforts to communicate the objectives and results of Better Regulation. This reflects largely the lack of a common strategy and coherent action plan, and limits the capacity to gather support and buy-in for reforms across the administration, as well as in parliament and in the public at large. While some targets have been set regarding the reduction of administrative burden on businesses, they have not been used effectively enough so far to communicate either within the administration or towards parliament and external stakeholders.

- **Recommendation 2.1: Bring the different elements of the policy for Better Regulation together in an integrated strategic plan for Better Regulation, with identified objectives and a clear communication strategy.** This strategic plan could take the form of a Government Resolution on Better Regulation (or any other comparable instrument) that would spell out the key building blocks of Better Regulation and bring together the provisions on better regulation that are now spelled out in different laws and resolutions. It should identify the lead institution(s) for co-ordinating implementation, give them a mandate to take and enforce decisions and set clear objectives. Regular reports on progress towards achieving these objectives would be provided to the government (see Recommendation 2.2). Having this single, comprehensive instrument would also help expressing high-level political support for the agenda and developing better communication towards stakeholders within and outside government. This instrument should be supported by a high-level institutional body to oversee and co-ordinate implementation (see Recommendation 3.1 below).

Ex post *evaluation of regulatory policy*

There is no policy in place for systemic evaluation of regulatory policy or particular regulatory quality tools in place in Lithuania. Some indicators of performance related to regulatory policy are mentioned in different strategic documents of the government. Quarterly reports are prepared by the Government Office based on the inputs submitted by individual ministries and submitted to the government. The quality of the information reported by the ministries varies. Annual ministrial reports on implementing the government programme are also published on the respective ministries' websites.

Lithuania closely monitors the World Bank's "Doing Business" indicators. Many reforms in Lithuania are motivated by improving its ranking in the Doing Business chart. While this might be useful in identifying some priority areas for reform (such as the issue of construction permits), it is also necessary to evaluate real outcomes for the society.

The Ministry of Economy was made responsible for reporting on the compliance with the cap on the overall level of administrative burdens on businesses set by the government in 2014. The data necessary for monitoring comes from the administrative burden evaluation reports submitted by individual ministries. The Government Office is conducting a review of the impact assessment process. Results are expected to be presented to the government in the course of 2015.

- **Recommendation 2.2: Set up a systemic framework for performance evaluation of regulatory policy and some of its elements.** Performance indicators for the implementation of regulatory policy and its programmes and tools should be set up-front. These indicators should give the government an overview of the progress made towards full implementation of a coherent, effective regulatory framework. They can help demonstrate measurable improvements that can be attributed against particular activities, and help highlight areas for improvement. The indicators should be qualitative and quantitative descriptions of whether the good regulatory practices described in policies have actually been implemented, for example the number of impact assessments that can be deemed fit for purpose. The OECD Framework for Regulatory Policy Evaluation may be used as guidance on setting up this framework. A high-level co-ordination body (see Recommendation 3.1) should be made responsible for annual reporting on regulatory policy to the government. These reports should be made public.

3. Institutional framework and capacities for regulatory policy

Within the Lithuanian government, the better regulation agenda is supported by a few key ministries and institutional bodies. The Government Office has responsibility for the general overview of law quality and use of impact assessment when preparing legislation. The Ministry of Economy leads the administrative simplification programme for businesses. Other key players are the Ministry of Justice, for law quality, the Ministry of Interior, leading administrative simplification for citizens and the Ministry of Transport and Communications in the area of e-government and electronic services. There is a small network of officials who work on the development of regulatory management policies and tools, but the diffusion and ownership of better regulation policies and tools across the administration appears limited.

While some capacities have been built up, the current fragmentation of responsibilities limits the capacity to develop further better regulation policies. While the Better Regulation Policy Unit of the Ministry of Economy has a mandate to plan and implement better regulation policy initiatives stemming from EU obligations and also some national initiatives, it has limited capacity and other government bodies have their own initiatives. No unit has a specific mandate to promote and ensure the implementation of better regulation policies across the administration, which goes in line with the lack of a comprehensive approach to regulatory management. Increased horizontal co-ordination and co-operation across the administration is needed for the roll-out of good regulatory management and tools throughout the administration.

Moving forward requires stronger political support and leadership from the centre and a clear mandate for a unit at the core of government to promote and roll out regulatory management policies through effective monitoring. Having a unit specifically in charge of regulatory management can not only improve co-ordination between existing ministries and agencies, but is essential to ensure that regulatory quality principles are successfully applied. Such a unit can also serve as an advocate for reform, as a co-ordinator, as expert and as a source of practical and technical support for the use of regulatory tools.

- **Recommendation 3.1: Establish a high-level co-ordination body to steer and oversee the implementation of the strategic plan for Better Regulation (Table 1).** This body should involve key ministers and/or deputy ministers and a wide range of stakeholders to identify and agree on key priorities for implementing the Better Regulation strategy recommended above (see Recommendation 2.1), discuss progress and take any corrective actions that are needed to advance implementation. Competences of the Better Regulation Supervisory Commission could be broadened so that the Commission could play such a role. In addition, representatives of stakeholders could become members of the Commission to bring the perspective of citizens and businesses and provide a reality check on progress in implementing the Better Regulation strategy and steps forward. To facilitate active participation, stakeholders should have the possibility to table proposals on issues that directly concern them. The Commission could operate on the basis of a "comply and explain" rule committing the government to accept a proposal or to clearly explain why the proposal was not accepted. The government should also consider giving this body a role in supporting the Government Office in assessing the quality of in-depth impact assessments (see Recommendation 5.2).

- **Recommendation 3.2: Establish a Better Regulation Unit within the Government Office to provide the daily operational support for the work of the high-level institutional body (Table 1).** The unit could take up primary responsibility for developing regulatory management policies and tools, ensuring co-ordinated and consistent approach in the implementation of these policies and tools, and providing support to all government ministries through training and methodologies, including on regulatory management tools such as regulatory impact assessment, administrative burden measurement and reduction (see Recommendation 5.3). Staff background should include expertise in law, economics, social sciences and public management.

Table 1. **Structure and functions of the recommended Better Regulation institutions**

High-level Co-ordination Body	Better Regulation Unit
Advisory body to the government; the existing Better Regulations Supervisory Commission's competences could be broadened to play this role	Within the Government Office, providing secretarial and operational support to the High-level Co-ordination Body
Composed of high-level officials from line ministries and the Government Office and including non-government stakeholders, for example business associations, consumer groups, trade unions	Staffed with civil servants with expertise in law, economics, social sciences, public management
Adopting the Better Regulation Strategy, setting priorities for regulatory policy	Developing regulatory management policies and tools, ensuring co-ordinated and consistent approach in their implementation
	Providing support to all government ministries through training and methodologies
Agreeing on the Priority List (and submitting it to the government for approval)	Developing and enforcing criteria for inclusion of proposed legislation into the Priority List
	Checking compliance with the obligation to conduct preliminary impact assessment before drafts are included in the Annual Legislative Programme
Solving conflicts and serving as sounding board on RIA assessment	Overseeing the quality of impact assessments
Reporting to the government on compliance with the obligation not to increase administrative burdens and identifying areas for improvement	Overseeing compliance with the obligation not to increase administrative burdens (as part of overseeing IAs) and preparing annual scorecard on progress
Reporting to the government on progress on *ex post* reviews of regulations	Co-ordinating the programme on *ex post* reviews of regulation
Reporting to the government on the performance of regulatory policy and its particular elements	

4. Transparency, consultation and communication

The practice of prior consultation in the development of regulations is anchored in the Lithuanian administration. A general requirement to consult is set in the Law on the Basics of Legislation, and provides that the result of consultation be attached to the draft law. In practice there is interaction between stakeholders and the government, in some cases at an early stage of development. The review also found a general awareness within ministries for the need to consult and the benefits which can be drawn from consultation.

The review however showed areas for progress, in particular with respect to the time allowed for consultation and the quality of feedback. In many cases the standard 10 or 15 day period does not allow stakeholders adequate time for responding and providing valuable inputs. A number of stakeholders expressed some dissatisfaction with the explanations provided on why inputs are not accepted. More feedback on the results of consultation and the use made of comments could encourage stakeholders to provide comments and public ownership of the policy under development. In addition, as ministries consult their network, the process runs the risk of excluding some stakeholders from the consultation. Publication of draft laws on the central registry allows comments in principles. However as no specific publicity is given, this has not created a significant avenue for effective consultation and outreach to the wider public.

Consultation currently lacks a baseline methodology and technical guidance to public officials on how to design effective public consultation and integrate the views of the public. Ministries, which initiate legislation, broadly consult stakeholders as they see fit, since they have no guidelines on consultation, beyond the legal requirement that a consultation should take place and feedback be provided. Enhanced sharing of experiences across ministries and strengthened guidance on conducting consultation could improve the efficiency of the process. Several interlocutors raised the need to establish more structured procedures regarding time, duration, scope, formats, and feedbacks.

The system still lacks a government-wide online consultation platform, which would facilitate access to ongoing consultations of all stakeholders, within and outside the administration, at an early stage of development of new regulation. Publication on the official registry of draft laws takes places at a rather late stage of development and is not pro-active enough to drive comments. The current project for e-democracy services can provide an opportunity to switch from disseminated sources of information to a single government-wide consultation portal, with consultations being announced as early as possible.

- **Recommendation 4.1: Develop public consultation guidelines, make use of ICT tools to facilitate consultation and allow more time for consultation.** Guidelines should provide ministries and other law making bodies with clear indications on, for example, when to consult, the clarity and scope of what is consulted, accessibility to data and information and responsiveness to stakeholder feedback. The Legal Act Register should be used as a support for an online consultation portal; the Register could be upgraded to ensure that stakeholders can receive notification on upcoming consultations and legal drafts according to their area of interests. The 10-15 days that are currently required appear not sufficient for stakeholders to make meaningful contributions. Requirements for longer consultation periods could help improve stakeholder participation. While there is no ideal length of time for consulting, a number of OECD countries allow for a period that ranges between 4 to 6 weeks. The UK consultation guidelines and the Danish consultation portal could serve as useful examples (see Chapter 4, boxes 4.1 and 4.2).

5. The development of new regulations

The requirements for impact assessment are largely in place. Since 2012, new legal requirements have been introduced for assessing impacts for any legislative act. These requirements apply to both the executive and the legislature, at the national and local level. The depth of the impact assessment is expected to be proportional to the significance of the legislative proposal. The assessment is expected to address a number of impacts, including impacts on the economy, the environment, society, regional development and business.

In practice, however, impact assessment remains a largely formal exercise to justify choices already made (with a strong preference for the regulatory option). Legislative proposals include an Explanatory Note that should reflect an assessment of the expected impacts of the legislation. This assessment, however, is rarely based on hard data or comparative analysis of alternative options. In most cases, it is prepared in parallel with the drafting of the legislative proposal and justifies the choice already made, rather than offering a basis for evaluating alternative solutions to a public policy problem.

The impact assessment is proving ineffective in slowing down a tendency to legislate (too) quickly and then amend the law, which entails the frequent and disruptive change of the regulatory environment. Between 2010 and 2013, Lithuania adopted on average 458 laws per year (a comparable country like Estonia adopted on average 115 laws per year). Most of these laws originate in the executive. On average, the government submitted to parliament about 300 legislative proposals per year between 2010 and 2013 (compared to approximately 100 in Estonia). These proposals are included in an Annual Legislative Programme that is sent to Parliament at the beginning of each parliamentary session. A more careful evaluation of the public policy problem and the possible options to address this problem could help reduce the legislative production and the frequent changes of the regulatory environment that can be disruptive for businesses and citizens.

- **Recommendation 5.1: Start the preparation of the impact assessment early in the decision-making process, before the inclusion of a proposal in the Annual Legislative Programme (Figure 1).** The identification of the problem and the consideration of meaningful alternative solutions should be performed early in the decision making process and include some simple back-of-the-envelope estimation of the potential impacts. This first preliminary assessment should include a justification that a regulatory solution is the most suitable option so that this preliminary assessment would serve as an early test of whether a problem needs to be addressed through legislation or some other non-legislative tool. This preliminary assessment should become a condition for the inclusion of the legislative proposal in the Annual Legislative Programme. Compliance with this condition should be monitored and enforced by the Government Office.

Criteria for identifying in advance proposals for more in-depth assessment are not yet clearly defined. Since 2013, the Government Office has prepared an annual Priority List of the legislative initiatives that need to be assessed in greater depth. This is useful in that it can help modulate the depth of the impact assessment (and therefore the resources invested in it) according to the potential impact of the proposed measure already in the planning phase. The initiatives are included in the list on the basis of a few ministerial proposals and a choice made by the Government Office among those who are to be included on the Annual Legislative Programme. The Priority List included 14 initiatives in 2013 and 26 initiatives in 2014. Given the 300 plus draft laws in the Annual Legislative Programme, a good share of high-impact measures that would deserve an in-depth assessment are likely to "slip through the cracks".

Figure 1. **Impact assessment process: State of play and proposed reforms**

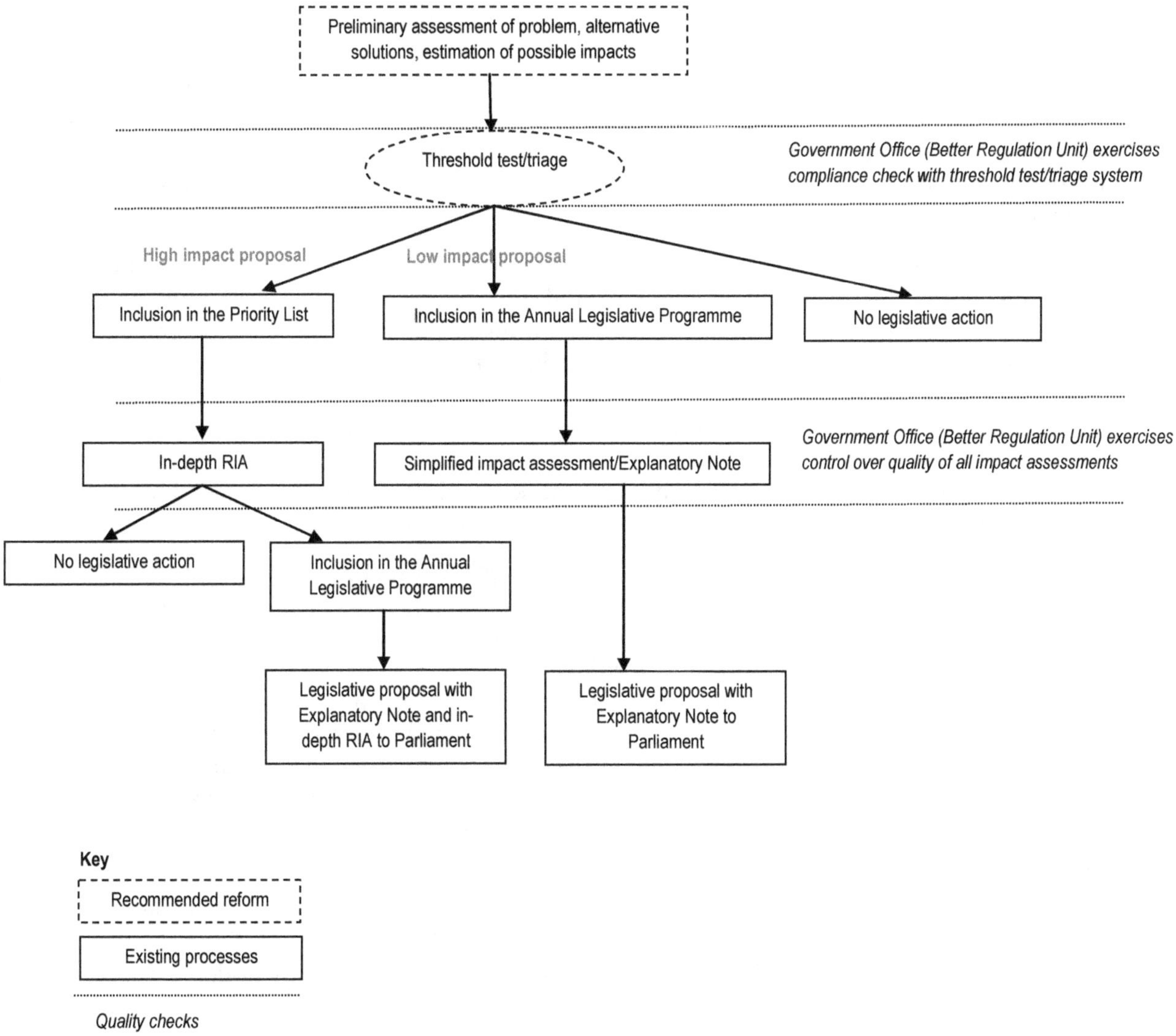

- **Recommendation 5.2: Consider the introduction of some threshold test or triage system to determine more systematically the legislative proposals that require an in-depth RIA (Figure 1).** The Priority List should systematically include the measures that are likely to have a significant impact on the economy and/or society. Some objective criteria could be set for the inclusion of the measures on the list (including, for example, number of people affected or monetary value of economic impact or impact on business, economic competition) and compliance with these criteria should be monitored and enforced by the Government Office. The high-level institutional body recommended above (see Recommendation 3.1) could serve as a sounding board by, for example, discussing a sample of these in-depth RIAs and/or arbitrating on any issue emerging from the assessment of impacts. The experience of Canada, Mexico and the United States could provide some useful examples (see Chapter 5, Box 5.2).

Multiple checks are conducted on draft government legislation, with a strong focus on legality (but no specific check is carried out on the quality of the impact assessment included in the Explanatory Note). Draft laws and regulations are first checked by each ministry's legal department before they are submitted to both the Ministry of Justice and the Legal Department of the Government Office for additional rounds of legality checks. A legality check is also conducted by the Legal Department of the *Seimas* for draft laws which are submitted to Parliament. These checks focus on compliance with legal requirements and conformity with existing laws, but relatively little attention is paid to the possible impact of the legislation and whether legislating is the most appropriate solution.

- **Recommendation 5.3: Streamline legal quality checks and strengthen quality checks on the assessment of impacts and options.** For example, there could be a more clear division of labour between the Ministry of Justice and the Government Office, with the Ministry of Justice focusing on legality and legal drafting (such as use of plain language and consistency of definitions) and the Government Office focusing on strategic focus, quality of impact assessment, consideration of alternative options for proposed legislation and the scope and extent of stakeholder engagement. This quality check should be mandatory and drafting institutions should be required to revise the draft proposal if necessary.

Even for more in-depth impact assessments, the depth and scope of the analysis is still limited and is used to back up a preconceived option. Initiatives included in the Priority List undertake a more in-depth RIA. Modulating the impact assessment is a good approach and needs to be supported as it allows focusing resources on the analysis of problems that can have the greatest impact on the economy and society. Since the introduction of the Priority List, 14 RIAs have been completed. The process is in the early stages of implementation and inevitably needs some fine-tuning. Particular attention should be paid to the quality of the analysis and the use of the analysis to assess the problem and truly evaluate alternative options. Investing in these critical areas in this early phase can pay off in the long term.

Controls on the quality of impact assessment are distributed across different institutions. Four institutions—the Government Office, the Ministry of Finance, the Ministry of Economy and the Ministry of Interior—check the quality of in-depth RIAs (but not necessarily the Explanatory Note for all the other legislative proposals). There is a network of impact assessment focal points within line ministries, who can provide advice on the preparation of impact assessments (but do not systematically check the quality of all impact assessments, including those not included in the Priority List).

- **Recommendation 5.4: Consolidate controls on the quality of impact assessment within a lead institution with some gatekeeping functions and strengthen filters and controls within sector ministries.** Some of the responsibilities for the control of the impact assessment could be consolidated in a specialised unit within the Government Office (see Recommendation 3.2) with **power to prevent a draft from going forward if the impact assessment does not meet quality requirements (adding a "gatekeeping" function which is not**

currently in place). This control should be gradually extended to all draft legislation (and not only those included in the Priority List). At the same time, a better regulation focal point within each sector ministry (for example, the focal points who are already expected to provide advice on the assessment of impacts) could exercise an internal control on the quality of impact assessment.

External stakeholders do not see the impact assessment as a useful tool to improve legislative proposals. The Explanatory Notes are used to consult with stakeholders. However, because they back up decisions that appear to have been already taken, they provide little room for meaningful feedback and contributions of stakeholders.

- **Recommendation 5.5: Use the preparation of the impact assessment as a tool for collecting feedback from stakeholders (and hence improving proposals and decisions).** Stakeholder should be consulted in the early phases of the preparation of the Explanatory Note and the in-depth RIA, in order to test different options. The formal and informal working groups and networks set up by sector ministries could facilitate this consultation.

6. The management and rationalisation of existing regulations

Reducing administrative burdens

The major part of the efforts of the Lithuanian government in dealing with the stock of regulations focuses on administrative burden reduction on businesses. These efforts were launched through a Better Regulation Programme in 2008 and included measuring administrative burdens in 7 priority areas and putting together suggestions for legislative changes that would lead to their reduction.

Despite the fact that legislative changes to achieve the 30% reduction goal have been developed and submitted to the government already in 2013, so far, only 5% reduction has been achieved. This is probably due to insufficient co-ordination between the executive and the legislative powers. Most of the proposals got stuck in the legislative process, especially in the *Seimas*, and have been abandoned and watered down. In addition, since the government decided to adopt a new Labour Code, it has been decided not to amend it before a new draft is prepared. This decision could to a large extent explain the low rate of reduction as the Labour Code accounted for a large share of the burden to be reduced.

- **Recommendation 6.1: Wherever possible, the government should try to implement legislative proposals aiming at reducing administrative burdens.** The new Labour Code, when prepared, should take into account the suggestions stemming from the project of reducing administrative burdens. Better communication with the legislative power could lead to implementing at least the majority of the simplification proposals, reducing administrative burdens for business significantly and restoring the trust of stakeholders and civil servants in the government's simplification efforts.

The programme on reducing administrative burdens has received a new boost from the new government through the adoption of a Law on Administrative Burden Reduction that came into force in 2013. This law created a new Better Regulation Supervisory Commission consisting of representatives of the government and stakeholders. The Commission, established in 2014, is supposed to provide the government with proposals on administrative simplification summarised in two-years Administrative Burden

Reduction Plans. The right given to the Commission to evaluate legislative drafts submitted to the government from the point of view of potential administrative burdens has not been used so far, which is not surprising given the high volume of draft laws prepared every year.

- **Recommendation 6.2: Ensure that the measures contained in the Administrative Burden Reduction Plan for 2014-15 are properly implemented.** The Better Regulation Supervisory Commission could become a high-level body co-ordinating implementation of regulatory policy (see Recommendation 3.1). It should also oversee the implementation and report to the government annually on the results of the implementation of the Action Plan as well as the overall reduction of administrative burdens and compliance with the cap on administrative burdens on businesses (see Recommendation 6.3).

Administrative burdens are also assessed *ex ante* when developing new legislative drafts. As of July 2014, any change of the level of administrative burdens must be expressed in monetary terms every time the new draft changes, eliminates or creates an information obligation for business. In 2012-13, the Ministry of Economy reviewed around 423 types of licences. In the beginning of 2014, the Ministry of Economy presented its suggestions on abolishing licensing and/or replacing them with declarations and these suggestions were approved by the government. The responsible ministries drafted most amendments of legal acts in their competence by the end of 2014, with the few remaining amendments expected to be ready by mid-2015. In total, 56 laws will need to be amended. As of June 2015, 7 laws had been amended by the *Seimas,* with 11 more under discussion. The government prepared 32 draft amended laws for the submission to the *Seimas*, while the remaining 24 drafts are expected to be ready in the nearest future.

An obligation to each individual ministry not to increase the overall level of administrative burdens caused by regulation in the ministry's competence was introduced in 2014. This is a form of a "one-in one-out" approach. Implementation of this measure is rather weak with quasi non-existent enforcement mechanism. The Ministry of Economy is formally responsible for reporting on this process and it does not have the necessary levers to ensure that other line ministries comply with this obligation. There are also problems in communicating this measure across the administration. At the time of the review, many interviewed ministries were not aware of this cap and therefore did not have any mechanisms to ensure compliance with it. The cap is set for each ministry individually.

- **Recommendation 6.3: Make sure that the cap on administrative burdens on businesses is properly implemented and enforced.** To make sure that administrative burdens are properly quantified as part of the *ex ante* assessment of impacts of new regulations, the quality control of RIAs should be strengthened. The Better Regulation Unit recommended above (see Recommendation 3.2) should be charged with overseeing compliance with the obligation not to increase administrative burdens, regularly reporting to the government and publicly, for example, through an annual scorecard highlighting progress for each ministry. The Unit should have sufficient capacity and authority to co-ordinate other ministries. The Better Regulation Supervision Commission (including external stakeholders) could review the annual scorecard report and identify actions for further improvement. The Commission could also serve as a "sounding board" for any impact assessment whose analysis of administrative burdens is considered particularly complex or problematic. To allow for some flexibility, off-setting of new administrative burdens by reducing burdens stemming from regulations in the competence of other ministries than the one drafting the new regulations should be made possible only in clearly selected cases. The Canadian system could be used as an example (see Chapter 6, Box 6.1).

In parallel with reducing administrative burdens on businesses, the Lithuanian Ministry of Interior was running a project on reducing administrative burdens on citizens. A methodology based on the Standard Cost Model was used.

Ex post *reviews of regulation*

There are some general requirements set by the Law on the Basics of Legislation to conduct monitoring and ex post reviews of existing regulations. Monitoring and reviews of existing regulations should be conducted by central and municipal administration institutions in the areas of their competence. The Ministry of Justice is responsible for co-ordinating these reviews. It issued the Description of Procedure for Conducting the Monitoring of Legal Regulation. This document set out the objectives, terms and conditions for *ex post* regulatory reviews and identified regulations to be reviewed.

The law is rather vague on how ex post reviews should be conducted and which institutions are obliged to conduct such reviews. The Ministry of Justice does not actively promote regulatory reviews in the sense of putting pressure on other ministries to review regulations in their area of competence. The annual reports produced by the Ministry only contain information on the number of reviews conducted each year. The actual results of these reviews are not analysed.

- **Recommendation 6.4: Based on the current programme**, set up by the Description of Procedure for Conducting the Monitoring of Legal Regulation, **introduce a more systemic programme of *ex post* reviews of regulations, including a timeline for the planned reviews, and guidance and methodologies form these evaluations.** A limited number of priority areas for reviews should be identified in co-operation with the stakeholders (e.g. through the Better Regulation Supervisory Commission). These priority areas should be linked with the government's priorities. The whole set of regulations in these priority areas should be reviewed in consultation with stakeholders, to see if they are still fit-for-purpose, based on clearly set criteria and under the leadership of the co-ordinating body in co-operation with responsible ministries. The recommended Better Regulation Unit (see Recommendation 3.2) should serve as the co-ordinating body. It should report annually on the results of such reviews to the Better Regulation Supervisory Commission that would review progress and propose areas for improvement to the government. These reviews should be publicly accessible.

Licensing reform

A programme to screen all licences and permits needed to start a business activity has been in place since 2012. The main goal of the process was to screen all licences/permits in order to assess their necessity and proportionality, to abolish the ones which are unnecessary and/or disproportionate and to identify licences that could be replaced by simple declarations. Another goal was to review and simplify administrative procedures for businesses to obtain a licence/permit and to enable obtaining a licence or permit using electronic means. In 2012-13, the Ministry of Economy reviewed around 423 types of licences. In the beginning of 2014, the Ministry of Economy presented its suggestions on abolishing licensing and/or replacing them with declarations and these suggestions were approved by the government. The responsible ministries drafted most amendments of legal acts in their competence by the end of 2014, with the few remaining amendments expected to be ready by mid-2015. In total, 56 laws will need to be amended. As of June 2015, 7 laws had been amended by the *Seimas,* with 11 more under discussion. The government prepared 32 draft amended laws for the submission to the *Seimas*, while the remaining 24 drafts are expected to be ready in the nearest future.

- **Recommendation 6.5: Speed up the process of adopting the amendments to implement the results of the review of licences.** Make sure that the process is finalised as soon as possible to simplify the licensing process in Lithuania. Make the necessary steps to enable electronic issuing of licences and develop an electronic registry of licences.

ICT and administrative simplification

There is a central government portal serving as a single point of access to all public and administrative services for the citizens and businesses – the E-Government Gateway. All services provided by central government institutions and municipalities are accessible via this portal. Electronic services in such areas as taxes, state social insurance, reports to police, legal entities registration, traffic information, libraries, services for patients and others, are being actively developed. The uptake of the electronic services in Lithuania is also increasing: in 2014, 41.5% of Lithuania's residents, and 100% of businesses, were using electronic services.

The Point of Single Contact for Services and Products (PSC) established in 2009 serves as a single point of contact in compliance with the EU Services Directive. The PSC is however not interconnected with the E-Government Gateway. In many cases, the website just provides information on regulations and administrative procedures; in some cases it enables to request a licence online and only in few cases the process is fully automatic. The State Enterprise Centre of Registers – a public entity responsible for administering the three main state registers (i.e. Real Property Register and Cadastre, the Register of Legal Entities and the Address Register) – is developing an electronic licensing registry in order to administer in one place the data and information on all licences that have been issued. All public institutions issuing licences and using licensing information systems will have to submit to this registry their information on licences that have been issued, revised or withdrawn starting on 1 September 2015.

There are, in addition, several examples of electronic services provided in particular areas of public service, such as the E-Service System for Insurers and the State Tax Inspectorate's "My STI" service. The approach to electronic services suffers from a lack of co-ordination among these different services. Many information systems of individual ministries are not interoperable. There is also a lack of co-ordination between the administrative simplification efforts and those focusing on using ICT and e-government approaches.

- **Recommendation 6.6: Ensure better co-ordination of e-government projects and with administrative simplification efforts.** The e-government initiatives should be co-ordinated by one body and summarised in one government-wide policy. Interoperability and inter-connectivity of all information systems and portals must be ensured. Projects in the areas of e-government and administrative simplification should be interlinked (ideally part of one wider policy) and thoroughly consulted. No digitalisation of public services and/or administrative procedures should be carried out without prior assessment of options for their simplification.

Common Commencement Dates

Lithuania is applying a similar approach to the so-called Common Commencement Dates. According to the Law on the Basics of Legislation, legal acts modifying or setting new legal requirements for economic entities should usually enter into force on 1 May or 1 November; however, they should never enter into force sooner than three months following their official publication. Similarly, some tax laws shall enter into force no sooner than following six months after their official publication.

7. Compliance, inspections and enforcement

Lithuania has recognised the importance of reforming inspections as one of the key drivers for reducing administrative burden and strengthening regulatory policy and governance. Inspection reform was one of the key priorities of the regulatory reform agenda launched in 2009. The reform was led by the Ministries of Economy and Justice, with strong political support and engagement. The team looked at the problems of the country and at existing international experience. The legal foundations of the reform were set by a Government Resolution in May 2010 and by the adoption of amendments to the Law on Public Administration at the end of 2010.

The provisions included in the 2010 Law on Public Administration are comprehensive and, in many ways, highly innovative. Significantly, the law refers to supervision rather than inspection to emphasise an integrated approach to promoting compliance. Inspections are not seen any more as an enforcement tool, but as complementary tools alongside advice (which comes first), and analytical work. Inspection institutions are required to provide methodological assistance to economic entities. This requirement has been the foundation for the development of inspectorates' call centres, in order to ensure that advice and guidance provided are of consistent quality (given the binding nature of this advice).

The provisions included in the law, however, suffer from some "weak spots" – but recent improvements have been made. While methods for planning inspection visits are left to secondary legislation as in a number of countries, the law does not define the foundations and principles on which these methods should be developed. The list of admissible grounds for "non-routine" inspections is vague and fails to link it to risk considerations. Recent amendments adopted in November 2014 established risk assessment as the foundation for inspections, meaning that supervisory institutions should focus on high risk cases, with risk defined as the likelihood of harm to values protected by legal norms, combined with the potential magnitude of such harm. This is a welcome development and should help further develop good practices in this direction, by providing a stronger legal basis for risk-based approaches.

The reform has also suffered from some implementation gaps and a relatively informal steering and co-ordination mechanism. Secondary legislation – the Government Resolution of May 2010 subsequently amended and strengthened in 2011 and 2012 – has been the source of all the implementation work on risk-based inspections planning, and checklists. It created an Expert Group gathering the key ministries and most important inspectorates to co-ordinate and guide the reform process. It gave the ministries of Economy and Justice some steering role. This has led to the adoption of comprehensive guidelines for checklists and risk criteria development (both based on best international practice), as a joint decision of the Ministers of Economy and Justice. However, this joint decision has a weak status and compliance with it remains mostly voluntary for inspectorates. Even with the recent amendments to the Law on Public Administration, such guidelines remain very important to ensure quality of implementation.

Governance of inspectorates is an aspect that has been nearly entirely missing from the reform so far. In most cases, inspectorates are under the direct responsibility of a ministry, and have no specific status that would ensure their stability, identity and long-term vision, and also avoid political meddling in their operations. Some of the best inspectorates (such as the State Food and Veterinary Service) have a special status, with, for example, specific reporting lines and fixed terms for their head. However, statutes including more collegial management, board of directors to ensure independence of the body and representation of stakeholders, and performance management considerations appear mostly absent.

The pace of reform implementation appears to have slowed down, with some key issues remaining unresolved. At the on-set of the reform, conscious choices were made to prioritise the actions that were considered most likely to produce quick results and impact, including checklists development, development of guidance and consultation activities, changes in enforcement and risk-based approaches. While work has been done on some key issues that were missing from the first phase of reform (for example, development of IT systems and consolidation), little results have been achieved so far, and there are a number of concerns, including inspectorates' mandates and goals and inspectorates' governance. Checklists are now widespread in Lithuania, but their quality is unequal. Some are really clear and focused, others are long lists of every possible requirement.

The slowing-down of the reform's pace appears to be confirmed by inspection data. For example, after a strong decrease from 2011 to 2012, the percentage of businesses covered by inspections increased strongly in 2014. The number of inspection visits per inspected business went down at first, but this has not been confirmed over time. In fact, between 2013 and 2014, inspections increased by 8%. The average duration of inspections for 2011 is estimated at somewhat above 3 hours, whereas in 2014 it was around 2 hours. Advance notification is complied with in 63% of cases in the latest survey, a number that has been roughly stable since 2012. Use of check lists has improved over time, in line both with the elaboration of more checklists (covering more agencies, and more economic activities), and with greater familiarity with the tool. The number of respondents who knew about the checklists went from 59% in 2013 to 75% in 2014. However, from 2012 to 2014, the percentage of respondents indicating that inspectors also checked points *not* included in checklists has increased strongly: from 40% to 49% in 2013 and 53% in 2014. This should not be a cause of major concern as checklists require regular improvements and revision. Nevertheless, it points to the importance of sustained implementation efforts and further action.

Professionalism and training of inspectors have been a missing element of reforms so far, one that is now important if the system is to make further progress. While many inspectors have good technical skills, and most of them have received some "on the job" training, the only somewhat more formal training plans have been introduced for call-centre consultants (and for some technical issues of EU interest, e.g. food safety). Rather, what is needed is a comprehensive vision of the "inspector" job: not only technical skills, but "core" skills (as in the Competency Framework developed by the UK's Better

Regulation Delivery Office), including risk management, communication and outreach, relations with businesses, investigation, enforcement.

- **Recommendation 7.1: Review goals and missions of inspectorates and consolidate inspectorates on the basis of new missions and a newly defined governance model.** The first priority should be reviewing all the existing inspectorates and seeing which ones have a clear, risk-based mission – and which ones have confused goals, or objectives defined only in terms of "enforcing legislation". Simultaneously, the government should develop a vision of which supervisory functions it needs to have, based on international experience and the country's priorities. These functions should, again, be defined in terms of risks being addressed. Before moving further with consolidation of inspection functions, the government should develop a model for inspection institutions, based on international experience and specifics of Lithuania's institutional and legal framework, to give inspectorates the desired autonomy, stability, transparency and responsiveness to stakeholders' interests.
- **Recommendation 7.2: Further develop and strengthen performance management and impact data collection.** Develop first a set of guidelines that will then result in: a set of clear performance indicators for every new (reformed, consolidated etc.) function, and mechanisms for data collection to support evaluation and risk assessment of inspectorates. This last point should also ensure that adequate information is collected by different structures (state and non-state) to serve for evaluation and analysis (e.g. data on causes of injuries and deaths to be collected in the health care system, etc.). The high-level performance management for inspectorates should be matched by criteria and processes that assess staff performance along the same dimensions.
- **Recommendation 7.3: Strengthen the reform co-ordination framework (including guidelines).** Develop a renewed reform co-ordination mechanism with strong decision making and steering powers, as well as a specific action programme with clear goals, objectives, benchmarks and timeline – and to give more strength to the reform's technical support team (in the Ministry of Economy), through more resources and more binding guidelines for reform implementation.
- **Recommendation 7.4: Continue development and implementation of risk-based approaches. Allocate resources based on data and risk analysis. Introduce a system for shared information management.** Risk-based planning/targeting still needs to be introduced in a number of institutions – and further strengthened/refined in others. Second, resource allocation and choice of instruments (outreach, education, visits, but also innovative schemes such as "sticker schemes" etc.) should also be made on the basis of risk – and this transformation is only just beginning in Lithuania. Finally, risk should also be the main criterion to decide what to inspect, and how to enforce. The current quality of checklists is often unsatisfactory in this regard, and this will require improvements, as well as further development of enforcement approaches and guidelines. Further progress in risk management by Lithuanian inspectorates requires both that those with already good information systems get more access to information and data from other agencies (to further improve their risk analysis, update their data more frequently etc.) – and that those still without such information systems get one. The most efficient and effective response to this

need is a shared information system with a single database and modular access, that would be at the very least shared by all inspectorates that currently have no good information system, and interfaced with the existing modern systems (e.g. Tax, Labour).

- **Recommendation 7.5: Review, improve and further roll out checklists and other tools.** There needs to be a thorough review of the existing stock (and of gaps), improvement where needed, and further development of checklists where they are missing and needed. Other tools also need to be developed: guidance documents, not only for businesses but, in many cases, for workers and the public, are one important example.
- **Recommendation 7.6: Build a framework for inspectors' professionalism.** There should be a set of skills and competences, as well as a training programme for new inspectors, and a system to regularly check the proficiency of existing inspectors, and update and upgrade their capacity over the course of their careers.
- **Recommendation 7.7: Consider addressing some institution-specific problems**, such as:
  - Consolidate the environmental supervision functions in one institution with a robust understanding of risk and sound, modern methods of compliance promotion.
  - Review allocation of resources in Fire Safety to ensure that more efforts are made to promote safety in residential buildings and that business inspections are more commensurate to their (quite limited) relevance for fire risks.
  - Introduce risk-based objectives and planning in public health supervision, and develop education and outreach to patients in the health care and medicines field.
  - Consider whether the Territorial Planning Inspectorate's function is still relevant in a modern regulatory system based on risk, considering that its role appears to duplicate other institutions and/or market mechanisms, and the case for allocating state resources to it is weak as it is not very clear what market failure it is supposed to address.

8. The interface between supra-national, sub-national and national levels of government

The interface between sub-national and national levels of government

Municipalities, Lithuania's only self-governing authorities, have significant responsibilities for delivering public services but limited regulatory responsibilities. Municipalities are relatively autonomous and provide a number of public services including pre-school, primary and secondary education, primary and secondary health care and public health services. Approximately 55% of their revenues come from central government's grants. They deliver construction permits and some business licences; the regulatory framework informing these permits and licences is, however, set at the national level.

While regulatory coherence does not appear to be a problem, business and citizens interact daily with municipalities and face some administrative burden originating from these interactions. The speed and simplicity of obtaining licences and permits can vary across municipalities, depending in part on municipalities' administrative capacity.

Better regulation reforms have introduced requirements for ex ante impact assessment, stakeholder engagement and administrative burden reduction for the 60 municipalities. However, there is limited control on the quality of regulatory processes at the municipal level as the government has limited levers to ensure municipalities' compliance with this obligation. As of December 2014, 41 municipalities had prepared an administrative burden reduction plan or included some reduction measures into municipality strategic plans. However, there is limited co-ordination and follow-up on the implementation of these plans and measures. This implementation gap might undermine the overall effectiveness of the better regulation reforms.

Consultations with municipalities for the preparation of draft legislation tend to be largely formal, with limited impact on the development of the legislation. The Association of Local Authorities (ALA), which represents all municipalities, participates in inter-ministerial meetings and shares draft legislation with municipalities to collect inputs (with limited interest from municipalities and little impact on the draft legislation). The ALA is also represented in the Better Regulation Supervisory Commission.

- **Recommendation 8.1: Explore mechanisms to more actively communicate with municipalities on the pay-offs of better regulation and involve municipalities more actively in the implementation of the Better Regulation agenda.** Business and citizens do not distinguish between the sources of administrative burden. Initiatives aimed at improving policy making at the central level should trickle down to the local level, where citizens and businesses are more likely to have daily interactions with the public administration, in order to maximise the impact of these initiatives. This would involve strengthening partnerships and co-operation with municipalities, for example, through some measurement of local burdens at the local level in partnership with the Association of Local Authorities. It could also involve the development of specific programmes targeted to municipalities (similar to Portugal's Simplex for Municipalities) with tangible incentives for participation and guidance and support for sharing good practices across municipalities. The experience of Denmark, Portugal and Sweden could be useful (see Chapter 8, boxes 8.1 and 8.2).

The interface between the national level and the EU

Negotiation

The process for co-ordinating the position of Lithuania in the negotiation process is standard and similar to many OECD countries which are members of the EU. Individual line ministries are responsible for drafting positions in their areas of competence. The Ministry of Foreign Affairs is in charge of co-ordinating the preparation of Lithuanian positions with regard to the legislative proposals within the European Union. Draft positions for the European Council and the Council of the EU meetings are adopted by the Governmental Commission on the EU Affairs and endorsed by the government.

A special information system called LINESIS enables online co-operation among state institutions involved in the negotiation process in real time. NGOs and social partners can get access to this system. The relative openness of such a system is rather rare among OECD countries.

A typical position should contain an impact assessment of the legislative draft which is rather rare even among OECD countries; however, the assessments are rarely of a sufficient quality. The obligation of impact assessment is stipulated in the Government Resolution No. 21 of 9 January 2004 "Regarding Coordination of European Affairs", which sets rules for a typical position.[1] This Resolution also introduces an obligation to conduct impact assessment according to the methodology adopted by the Government Resolution No. 276.

- **Recommendation 8.2: Make sure that a proportionate analysis of impacts is carried out in the process of preparing relevant positions to draft EU legislation that might have significant impacts on Lithuanian society and economy. Criteria for when such assessment is necessary should be set by a government resolution.** The EU Department of the Ministry of Foreign Affairs together with the European Law Department of the Ministry of Justice should be made responsible for enforcing such obligation in co-operation with the Better Regulation Unit recommended above (see Recommendation 3.2).

Transposition

The process of transposition and implementation of the EU law in Lithuania is highly centralised and well regulated. The European Law Department of the Ministry of Justice is the main institution co-ordinating and monitoring the transposition using the electronic system LINESIS. One government institution is always chosen as the one responsible for transposition. Within 3 weeks after the assignment, the responsible institution has to come up with a description of concrete measures needed to implement the draft and the deadlines for their preparation and adoption. The European Law Department supervises how the institutions are following the plan and the deadlines. It is required to complete and attach a correlation table to every single draft legal act which is implementing the EU legal act. The European Law Department then reviews the table with its EU law legal experts. All the correlation tables must be uploaded to LINESIS. The right to conduct *ex post* reviews of the existing legislation for their consistency with EU legislation is used rather scarcely.

One of the issues of the transposition process is the fact that the civil servant(s) that was/were participating in the negotiating process on a particular piece of legislation at the EU level is not involved in its transposition. Therefore, the institutional memory the person might have is not fully used. This is, however, a general problem in many other EU member states.

Special attention is paid to the issue of gold-plating. The European Law Department is responsible for reducing administrative burdens during the process of EU law transposition. To better formalise the process of preventing gold-plating, the European Law Department prepares a set of recommendations for public institutions and a concrete methodology for preventing creation of unnecessary administrative burdens in the process of EU law implementation.

1. www.e-tar.lt/portal/lt/legalact/tar.db68bca9e3a0/tais_465634.

- **Recommendation 8.3: Finalise and implement the recommendations and the methodology for preventing creation of unnecessary administrative burdens in the process of EU law implementation and make it binding to all ministries and other institutions.**

9. Territorial planning and construction permits

Rationale for and commitment to a comprehensive reform

The government of Lithuania appears to have good understanding of the importance of leveraging the governance of construction and territorial planning to foster economic development, new job creation and capital attraction. This is critical in post-crisis times. The government has made the reform of Lithuania's business environment one of its mandate's priorities. Such a commitment is grounded in the acknowledgment that several factors contribute to the decisions by foreign and domestic developers when determining possible investments in the country. The quality of the regulatory framework features prominently among those factors, calling national and local public authorities to provide the basic conditions for investment and business to thrive.

To achieve this, the government correctly identified the reform of the construction permit procedures in particular as one of the principal strands of action, since this sector of administrative activities is particularly prone to achieve important spill-over effects. The reform of the construction and territorial planning procedures fits the above mentioned rationale and explicitly seeks to achieve greater economic efficiency while preserving agreed safety and health standards. Not only do excessively complex or burdensome permit procedures tend to reduce the attractiveness of an economy; they may also jeopardise the actual main objective of building permits – to ensure the health and safety of the community. Construction permits moreover form an integral part of the (urban) territorial planning vision and management. They are critical for public authorities to strategically exploiting their comparative advantages and organise society, the economy and the territory accordingly. This has become particularly relevant over the past decades when – in Lithuania and all OECD countries alike – territorial development has tended to occur mainly in urban and metropolitan areas.

The government commitment to reforming this specific administrative area reflects stakeholders' concerns as well as international statistical evidence. The feedback from private sector organisations appears to have been the main trigger for action. Over the past years, stakeholders' concerns have focused especially on the excessive length and complexity of the permit procedures as well as the low predictability and accountability of administrative decision-making. The same sense of urgency for reform action does not appear to be provided by the related Doing Business index, the other main source of reform action. The index has considered Lithuania among the regional leaders since 2012-13 and in 2015 it ranks the country within the top 25 in the world. This notwithstanding, the government has centred both the design of its reform and the communication thereof around the improvement in that particular ranking.

At the same time, the potential of inserting the reform into a wider agenda appears to have been grasped by the government to a noticeable extent. Lithuania has significantly amended its Construction Law in 2010; revised the Law on Territorial Planning in 2014; and it is currently working on modernising the Law on Infrastructure (with final adoption of the law indicatively expected by the end of 2015). This set of initiatives aims at tackling important governance elements, ranging from zoning, infrastructure design and management to energy efficiency policies and green building. Against this background, the changes brought about to the construction permit legal framework to date appear to be seen by the government as one piece in the puzzle of reform that, taken together, are likely to yield territorial development. Overall, the reforms all seek to increase the responsibility and accountability of public authorities at all levels of government to achieve ever more efficient public service delivery. Nevertheless, while broader (legislative) reforms have been undertaken over a few years, a number of fronts are still open to complete the reform endeavour.

Effectiveness of the reform and the monitoring of its performance

The construction permit reform undertaken by the government builds on several international good practices and has already achieved remarkable change. Among the critical success factors are the simplification, clarification and digitalisation of the procedures. To date, the government has already introduced significant simplification amendments to the construction permit legal framework, reducing the overall number of days, procedures and institutional actors involved to such an extent that Lithuania stands among the top three economies in the region and the top 15 economies in the world in terms of ease to dealing with construction permits (Doing Business 2015 data). This is a remarkable achievement, which was in part made possible by the introduction of the "silence-is-consent" clause; the clarification of both definitions and procedural requirements, which allowed for a better operationalisation of risk-based approaches; the consistent update and consolidation of affected legal bases; as well as the digitalisation of the procedure and the upgrade of the information system Infostatyba. All such reform interventions represent international good practices and have been welcomed by stakeholders.

Achievements to date as reported by the government are impressive, but the actual impact of the reform is yet to be noticed in the economy. This may question the overall effectiveness of the reform measures in the long run. The Lithuanian business community at large has broadly welcomed both the sense of direction given by the government to the reform and the initial achievements. However, perception surveys are less enthusiastic and immediate statistical evidence on the performance of the Lithuanian construction market do not necessarily corroborate the improvements in the Doing Business rankings. While this may clearly depend on the still relatively recent legal and administrative changes, the fact that the reform was not based on a robust assessment of the administrative burden and compliance costs actually imposed on developers might constitute a major limitation of the effectiveness of the measures launched. While administrations are requested to evaluate the administrative burden of legal amendments (including reform proposals) and send evaluations to the Ministry of Economy, such an obligation was not fulfilled in the case of the construction permit reform and the government and the *Seimas* approved amendments to the construction law framework without any preliminary impact assessment. The reform could moreover not benefit from the inputs by the Better Regulation Supervisory Commission, which was created only after completion of the legal and procedural changes. Associating the effectiveness of the reform to improvements in Lithuania's relative performance in the Doing Business index is a useful metric for success that is easy to communicate and instil investors' confidence. Not grounding sufficiently the success of the reform in "hard evidence" related to the country's construction market and to the economy could however lead to partial results.

- **Recommendation 9.1: Pursue the strategic commitment to achieve economic growth and competition through a comprehensive and sustainable territorial planning, infrastructure and construction law reform.** Private sector stakeholders seek further improvements in the legal and administrative regimes but at the same time they expect greater predictability, legal certainty and stability and "informed change" so as to best plan investment and implement development projects.
- **Recommendation 9.2: Consider further reforms areas that remain to be tackled, in order to complement and reinforce what has been done in the construction sector to date.** In particular, attention might be given to issues related to public land ownership; public procurement procedures in the construction and real estate sector; and procedures related to the Environmental Impact Assessment. The example mentioned in the chapter of the shortcomings in the current procedures to get electricity illustrates the comprehensive approach that reforms should follow if they are to concretely make a difference. The ongoing debate on a new Infrastructure Law may constitute a good opportunity to address some of these issues.

Governance of the reform

The governance of the reform has relied mainly on frequent yet informal dialogue with key actors within the public administration and among stakeholders. While this has had some merits in terms of flexibility and speed in designing the reform, concern has been expressed about the actual capacity of the reformed system to both mainstream change and build institutional learning. The government has reportedly consulted intensively when determining the direction of the reform. Nonetheless, in doing so it has relied mainly on informal dialogue with affected parties. At the same time, the reform has allegedly not taken sufficient account of the likely difficulties that the municipalities would have faced in implementing the new deadlines and procedural requirements. Allowing a transition period for local civil servants and decision-makers to adjust to changes is structural for any reform initiative of this type – and in our case it has been largely accepted by all parties involved (both the government and the private sector). However, the mechanisms in place to ensure as much as possible a smooth adaptation in peripheral municipalities are reported to be underperforming. In particular, municipalities denounce difficulties in getting timely instructions or clarification on formal requests for assistance from the government. The Ministry of Environment fulfils for instance a crucial help desk function through the State Territorial Planning and Construction Inspectorate (despite the relatively limited resources allocated to it), but it is formally not required to issue an opinion when seized about a legal interpretation query. In addition, the ministry considers several procedural or substantial complaints related to the construction permit procedures and it autonomously reviews a number of decisions. While data are collected, there seems to be no dedicated feedback mechanism that allows capitalising on such an analysis and knowledge, thereby missing out the opportunity for a continuous refinement and upgrade of administrative performance.

Further, wider governance issues emerge when considering the broader territorial planning and development policy. They notably refer to multi-level (vertical) co-ordination gaps in the allocation of funds, which in turn depend to a great extent also on the only partially solved inter-ministerial (horizontal) mismatch between local level "strategic planning" considerations (currently managed by the Ministry of Interior) and "territorial planning" (under the responsibility of the Ministry of Environment).

Discrepancies are reported to still exist between the two exercises, which consider uneven time horizons, and rely on different budget sources and levels of socio-economic strategic analyses.

- **Recommendation 9.3: Streamline and strengthen the governance underpinning the various institutions responsible for strategic planning and territorial planning, so as to achieve efficient and sustained socio-economic development**. The government might envisage revisiting the internal and multi-level co-ordination arrangements, as well as the procedures and to develop the related budgets, to ensure a structured mid-term approach to market improvement and prosperity in the country.

Future reform perspectives

Additional reform initiatives are currently being discussed, which raises the overall potential impact of the reform even further. Particular attention is to be put on leveraging the interface between public and private actors and market-informed solutions. The reform has still potential for improvement and current ideas are being debated between the government and stakeholders in order to identify and fully exploit policy synergies. Among such areas are in particular the revision of the liability and insurance regime; the rationalisation of enforcement, inspection and controlling practices; and the performance of oversight and arbitration mechanisms.

The ongoing debate on how best to accomplish the construction permit reform constitutes a promising basis to overcome some difficulties that the reform has so far faced and which remain pending. In particular, difficulties persist in relation to the reportedly still significant ambiguity of legal (implementing) texts and the related administrative discretion in interpreting the provisions; the limited technical performance of Infostatyba and its partial inter-operability with other public databases and one-stop shop platforms; and the different levels of skills and organisation across municipalities in accommodating to the changes – from coping with the digitalisation of the procedures to, more structurally, bearing full responsibility for territorial planning and developing strategies.

- **Recommendation 9.4: Consolidate the specific reform of the construction permit by intensifying the support to implementing administrations, upgrading Infostatyba, and leveraging market-based forces.** While correctly promoting responsible public service delivery from local authorities, the government could reinforce its help desk and legal counselling function to minimise discretional or delayed decisions through the construction permit procedures. If deemed necessary, revising the current implementing regulations and making related guidance (charters of services) uniform might be taken into consideration. The government might envisage optimising the potential of Infostatyba through technical upgrades that improve the software's capacity and inter-operability with other e-government tools. The government is furthermore invited to evaluate the merit of revising the liability and insurance regime and rationalising enforcement, inspection and controlling practices (see also Recommendation 7.7).

- **Recommendation 9.5: Ensure concrete effectiveness of the simplification and digitalisation measures already implemented.** Doing Business rankings are immediate indicators of the overall performance of a public administration but they might come short in terms of gauging the real challenges faced by business and citizens when applying for permits. The government could consider developing a dashboard of indicators pertaining to the construction market trend which may inform more precisely on the concrete impact that the reform has on business activities. Proceeding to a measurement of the administrative costs incurred by the applicants may also enhance the effectiveness of the reform.

Chapter 1

Governance and well-being in Lithuania: The context of regulatory policy reform

This chapter describes the main public governance reforms and economic and social trends that have marked the country since its independence in 1991. It points to some of the challenges related to the development of a regulatory environment and public institutions that support investment, growth and well-being.

Public governance: From communism to EU accession

After regaining independence in 1990, Lithuania was confronted with a public administration with little internal coherence. Lithuania partly addressed these challenges through a series of reforms of the public administration and a clear commitment to EU integration. The treatment has been effective, but some of the symptoms, such as limited horizontal co-ordination and a relatively weak Centre of Government, are still evident.

The communist heritage

Under communism, ministries worked in silos, which resulted in little coherence and co-ordination among them. Political and strategic decisions were taken mostly within the communist party, as opposed to the administration (Synnerström, 1997). Closely related to the lack of coherence and co-ordination was the lack of co-ordinated staffing and personnel management. Each public institution was an independent employer, and there were no common standards for selection, recruitment, promotion, or personnel management. In addition, the concept of management functions was virtually absent. Officials working for the administration were considered "specialists". There were no standard requirements or professional criteria for the respective positions in the state administration, which impeded job mobility across institutions (Synnerström, 1997). Furthermore, due to the hierarchical and legalistic nature of the system, it was more important for officials to comply with the formal rules than to ensure the actual implementation of programmes (Nakrošis, 2001).

Post-communist government institutions

The constitution adopted by referendum in 1992 radically changed the governance system, abandoning the primacy of the communist party over the state. The President of the Republic, directly elected for a period of five years, is the head of state. The President appoints and dismisses the Prime Minister, with the approval of the *Seimas*, the Lithuanian parliament. The unicameral *Seimas* is composed of 141 members elected for a period of four years through direct, mixed-system elections.[1]

The executive and state agencies

The Law on the Government adopted in 1994 defines the composition, competences and roles of the executive, known as the Government of the Republic of Lithuania.[2] The Government of the Republic of Lithuania consists of the Prime minister and ministers. According to the Concept of the Improvement of the Structure of the Executive Power System,[3] the executive power consists of: ministries, agencies under the ministries, government agencies, public bodies, whose owner or stakeholder is the state and the state enterprises whose owner's rights and obligations are implemented by state agencies. There are also public and private limited liability companies controlled by the state. In 2013, 810 public sector organisations operated in Lithuania: 537 state budgetary agencies, 81 state enterprises, 134 public agencies, and 58 public and private limited liability companies. The group of state budgetary agencies consisted of: 14 ministries, 14 government agencies, 99 agencies under the ministries, and 411 other state agencies.[4]

The 14 relatively autonomous ministries in Lithuania shape public policy, organise, co-ordinate and control its implementation in the spheres of administration assigned to the minister. The functions of the public policy implementation may be assigned to the ministry only in the cases laid down by the law and for a set period of time. According to the Law on the Government, the government agencies and agencies under the ministries are responsible for the implementation of public policy.

Both the agencies under the ministries and the government agencies are budgetary institutions, i.e. financed through the state budget. The differences mainly lay in the appointment and accountability of the agency head, as well as in the agencies functions and organisation of their activities:

- **Government agencies** participate in the shaping of a policy in the area of administration assigned to the minister and implement such policy. The **directors of government agencies are appointed by the government** on the recommendation of the minister of an appropriate sphere of administration. There is no control by the parliament or the office of the President over this appointment. However, while the appointment lies in the hands of the government, directors are not generally replaced when a government changes. The director of the agency is accountable to the government and the ministers whose areas of competence are related to the activities of the agency.
- Agencies under the ministries implement public policy in the spheres of administration assigned to the minister and also attend to the shaping and implementation of such policy. An agency may participate in the shaping of the public policy in the policy area assigned to the minister. The **heads of the agencies under the ministries are appointed according to the Law on Civil Service for a period of four years**, with the possibility to extend their term of office by another four years. The head of the agency is recruited and dismissed by the relevant minister. The appointment follows the successful participation in a civil service competitive exam. The head of an agency is directly subordinated and accountable to the minister.

Lithuania has been successful in clearly separating political and professional functions and de-politicise the Civil Service. In each ministry, a career civil servant, the Chancellor of the Ministry, heads the administration. Vice-ministers are also civil servants. A Civil Service Law adopted in 1999 (and replacing a Law on Officials adopted in 1995) has supported the principle of impartiality and legal accountability of the civil service. The new Civil Service Law adopted in 2002 has reinforced these basic principles of the Civil Service and introduced some changes on the status of a civil servant, his responsibility, remuneration, social and other guarantees, as well as the legal basis for the management of the Civil Service.

Deconcentrated and decentralised levels of government

At the beginning of the 1990s, Lithuania had 581 municipalities, which limited familiarity and capacity for self-government. Municipalities were progressively reduced to 60 and made more democratic and open. A Law on Local Self-Government, adopted in 1994, regulates the functions and powers of municipalities.

In addition to municipalities, Lithuania was also divided into 10 territorial administrative counties with an appointed governor and a county administration. In 2010, the county administrations were abolished and functions were transferred to either municipalities or the central government. Counties still exist as territorial units. Chapter 8 on the interface between supra-national, sub-national and national levels of government provides an overview of the regulatory powers of municipalities and their role in supporting the regulatory policy agenda in Lithuania.

EU accession and the drive for strategic planning and evidence-based policy making

Lithuania's accession to the EU resulted in a number of considerable changes, including for the public administration. The EU accession process provided an incentive to strengthen the capacity of the public administration for forecasting, planning, organising, co-ordinating, controlling, and assessing outcomes.

In order to prepare for EU accession, between 1998 and 2003, Lithuania worked with the Institute of Public Administration of Canada (IPAC) and the Ontario Public Service (OPS) to introduce reforms aimed at strengthening planning, co-ordination and use of evidence in the policy-making process. A national programme on better regulation was prepared in 2007 and adopted in 2008. The reforms also introduced a number of new management tools and processes, including:

- A **Strategic Planning Committee** chaired by the Prime minister, to oversee the priority-setting and budget process and review major policy issues;
- A strategic planning system, including
  - a government priority-setting exercise in advance of the budget process;
  - preparation of individual ministry strategic plans to reflect the government's strategic priorities and ministry service-delivery priorities; and
  - public release of ministry strategic plans and public report of results achieved against targets;
  - An **integrated fiscal-planning system**, including
  - a macroeconomic plan developed in tandem with the priority-setting exercise; the plan included realistic aggregate revenue, expenditure and deficit targets, as well as a fiscal envelope to fund the strategic priorities;
  - individual ministry budget ceilings accompanying the budget circular's instructions to ministries and agencies; and
  - instructions requiring ministries to demonstrate how their budget requests supported the government's strategic priorities;
- A **restructured Centre of Government, the Government Office,** to reflect a shift in focus from an administrative to a strategic/analytic organisation, including the creation of a Strategic Planning Unit to co-ordinate the planning process and liaise with the Ministry of Finance.

The reforms were introduced under the first Kubilius government and, although the government stayed in power only from 1999 to 2000, the following governments continued the reforms aimed at connecting strategic planning, priority-setting, and fiscal planning. In 2003 the first report on ministries' performance was submitted to the *Seimas*. Furthermore, impact assessment reports were introduced, in order to base ministerial policies on greater evidence and move away from an overly legalistic approach to policy making.

Over time, however, reforms lost momentum. In 2009, the second Kubilius government assessed the reform progress rather negatively. Strategic planning had become an administrative rather than a political exercise. Furthermore, there appeared to be no meaningful evaluation system in place. Consequently, a new wave of reforms aimed at strengthening the efficiency and effectiveness of the public administration and, more broadly policy making, were introduced. Some of these reforms, in particular those related to regulatory policy, will be reviewed in the following chapters.

Growth and well-being: Economic performance, public finances and social challenges

Lithuania has been rapidly catching up with other EU countries. However, a large convergence potential remains. In 2013, GDP per capita was only 57% of the average GDP per capita in the 28 EU countries (Figure 1.1 and Box 1.1).

Figure 1.1. **Gap in GDP per capita with EU average**

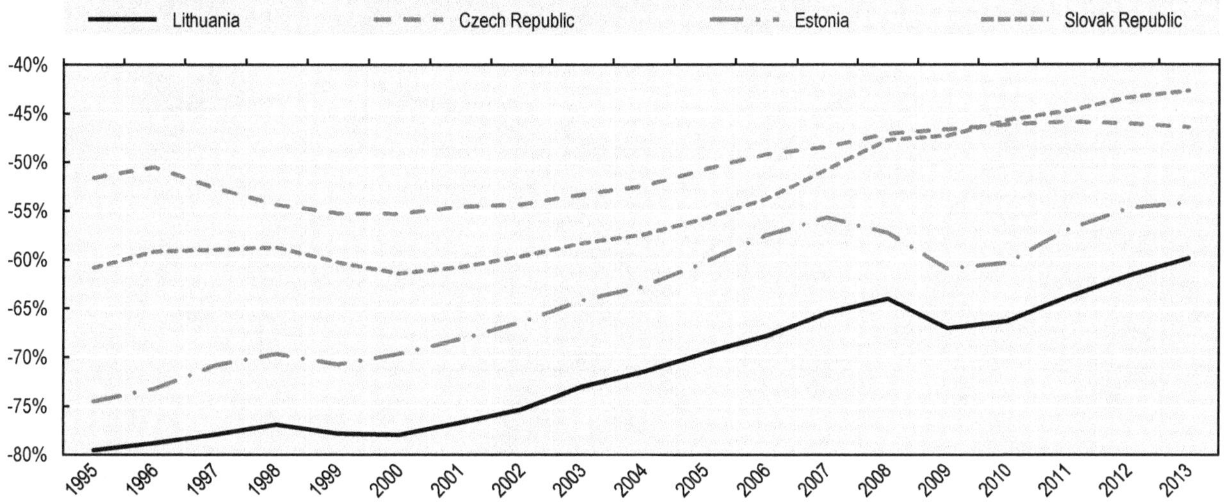

Note: Percentage gap with respect to the simple average of the GDP per capita of the 28 EU countries (in constant 2005 PPPs).
Source: World Bank World Development Indicators database, http://data.worldbank.org/indicator/ny.gdp.pcap.kd.

Box 1.1. Lithuania and comparable economies

The review uses as reference points for comparing Lithuania's socio-economic performances three EU members which are also OECD members: the Czech Republic, Estonia and the Slovak Republic. While there is some variation in the size of the economy and the population (see table below for reference), these countries share some geographic proximity (Central and Eastern Europe), recent history (former communist countries joining the EU in 2004) and economic structure (open catching-up economies).

Country	Population (2013, million people)	GDP (2013, million euros)
Lithuania	2.97	34 955
Czech Republic	10.51	156 932
Estonia	1.32	18 738
Slovak Republic	5.41	73 593

Source: Eurostat database, http://ec.europa.eu/eurostat/tgm/table.do?language=en&pcode=tps00001 and http://appsso.eurostat.ec.europa.eu/nui/show.do?dataset=nama_10_gdp.

Economic performance

The country was hit particularly hard by the economic crisis. Between 2008 and 2009, GDP dipped by almost 15 percentage points (Figure 1.2). The recovery has been as impressive as the recession. The economy has regained steam rapidly, largely pushed by exports. Lithuania has gained global market share, upgraded product quality, and reoriented away from traditional markets, mostly former Soviet Republics and Russia. However, success has relied to a large extent on labour intensive exports and was facilitated by favourable trading partner growth (IMF, 2014). For example, Lithuania performs worse than all its peers in attracting foreign direct investment (Figure 1.3).

Figure 1.2. **GDP, percentage change over previous year**

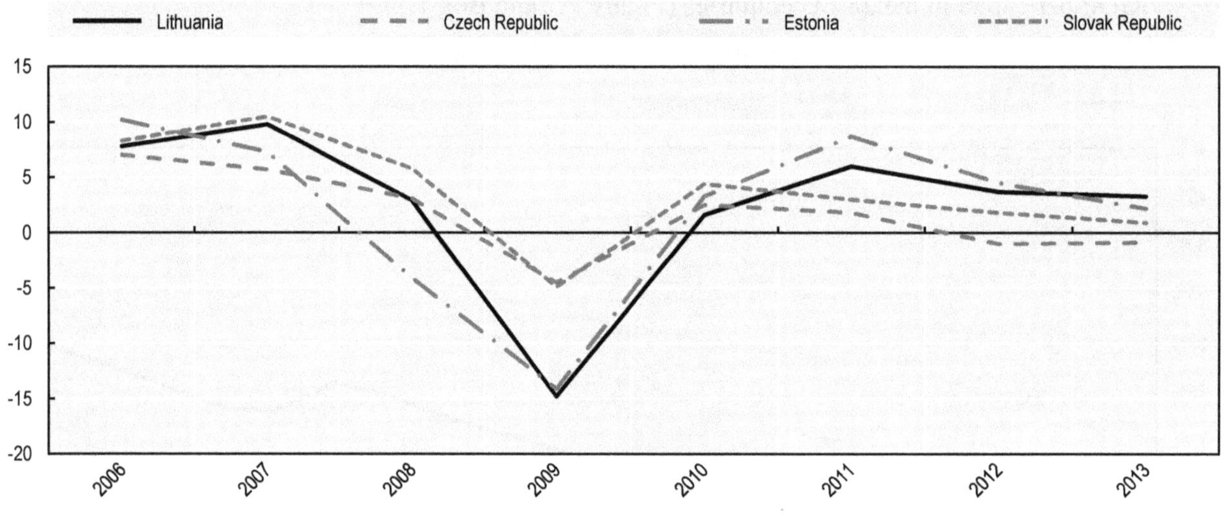

Source: Eurostat database, http://appsso.eurostat.ec.europa.eu/nui/show.do?dataset=nama_gdp_k&lang=en.

Figure 1.3. **FDI inward stocks**

2010-13 average, share of GDP

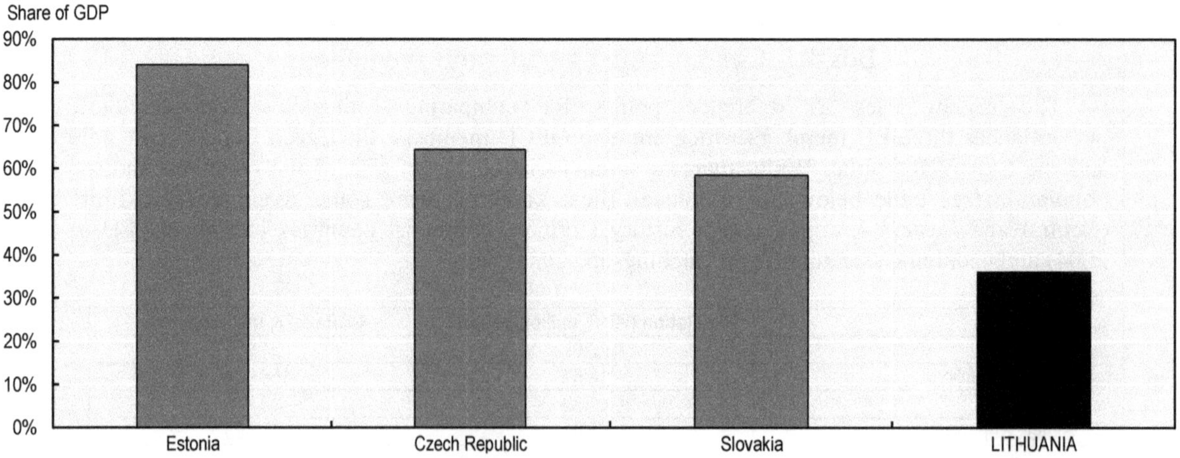

Note: Inward stocks measure all direct investment held by non-residents in a given country.

Source: Eurostat database, http://appsso.eurostat.ec.europa.eu/nui/show.do?dataset=bop_ext_intpos&lang=en.

The unemployment rate has decreased significantly from its peak of 17.8% in 2010, reaching 10.7% in 2014 (Figure 1.4). Despite the good economic performance, however, unemployment remains relatively high. Moreover, while before the economic crisis the unemployment trend closely followed Estonia, since the recovery, Estonia appears to have been more successful in bringing people back to work. While also confronted with significant challenges, Estonia appears to benefit from some framework conditions, including a business-friendly environment and governance that are conducive to sustained growth (Box 1.2).

Figure 1.4. **Unemployment rate**

As % of labour force, annual average

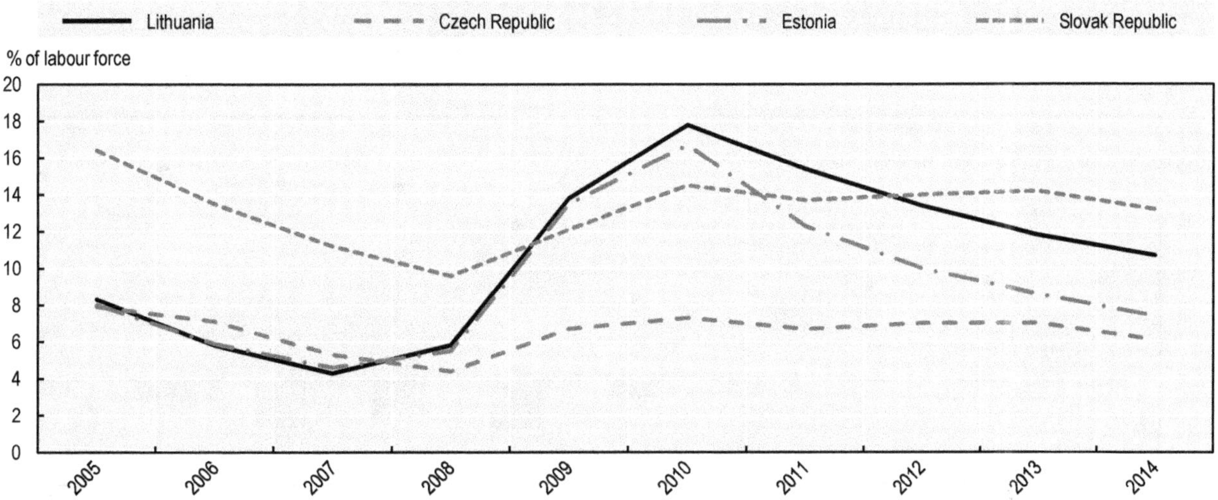

Source: Eurostat database, http://appsso.eurostat.ec.europa.eu/nui/show.do?wai=true&dataset=une_rt_a.

Box 1.2. Estonia's economic performance and the role of a growth-friendly business environment

Like Lithuania, Estonia experienced a sharp output contraction in the aftermath of the 2008 and 2009 economic crisis. In the following years, the economy has recovered quickly and, despite persistent socio-economic challenges including labour market conditions and a slow-down in 2012, Estonia appears to benefit from framework conditions that are conducive to sustained economic expansion. These conditions include:

- Product and labour market regulation are business-friendly and are backed up by an effective public administration, transparent governance and efficient law enforcement.
- Low and simple corporate taxation supports entrepreneurship;
- A solid banking sector and the strong fiscal position support growth;
- Literacy, numeracy and science competences among Estonian youth are among the strongest in the OECD. Numeracy and literacy skills of the adult population are also above average.

Source: OECD (2015a), *OECD Economic Surveys: Estonia 2015*, OECD Publishing, Paris, http://dx.doi.org/10.1787/eco_surveys-est-2015-en.

Public finances

In 2008, public-debt-to-GDP ratio declined to approximately 15% in 2008 thanks to a deficit that hovered around 1% of GDP and sustained economic growth. Consolidation, however, proved cyclical and the crisis triggered a fiscal deficit of almost 10% of GDP in 2009, which was reduced to approximately 7% in 2010, sliding back however to approximately 10% in 2011. Public finances have been brought back on track through a multi-year consolidation effort that has stabilised public debt at 40% of GDP, fiscal deficit at 2.6% of GDP and ushered Lithuania into the euro zone (Figure 1.5).

Figure 1.5. **Fiscal balance and public debt**

As % of GDP

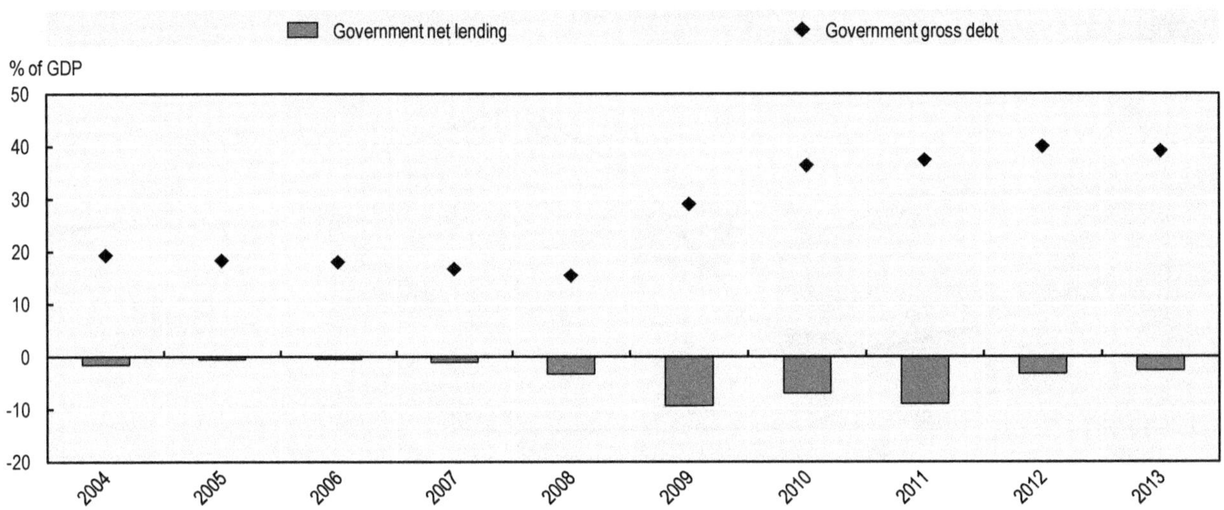

Source: Eurostat database, http://appsso.eurostat.ec.europa.eu/nui/show.do?dataset=gov_10dd_edpt1&lang=en.

Figure 1.6. **Public expenditure consolidation**

2009-2012

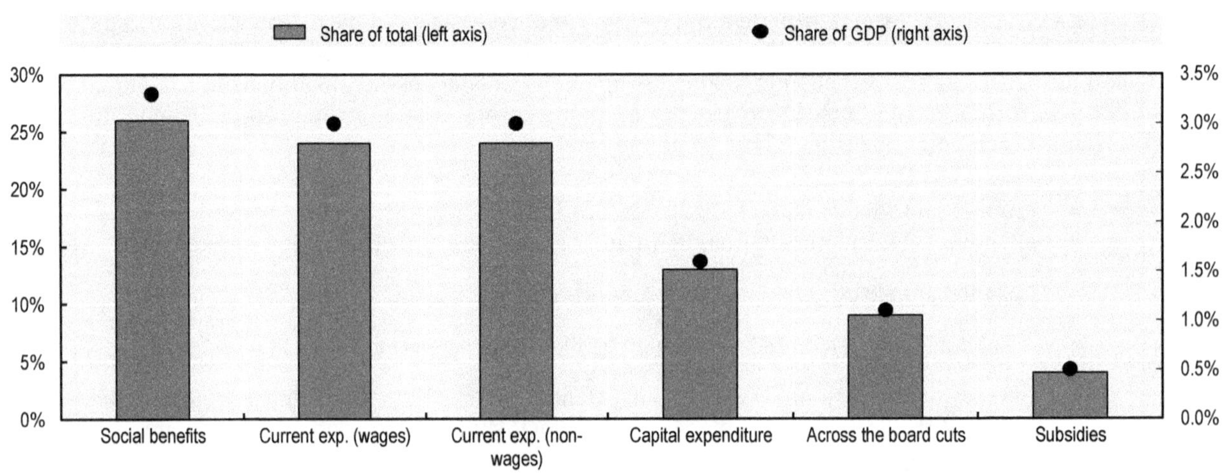

Source: IMF (2014), "Republic of Lithuania: 2014 Article IV Consultation: Selected Issues", IMF Country Report No. 14/114, www.imf.org/external/pubs/cat/longres.aspx?sk=41538.0.

The consolidation programme has significantly reduced government spending. Public expenditure was cut by 13% of GDP over the period 2009-2012. Social benefits and current expenditure (both wages and non-wages) accounted for almost three-quarter of the consolidation measures (and approximately 9% of GDP). Capital expenditure was reduced by 1.6% of GDP (Figure 1.6). In 2012, general government expenditure accounted for 36% of GDP in 2012, the lowest share compared to the Czech Republic (44.5%), Estonia (39.5%) and the Slovak Republic (37.8%) (Figure 1.7).

Figure 1.7. **General government expenditures**

As % of GDP

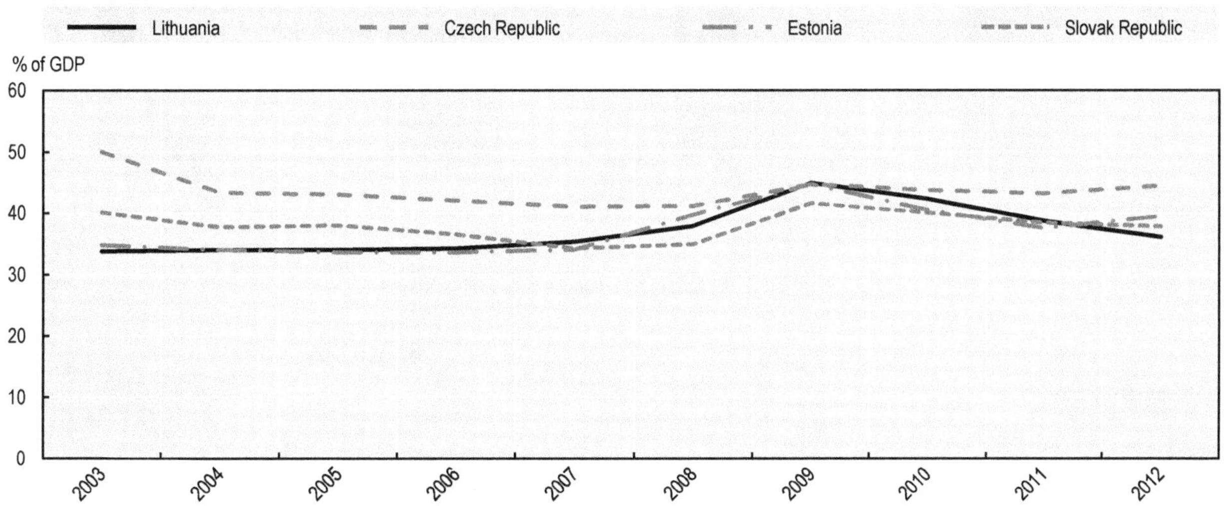

Note: General government includes central and local governments and social security funds.

Source: Eurostat database, http://appsso.eurostat.ec.europa.eu/nui/show.do?dataset=gov_a_exp&lang=en.

Poverty and population flows

Lithuania is confronted with a number of social challenges that calls for a good calibration of public policies to ensure that economic performance—impressive so far—is inclusive and sustainable over time. For example, 30% of the population is at risk of poverty or social exclusion, six percentage points above the average for the 28 EU countries and between 7 and 16 percentage points above its OECD and EU peers (Figure 1.8).

Emigration is another challenge that could affect the long-term welfare of the country. In 2010, Lithuania experienced an unprecedented peak in emigration. This increase in the number of registered emigrants might in fact represent a more realistic snapshot of the state of play (rather than a real increase in the number of emigrants) since this year it was introduced a statutory obligation for all permanent residents of the country to pay compulsory health insurance (providing thus an incentive to those who had already emigrated to declare their status as emigrants). This trend has continued through 2013, albeit at a slower pace (Figure 1.9). Immigration flows are minimal. The emigrants have been disproportionally young and more educated than those who have remained, depriving the country of a qualified labour force (Sipavičienė and Stankūnienė, 2013).

Figure 1.8. **People at risk of poverty and social exclusion**

Share of total population, 2013

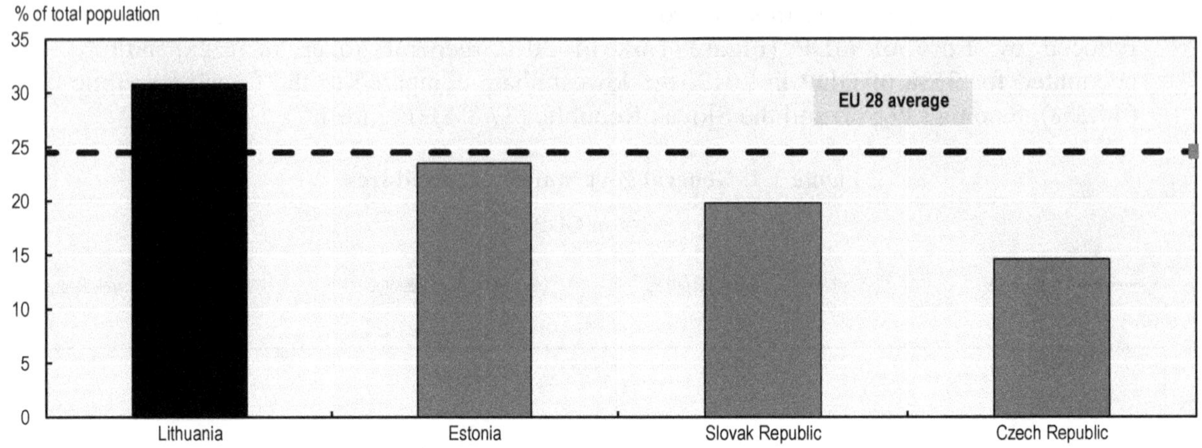

Source: Eurostat-SILC database, http://appsso.eurostat.ec.europa.eu/nui/show.do?dataset=ilc_peps01&lang=en.

Figure 1.9. **Emigration and GDP growth**

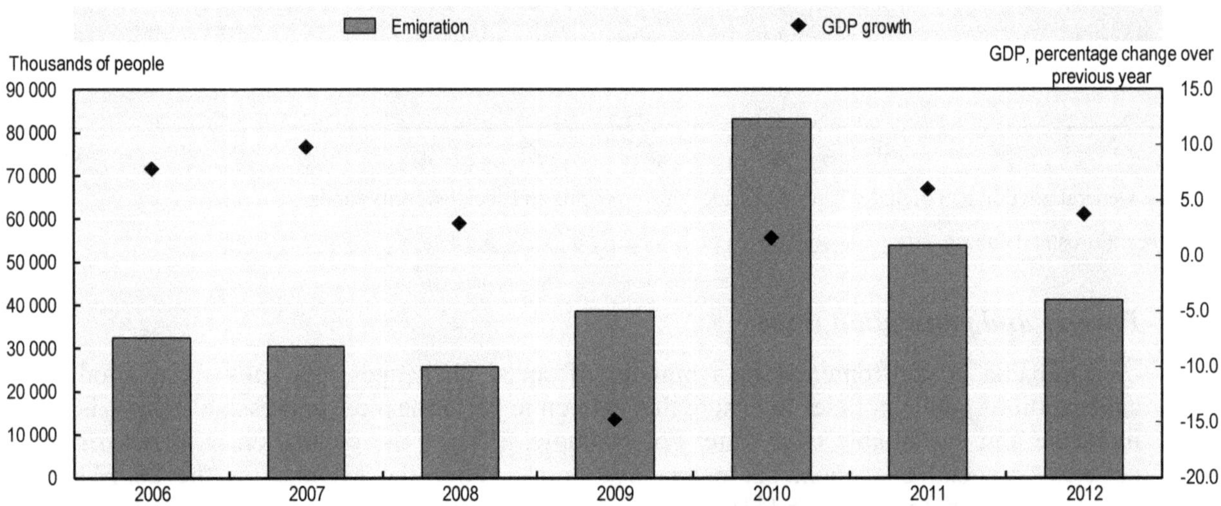

Source: Eurostat database, http://appsso.eurostat.ec.europa.eu/nui/show.do?dataset=migr_emi2&lang=en.

Fit-for-purpose public policies and institutions?

This section looks at three public policy areas – trust, tax administration and the business environment – that can help support inclusive and sustainable growth.

Trust

Trust in government can help increase the efficiency and effectiveness of government operations, including regulatory policy implementation. A decline in trust can lead to lower levels of compliance with regulation. Citizens and businesses can also become more risk averse, delaying investment, innovation and employment decisions that can help regain competitiveness and support growth (OECD, 2013).

Trust in the national government – 34% of Lithuanians tend to trust the national government – is lower than trust in other public services such as education and is lower than in other OECD countries which are also members of the EU. Trust in the judicial system is particularly low (30% of Lithuanians tend to trust the judicial system compared with 50% in other OECD-EU members). Nevertheless, Lithuania has improved its position since the crisis, with trust in the national government rising from 27% to 34% compared with other OECD-EU members where it increased only from 34% to 36% (Figure 1.10).

Figure 1.10. **Satisfaction and confidence with public institutions and services**

Lithuania and OECD-EU countries, 2014

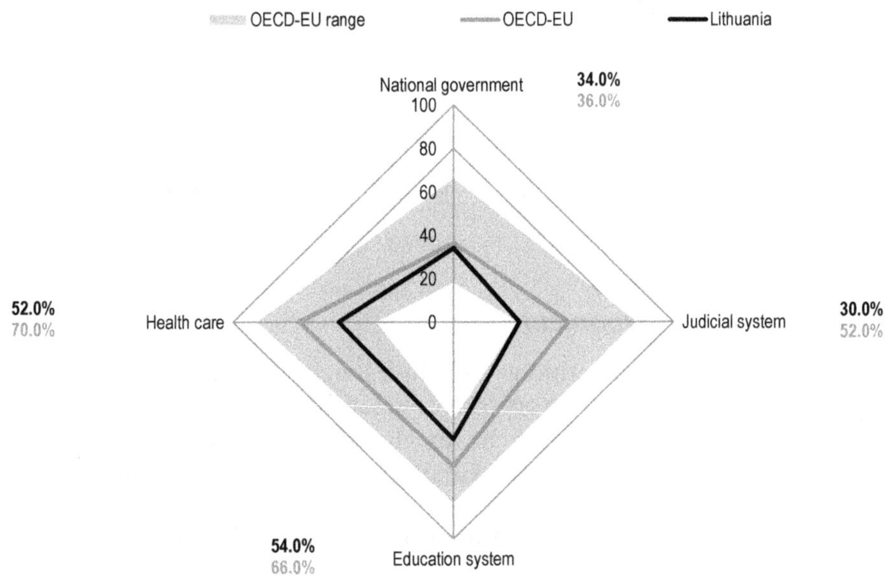

Source: Gallup World Poll (n.d.), www.gallup.com.

Tax administration

The difference between the VAT Tax liability and the VAT that is in fact collected is relatively large (36%) in Lithuania, 20 percentage points above the average for 26 EU countries (and second worst only to the Slovak Republic among some of Lithuania's OECD peers). This suggests room for improvement in the tax administration, with significant potential impact on the government's revenues (Figure 1.11).

Figure 1.11. **VAT Gap (2012)**

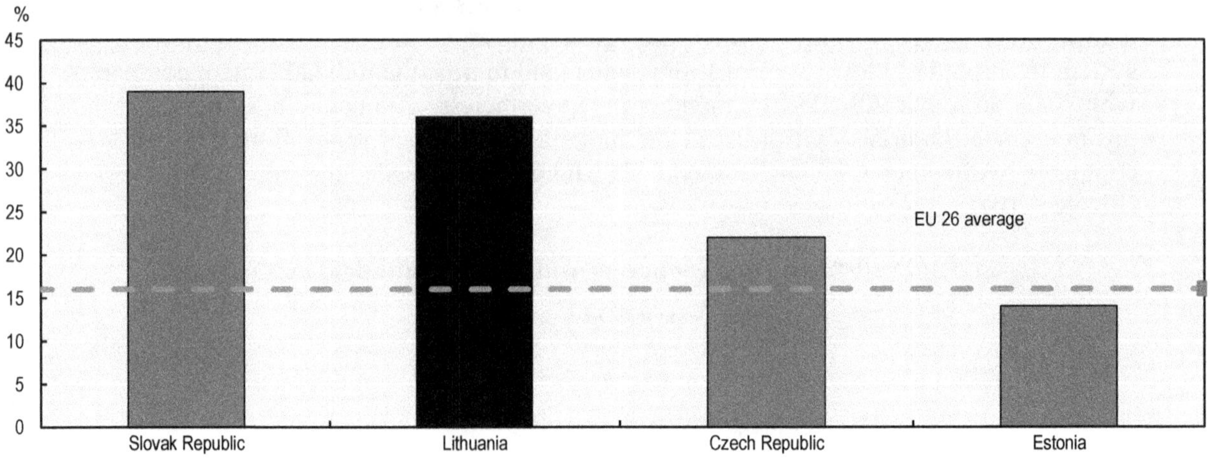

Note: The VAT Gap is the difference between the VAT Collections (as recorded by Eurostat) and the amount theoretically due, i.e. VTTL (VAT Total Tax Liability). The latter is the total amount of estimated VAT payments on the basis of national accounts aggregates and the existing structure of rates and exemptions.

Source: European Commission (2014), "2012 Update Report to the Study to quantify and analyse the VAT Gap in the EU-27 Member States", September, http://ec.europa.eu/taxation_customs/resources/documents/common/publications/studies/vat_gap2012.pdf.

Regulation and business environment

Regulation can hamper competition and investment. Overall, product market regulation (PMR) in Lithuania is not very pro-competitive when compared to a close competitor like Estonia. State involvement in the economy remains considerable. Moreover, more can be done to improve the overall regulatory system (Figure 1.12).

Figure 1.12. **Product Market Regulation indicator (2013)**

2013, index scale of 0-6 from least to most restrictive

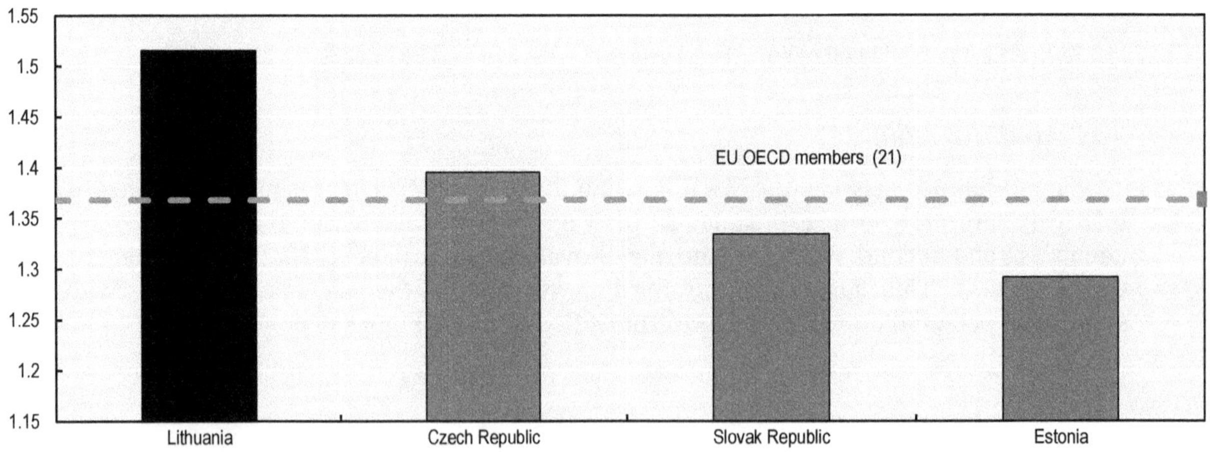

Source: OECD (2013), Product Market Regulation Database, www.oecd.org/economy/growth/indicatorsofproductmarketregulationhomepage.htm.

In *Doing Business 2015*, Lithuania ranks 24th (out of 189 countries); this is the same rank Lithuania had in 2014. Lithuania ranks particularly high in registering property (9th), as well as starting a business (11th), enforcing contracts (14th) and dealing with construction permits (15th), where its rank has improved significantly following reforms introduced between 2013 and 2014. It scores the lowest on providing electricity to business (105th), protecting minority investors (78th) and resolving insolvency (67th) (Figure 1.13).

Figure 1.13. **Lithuania's ranking in the Doing Business data**

Doing Business 2015 compared to 2014

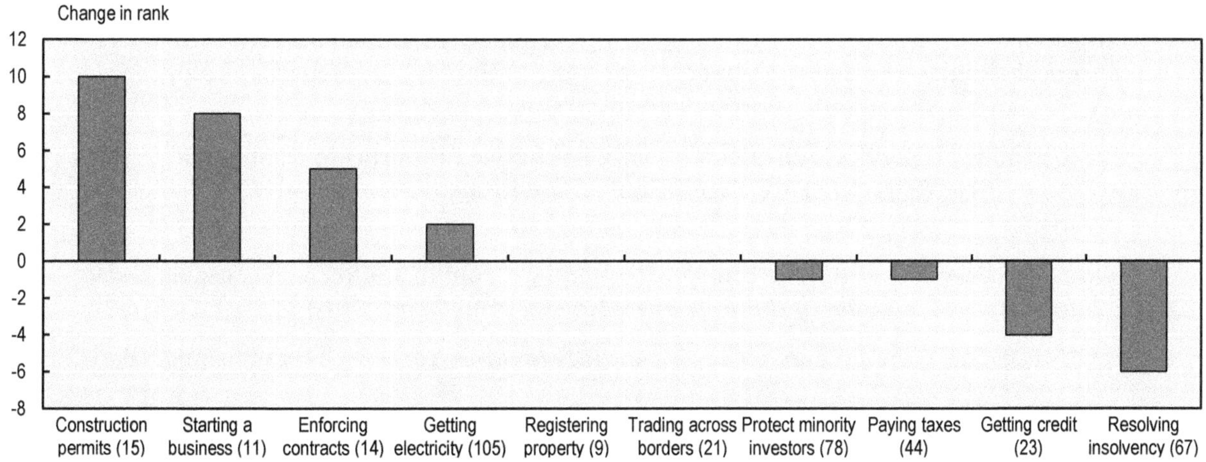

Note: In parenthesis, Lithuania's rank in *Doing Business 2015*.

Source: *Doing Business 2015*, www.doingbusiness.org/data/exploreeconomies/lithuania#starting-a-business.

Notes

1. Chapters V-VII, Constitution of the Republic of Lithuania, http://www3.lrs.lt/pls/inter3/dokpaieska.showdoc_e?p_id=275302&p_tr2=2.

2. Law on the Government, http://www3.lrs.lt/pls/inter3/dokpaieska.showdoc_e?p_id=449184&p_tr2=2.

3. Concept of the Improvement of the Structure of Executive Power System, http://www3.lrs.lt/pls/inter3/dokpaieska.showdoc_l?p_id=382452&p_tr2=2

4. Public Sector Analysis 2013, Ministry of Interior.

Bibliography

European Commission (2014), "2012 Update Report to the Study to quantify and analyse the VAT Gap in the EU-27 Member States", September, http://ec.europa.eu/taxation_customs/resources/documents/common/publications/studies/vat_gap2012.pdf.

International Monetary Fund (IMF) (2014), "Republic of Lithuania: 2014 Article IV Consultation: Selected Issues", IMF Country Report, No. 14/114, www.imf.org/external/pubs/cat/longres.aspx?sk=41538.0.

Meyer-Sahling, J. (2009), "Sustainability of Civil Service Reforms in Central and Eastern Europe Five Years After EU Accession", *Sigma Papers*, No. 44, OECD Publishing, Paris, http://dx.doi.org/10.1787/5kml60pvjmbq-en.

Nakrošis, Vitalis (2001), "Lithuanian public administration: A usable state bureaucracy?", *Journal of Baltic Studies*, No. 32, Issue 2, pp. 170-181.

OECD (2015a), *OECD Economic Surveys: Estonia 2015*, OECD Publishing, Paris, http://dx.doi.org/10.1787/eco_surveys-est-2015-en.

OECD (2015b), *Lithuania: Fostering Open and Inclusive Policy Making*, OECD Public Governance Reviews, OECD Publishing, Paris.

OECD (2013), *Government at a Glance 2013*, OECD Publishing, Paris, http://dx.doi.org/10.1787/gov_glance-2013-en.

Sipavičienė, A. and V. Stankūnienė (2013), "The social and economic impact of emigration on Lithuania", in OECD, *Coping with Emigration in Baltic and East European Countries*, OECD Publishing, Paris, http://dx.doi.org/10.1787/9789264204928-6-en.

Synnerström, S. (1997), "Professionalism in Public Service Management: The Making of Highly Qualified, Efficient and Effective Public Managers", Proceedings from Regional Conference on the Public Service in Transition. http://unpan1.un.org/intradoc/groups/public/documents/nispacee/unpan007278.pdf.

Chapter 2

Regulatory reform and policies in Lithuania

This chapter identifies the drivers of regulatory policy and assesses the communication with stakeholders on strategy and policies. It also looks at the policies, processes and institutions for evaluating the efficiency and effectiveness of programmes and policies aimed at improving the regulatory environment. It reviews the role of e-government in support of regulatory policy and governance.

Drivers of the agenda for Better Regulation in Lithuania

In 2008 the Lithuanian government adopted a Programme for Better Regulation as a government resolution. This was a major step following a government resolution of 2003, which had introduced the requirement to make *ex ante* impact analysis when preparing new legislation. For the first time the 2008 programme defined main principles and objectives for Better Regulation. It set three core areas for action: to strengthen capacities for Better Regulation in the administration, to improve the quality of the law-making process through the effective development of *ex ante* impact analysis and enhanced external consultation with stakeholders, and to reduce administrative burdens on businesses and citizens, as well as other regulatory costs. These general orientations have given way to different initiatives, which have not been strongly interrelated.

An important driver for the adoption of measures for Better Regulation in Lithuania has been the implementation of EU agenda for Better Regulation in Lithuania. This has in particular influenced the development of initiatives for the reduction of administrative burdens. Better Regulation has also been promoted to enhance the business environment of Lithuania, as seen in frequent references to international benchmarks. The programme of the government for the years 2012-16 identified the reduction of administrative burdens for businesses, the simplification of licensing requirements and inspection as priority measures for improving the business environment. Similar measures as well as a measure for gold-plating identification were established in the government priorities for 2014.[1] While administrative simplification is considered as a way to improve the regulatory environment for business, there is little discussion on how better regulation can promote growth and competitiveness of the economy.

Reforms to improve the law-making process have been made partly as a concern for legal quality, but the discussion on these issues tends to broaden. The review found a largely shared perception that an overproduction of laws limits the capacity to produce high quality legislation (see Chapter 5 on the development of new regulation). The review also found a large awareness that the production of high quality legislation requires stronger outreach to external stakeholders and the public at large. This view is reflected in Lithuania's Progress Strategy "Lithuania 2030", which states that the rapidly changing environment and growing need for self-governance call for an adjusted model of governance, including increased openness and collaboration with citizens. Many voices, within and outside the administration, call for increased efforts to improve public consultation when making new legislation.

Key measures for Better Regulation in Lithuania

In 2012 two major new laws were adopted in the area of better regulation. The first one was the Law on the Basics of Legislation of 18 September 2012, and the second one was the Law on Administrative Burden Reduction of 8 November 2012. The government has also adopted several important government resolutions in connection with better regulation (Box 2.1). While the government has continued the initiatives launched following the 2008 Better Regulation Programme, it has not taken a global approach to better regulation policy. Measures have been largely taken independently from each other.

Box 2.1. Main Better Regulation measures in Lithuania

- 26 February 2003: Government Resolution No. 276, introducing the requirement to make an impact assessment when preparing new legislation.
- 4 March 2009: Government Resolution No. 161 "Regarding Setting of the Target for National Administrative Burden for Businesses Reduction and Priority Areas for National Administrative Burden for Businesses Reduction".
- 23 February 2011: Government Resolution No. 213 "Regarding Adoption of Methodology for Identifying and Evaluating Administrative Burden for Citizens and Other Persons".
- 11 January 2012: Government Resolution No. 4 "Regarding Adoption of Methodology for Identifying Administrative Burden for Businesses".
- 18 September 2012: Law on the Basics of Legislation (XI-2220), which set out the main principles of legislation, stages of a legislative process, as well as rights and obligations of state and municipality institutions and entities, and other persons, that take part in the legislative process.
- 8 November 2012: Lithuanian Republic Law on Administrative Burden Reduction (XI-2386) (with some amendments introduced in January 2014), which defines the concept of administrative burden, as well as principles and measures of reduction of these burdens, foresees compulsory burden reduction at the municipal level, as well as the creation of the Better Regulation Supervisory Commission.
- 17 April 2013: Government Resolution No. 337 "Regarding Adoption of the Rules of Procedure of the Government of the Republic of Lithuania", by which Government's Rules of Procedure were recast, that sets out the main principles of drafting government legal acts and carrying out their legal, impact assessment and other content and quality control before sending them for the government's adoption.
- 23 October 2013: Government Resolution No. 964 "Regarding Amendment of 18 July 2012 Government Resolution No. 937 "Regarding Adoption of Description of Licensing Basics", which established main principles for evaluating justification of a need for licensing any economic activity, preparing draft laws that regulate licensing of specific economic activities and draft licensing rules, models of issuing licences, as well as terms and criteria for evaluating legal regulation efficiency.

Following the 2008 Programme for Better Regulation, the first major area of action was the improvement of the framework for preparing new legislation. The 2012 Law on the Basics of Legislation set out the main principles of legislation and stages of a legislative process. An important amendment to the Law on the Basics of Legislation came into force on 1 January 2014, replacing the Official Gazette for the official publication of legal acts with the electronic Legal Act Register. Additional measures were taken to improve the methodology for conducting impact assessment and ensure its implementation. The government chose to introduce a proportionate *ex ante* impact assessment process and introduced a List of Priority Initiatives that should be submitted to a more in-depth impact assessment. Regarding the preparation of secondary legislation, the procedures for drafting government resolutions were recast by a 2013 Government

Resolution, which enhanced quality control requirements, including by strengthening the requirement to make *ex ante* impact assessment (see Chapter 5 on the development of new regulation).

The second major area of action for Better Regulation has been the simplification of administrative burdens. While the government has launched initiatives for reducing burdens on citizens, efforts have mainly addressed businesses, with a target of 30% reduction in seven priority areas set by law in 2009. In 2013 a new law came into force, which further elaborated principles for the reduction of administrative burdens, created a consultative commission (the Better Regulation Supervisory Commission), and extended the scope of the administrative burden reduction programme to local governments. In July 2014 the government approved the administrative burden reduction plan for 2014-15,[2] which encompassed 92 measures (see Chapter 6 on the management and rationalisation of existing legislation). It also set a net target of zero growth of administrative burden on all central government bodies.

Specific action has been taken to simplify licensing and permits, and a broad reform has been engaged to improve enforcement.[3] In 2012-13, the Ministry of Economy completed the screening of all licences and permits to start a business, and in 2014 it put forth propositions for reforms. Measures regarding enforcement policy have included the development of risk assessment management and the use of key performance indicators to review the operational results of inspection authorities.

Guiding principles

The 2012 Law on the Basics of Legislation set a legally binding obligation on all government bodies to follow general principles regarding the regulatory framework, which had been initially outlined in the 2008 Programme for Better Regulation. The law defines seven principles:

- ***Necessity***, which means that new regulation can be developed and adopted only when the aims cannot be achieved by other means.
- ***Proportionality***, which means that the chosen regulatory measure must contain the lowest possible administrative and other burdens, not to create legal restrictions more than is necessary to achieve the objectives of the regulation.
- ***Respect for individual rights and freedoms***.
- ***Openness and transparency***, which means that the legislation must be public, legislative decisions cannot be taken without public knowledge and opportunities to participate.
- ***Efficiency***, which means that the draft legislation must assess all the possible regulatory alternatives and choose the best of them.
- ***Clarity***, which means that regulation must be concise, comprehensible, accurate, clear and unambiguous.
- ***Consistency***, which means that lower level regulation should not conflict with higher level regulation and secondary regulation necessary for the implementation of law should be adopted to come into force together with the law.

Communication on Better Regulation policy

The government publishes strategic progress reports on its general programme, as part of an institutionalised methodology for strategic planning established in 2012. It has not developed specific efforts to communicate on the objectives and results of initiatives for Better Regulation. The targets regarding the reduction of administrative burden on businesses have been used so far in a limited way to communicate either within the administration or towards parliament and external stakeholders.

E-government and Better Regulation

Measures for the development of Better Regulation have made a large use of ICT. The legislative framework is supported by the Common Legislative Information System, which provides openness and transparency of the legislative process and ensures accessibility of existing legislation. It covers all central government bodies but is not systematically used by municipalities. Some administrative procedures are available on the internet (such as tax reporting), and record a good take—up. The Lithuanian Digital Agenda adopted in 2014 foresees the provision of an increased number of public services online, including solutions to increase the openness of public governance processes. There are also plans to issue some licences and permits online in the future. The government has developed a single governmental portal (www.epaslaugos.lt) and a common back-office platform. However there are still many databases run by different ministries, which do not communicate with each other (see also Chapter 6 on the management and rationalisation of existing legislation).

Ex post evaluation of regulatory policies

There is no policy in place for the systemic evaluation of regulatory policy or particular regulatory quality tools in place in Lithuania. This is, nevertheless, the case in many OECD countries even though some attempts exist, especially in case of evaluating RIA programmes and administrative simplification and burden reduction programmes (Table 2.1).

In general, some indicators of performance related to regulatory policy are mentioned in different strategic documents of the government (*Priority Measure for Implementation of Government of the Republic of Lithuania Programme for the years 2012-16; government priorities for 2014*). Reporting on implementation of these strategic documents is described in the Strategic Planning Methodology.[4] Every institution implementing/participating in the implementation of government priorities has to submit information about the progress in implementing a particular government priority quarterly to the Government Office, which then prepares a summary report and submits it to the government. The quality of the information reported by the ministries varies. After the approval by the government the report is published on the government website. Annual ministries reports on implementing the government programme are also published on the respective ministries' websites.

Lithuania also closely monitors the World Bank's "Doing Business" indicators. These indicators are used as a benchmark with the aim to improve business conditions in Lithuania. Many reforms in Lithuania are motivated also by improving its ranking in the Doing Business chart. Using indicators developed by international organisations might be helpful in identifying priority areas for reform. On the other hand, some reforms might help a country to climb the chart, however, the real-life effects for citizens and businesses in the country are hardly visible (one example could be shortening the time needed to register a business from several hours to fifteen minutes). It is therefore always necessary to set ambitious goals indicating the desired outcomes for the society and evaluate the performance of reforms against these goals.

Table 2.1. **Countries publishing performance reports by policy tool/programme**

	Reports published online on the performance of the following regulatory management tools and programmes (i.e. how they function in practice):			
	Regulatory Impact Analysis on draft regulations	Consultation practices on draft regulations	*Ex post* analysis of existing regulations	Administrative simplification and burden reduction programmes
Australia	●	❍	●	❍
Austria	●	❍	❍	●
Belgium	●	❍	❍	●
Canada	❍	❍	❍	❍
Chile	❍[1]	❍	❍	❍
Czech Republic	●	●	❍	●
Denmark	❍	❍	❍	●
Estonia	●	❍	❍	❍
EU	●	●	●	●
Finland	●	❍	❍	●
France	●	❍	❍	●
Germany	●	❍	●	●
Greece	❍	❍	❍	❍
Hungary	❍	❍	❍	❍
Iceland	❍	❍	❍	●
Ireland	●	❍	❍	❍
Israel	❍	❍	❍	❍
Italy	●	❍	❍	●
Japan	●	●	❍	❍
Korea	❍	❍	❍	❍
Luxembourg	❍	❍	❍	❍
Mexico	●	●	❍	●
Netherlands	❍	●	❍	●
New Zealand	●	❍	❍	●
Norway	●	❍	❍	❍
Poland	❍	❍	❍	●
Portugal	❍	❍	❍	●
Slovak Republic	●	❍	❍	❍
Slovenia	●	●	❍	●
Spain	❍	❍	❍	❍
Sweden	●	❍	❍	●
Switzerland	●	●	❍	●
Turkey	❍	●	❍	●
United Kingdom	●	❍	●	●
United States	❍	❍	❍	●
OECD34+EU	**20**	**8**	**4**	**21**

● Yes ❍ No.

1. Although Chile does not have a performance report on their RIA system, the status of RIAs can be tracked on www.e-seia.cl/busqueda/buscarProyectoAction.php?modo=ficha&nombre=&sector=&regiones=14&presentacion=EIA&buscar=true&popup=1.

Source: OECD (2014), *OECD Framework for Regulatory Policy Evaluation*, OECD Publishing, Paris, http://dx.doi.org/10.1787/9789264214453-en.

Reporting on administrative burden reduction

The results of the administrative burden reduction project are monitored and evaluated in quantitative means following requirements set in the Government Resolution "*Regarding Adoption of Methodology for Identifying Administrative Burden for Businesses*". Recent amendments to this Resolution set an obligation not to increase the overall administrative burdens to businesses which is applied individually for every governmental institution – a level of administrative burden caused by each institution's regulation for each calendar year has to remain unchanged or to decrease. The Ministry of Economy was made responsible for the supervision of the change in overall level of administrative burden on businesses. The data necessary for monitoring comes from the administrative burden evaluation reports submitted by individual ministries to the Ministry of Economy (see also Chapter 6 on the management and rationalisation of existing regulation).

Plans on evaluating RIA

Regular discussions between the Government Office, the Ministry of Economy, the Ministry of Finance and the Ministry of Interior help identify challenges, constraints and achievements in the area of impact assessment and identify areas where improvements are needed. The Government Office is conducting a review of the impact assessment process in consultation with the other institutions like the Ministry of Economy, the Ministry of Finance and the Ministry of Interior, in order to take stock of the use of impact assessment. Results are expected to be presented to the government in the course of 2015.

Notes

1. Government Resolution No. 931, adopted on 9 October 2013, https://www.e-tar.lt/portal/lt/legalact/tar.0f673b2d9bed.
2. https://www.e-tar.lt/portal/lt/legalAct/af2bf32005da11e4b836947d492f2f50.
3 18 July 2012 Government Resolution No. 937, "Regarding Adoption of Description of Licensing Basics", amended by 23 October 2013 Government Resolution No. 964, https://www.e-tar.lt/portal/lt/legalact/tar.62b1abb28b06.
4. Government Resolution No. 827 from 6 June 2002.

Bibliography

EU (2014), "Regulatory Fitness and Performance Programme", COM(2014)368 final, http://ec.europa.eu/smart-regulation/docs/com2014_368_en.pdf.

EU (2010), "Smart Regulation in the European Union," COM(2010) 543 final, http://eur-lex.europa.eu/legal-content/en/all/?uri=celex:52010dc0543.

OECD (2014), *OECD Framework for Regulatory Policy Evaluation*, OECD Publishing, Paris, http://dx.doi.org/10.1787/9789264214453-en.

OECD (2012), "Recommendation of the Council on Regulatory Policy and Governance", www.oecd.org/gov/regulatory-policy/2012recommendation.htm.

World Bank (2014), *Doing Business 2015: Going Beyond Efficiency*, The World Bank, Washington, D.C., www.doingbusiness.org/~/media/giawb/doing%20business/documents/annual-reports/english/db15-full-report.pdf.

Chapter 3

Institutional framework and capacities for regulatory policy in Lithuania

This chapter maps the different and interlocking roles of the entities involved in regulatory management and the promotion and implementation of regulatory policy and governance, as well as training and capacity building within government.

Key players for regulatory management in the executive

Institutions

In the context of a highly decentralised rulemaking process, the responsibility for regulatory management tools and policies in the Lithuanian administration is spread across ministries. A few government bodies however play a more prominent role in regulatory management.

The **Government Office** co-ordinates and supervises the law-making process when draft laws are initiated by the executive. It is in charge of preparing the annual legislative programme and supervises the law-drafting process, which is decentralised in ministerial departments. It reviews all draft laws drafted by ministerial departments after inter-ministerial consultation and consultation of stakeholders has taken place. The Government Office also reviews all government draft resolutions. It has a responsibility for the development of the impact assessment system in co-operation with the Ministry of Economy and the Ministry of Interior. It has a small unit, called the "Strategic Planning and Monitoring Unit", in charge of impact assessment development and implementation. The unit defines requirements and methodologies on impact assessment, and elaborates the list of priority legislative initiatives that are subject to full impact assessment, following submissions by line ministries. It monitors the overall quality of impact assessment and provides support and advice to public sector institutions through guidelines and training. Officials in sectoral units of the Government Office also take part in the quality monitoring of impact assessment.

The **Ministry of Economy** is in charge of co-ordinating initiatives in the field of administrative simplification for business as part of the Better Regulation programme launched in 2008, which has focused on the reduction and prevention of administrative burdens on businesses, and the simplification of licences and permits. The Ministry has elaborated annual plans for the implementation of the programme, developed methodologies and provided guidance to other ministries. It has also some specific responsibilities regarding impact assessment as it reviews the results of impact assessment on the economy done by other ministerial departments, including impact on competitiveness, SMEs and administrative burdens on business.

The **Ministry of Justice** reviews all draft laws and government resolutions, and submits its legal opinion, with the exception of those related to international treaties and agreements. It is also in charge of co-ordinating *ex post* evaluation of legal regulations.

The **Ministry of Interior** is responsible for developing the administrative burden policy for citizens. It is also responsible for e-government together with the **Ministry of Transport and Communications**. It also exercises public administration functions related to the development of local governance and regional development.[1]

The **Ministry of Foreign Affairs** has the leading role with regard to EU legislation. It co-ordinates position of line ministries in their own field of responsibility. The Ministry of Justice and the European Law Department under the Ministry of Justice perform monitoring and supervision during the transposition of EU legal acts.

Co-ordination

The Rules of Procedure of the Government of the Republic of Lithuania provide for all proposals of laws, government resolutions and other legal texts that go to the government to be agreed with ministries, government agencies, and other institutions and bodies within their respective competencies. During the process of drafting laws and resolutions, co-ordination is led by the ministry that is responsible for the draft and takes place through a formal consultation process. The Government Office examines all drafts after this consultation stage, and comments and remarks can also be discussed at the ministerial meeting of vice-ministers and chancellors. As the Prime Minister sets the agenda of the Cabinet meeting, the Government Office can play a gatekeeping role in the law-making process for laws and resolutions initiated within the executive.

In some cases, *ad hoc* joint working groups are established and inter-ministerial meetings are organised to resolve disagreements before drafts are submitted to the Cabinet. Informal co-ordination can also take place, through direct contacts between officials and unofficial meetings, but a formal culture tends to prevail and line ministries usually keep a lot of autonomy.

With respect to better regulation policies, no formal inter-ministerial co-ordination mechanism has been established, whether at the political or administrative level. This reflects the lack of a global approach to regulatory policy. As seen above, the responsibility for co-ordination is allocated to different ministries by subject (administrative burden reduction on business, administrative burden reduction on citizens, impact assessment, *ex post* review). These departments and unit ensure co-ordination between themselves and with other parts of the administration mainly through direct contacts. The Better Regulation Supervisory Commission, which has been established in the area of administrative burden reduction, does not play any specific role in the elaboration and supervision of the better regulation agenda. Composed of 19 members, half of whom are government officials and half are representatives of stakeholders, it is mainly an advisory body charged with making proposals.

Other players

Parliament

Members of Parliament, called *Seimas*, have the right to initiate new legislation, and the Parliament is relatively independent in setting the legislative agenda. All draft laws proposed by the government or initiated by the parliament are assessed by the legal department of the parliament and are subject to consultation through formal hearings and more informal consultation of stakeholders. Draft laws initiated by members of parliament are subject to similar procedures as those initiated by the executive, but there is no requirement for any impact assessment. Requirements regarding consultation on draft laws initiated by members of Parliament are also limited as the Parliament Statute only provide that interested persons may participate and submit their comments in committee hearings, and that a summary of these comments be sent to the main committee. The adoption of amendments during the last stage of voting can reduce the effectiveness of the process for making high quality legislation, either initiated by the executive or the legislative. Awareness and interest in regulatory management policies seem limited, although some voices in Parliament call for the development of in-depth analysis of the potential impact of major legislative initiatives, broader consultation and increased monitoring of existing legislation.

National Audit Office

The National Audit Office is accountable to the *Seimas* and the President of the Republic. The auditor general is appointed by the *Seimas* based on a nomination by the President. Reports of the Office are examined at the parliament's Committee on Audit. The National Audit Office has not been involved in the review of better regulation related polices.

Local governments

Lithuania is a unitary state with one level of local self-government. Municipalities act independently within their competence defined by the Constitution and laws, in particular the Law on Local Self-Government. The Association of Local Authorities in Lithuania represents the common interests of municipalities, in particular in relation to the government.

Municipalities have significant responsibilities for service delivery but limited regulatory responsibilities. They deliver construction permits and some business licences. The law on administrative burden reduction, which came into force in 2013, put a duty on municipalities, for the first time, to formulate and implement reduction plans. The Association of Local Authorities has been consulted on initiatives regarding administrative burden reduction and is a member of the Better Regulation Supervisory Commission (see Chapter 8 on the interface between supra-national, sub-national and national levels of government).

Resources and training

Resources

A small number of officials directly work on regulatory policy, as one unit or part of a unit is dedicated to regulatory management issues in the Government Office, the Ministry of Economy, the Ministry of Justice and the Ministry of Interior. The Strategic Planning and Monitoring Unit of the Government Office has two full-time officials, one economist and one lawyer. The Ministry of Economy also has a small part of a unit working on administrative burden reduction.

A large number of officials are however involved in the development of regulation and its implementation as the law-making process is decentralised in each government institution. Around 70% of civil servants in government administration take some part in policy development and legislative drafting process. Nearly 9 000 officials are involved in the enforcement of regulations (consultation, inspection, information assessment, and the application of sanctions). The total number of civil servants was 29 700 at the end of 2013, of which 17 400 were in state public administration.

Training and support material

Training of civil servants is regulated by the Law on Civil Service[2] which lays down the basic provisions. The Strategy for the Training of Civil Servants for 2014-17 has established priorities for the training of civil servants, with respect to competencies of civil servants (management, leadership and change management, communication, analytical skills, prevention of corruption and professional ethics) and targeted servants. There are four target training groups: high and middle level managers, civil servants who provide services to citizens, civil servants who occupy positions with high risk of corruption and civil servants in charge of corruption prevention and control functions. Nearly half of all state and local civil servants participated in a training programme in 2013.While training is decentralised and organised by the ministry or agency (under the ministries and under the government), which has hired the civil servant, training compulsory training programme for high and middle level managers is organised centrally by the Ministry of Interior. In addition all new public servants follow an introductory programme, which includes training on the preparation and drafting of legal acts. The programmes have a general format and do not specifically address impact assessment, stakeholder engagement or *ex post* evaluation. In 2013 the introductory programme was followed by 569 civil servants participating in policy formulation and legal drafting.

The Government Office and the Ministry of the Economy have provided specific programmes related to regulatory management and Better Regulation:

- During 2009-2011, the Government Office provided training on impact assessment to civil servants across state administration.[3] The training scheme targeted civil servants drafting regulations, and heads of strategic planning departments. About 120 civil servants followed this programme. The programme covered the following topics: process of *ex ante* impact assessment (steps and participants, principles, impact assessment aspects), analysis methods, cost-benefit analysis, *ex post* impact assessment (steps and methods, design of *ex post* impact assessment), counterfactual analysis, theory-based evaluation.
- The Ministry of Economy organises special training on the measurement of administrative burdens at least once a year. It also provides ongoing support to civil servants regarding concrete measurement issues and questions via telephone, e-mail or live consultations.
- With the support of EU structural funds, the Ministry of Economy has also organised outsourced training for inspectors in the fields of risk management, checklist preparation and application, the use of key performance indicators in operational analysis, and telephone consultation. Six hundred employees from the full spectrum of inspection authorities participated in this training throughout 2014.

A number of support materials have been produced in the area of law drafting and administrative simplification. Methodologies have been mainly provided through government resolutions and ministerial orders.[4] A number of documents provide specific guidance on subjects relating to regulatory quality. The Ministry of the Economy has produced an informative training publication on administrative burden reduction.[5] The Government Office has provided guidance on social cost-benefit analysis and *ex post* evaluation.[6] The Ministry of Finance has published recommendations on Implementing Methodology for Programme Evaluation.[7] While the Minister of Justice has issued recommendations for drafting legal acts, no practical guidelines have been published that encompass the whole law-drafting process, including quality of legal drafting, impact assessment, engagement of external stakeholders, *ex post* evaluation (see Chapter 5).

Notes

1. Ministry of Interior, Interior Affairs System, www.vrm.lt/interior_affairs_system126 (accessed on 30 March 2015).

2. http://www3.lrs.lt/pls/inter3/dokpaieska.showdoc_l?p_id=471047.

3. The training programme (in Lithuanian) on impact assessment is available on the Government website: www.lrv.lt/bylos/vort/vort-3/mokymu%20programa.pdf.

4. Such as 16 October 2012 Government of the Republic of Lithuania Resolution No. 1276 "Regarding Amendment of 26 February 2003 Government Resolution No. 276, "Regarding Adoption and Implementation of Methodology on Impact Assessment of Draft Legislative Acts"; 23 February 2011 Government Resolution No. 213 "Regarding Adoption of Methodology for Identifying and Evaluating Administrative Burden for Citizens and Other Persons"; 11 January 2012 Government Resolution No. 4 "Regarding Adoption of Methodology for Identifying Administrative Burden for Businesses".

5. Available in Lithuanian, www.ukmin.lt/web/lt/verslo_aplinka/geresnis_reglamentas/administracines_nastos_vertinimo_ir_mazinimo_praktine_informacija.

6. www.lrv.lt/bylos/VORT/VORT-3/metodines_gaires.pdf, available in Lithuanian.

7. www.finmin.lt/finmin.lt/failai/veiklos_kryptys_biudzetas/Programu_vertinimas/PVrekomendacijos2011.pdf, available in Lithuanian.

Bibliography

Government Office (2011), "Social Cost-Benefit Analysis: Methodological Guidelines" in Lithuanian, www.lrv.lt/bylos/vort/vort-3/metodines_gaires.pdf.

Ministry of Finance (2011), "Programme Evaluation Application Procedures Recommendations" in Lithuanian, www.finmin.lt/finmin.lt/failai/veiklos_kryptys_biudzetas/Programu_vertinimas/PVrekomendacijos2011.pdf.

OECD (2012), "Recommendation of the Council on Regulatory Policy and Governance", www.oecd.org/gov/regulatory-policy/2012recommendation.htm.

Chapter 4

Transparency, consultation and communication in Lithuania

This chapter examines how Lithuania secures transparency in the regulatory environment, both through public consultation in the process of rule making and public communication on regulatory requirements.

Public consultation on regulations

Formal requirements

The 2012 Law on the Basics of Legislation sets general requirements for transparency of the legal framework and for public consultation in the law-making process. Openness and transparency is one of the legislative principles set out by the Law on the Basics of Legislation, whose Article 3 specifies the need for legislation to be public, for the public to be informed about the preparation of new or amended texts, including regulatory impact assessment, and to be given the possibility to provide comments.

Article 7 of the law spells out three main principles for public consultation, which are: appropriate timing, proportionality, and efficiency. The law also requires that information about the results be provided to parliament, or to government in case of a government resolution. The body which initiates the draft law has the right to decide whether the consultation is necessary in view of the scope of the project. It also has the right to decide on the extent of consultation, under the general requirement of efficiency. This means that consultation should focus on substantive issues. In case of labour-related legislation, the Tripartite Council, which gathers trade unions, business representatives, the executive and the parliament, must be consulted.

The law does not provide detailed requirements on the consultation process and leaves it to the initiating body to define how consultation should be conducted. There is no standard process for consultation, with respect to planning, choice of methodology, analysis and evaluation. The only specific requirement is that the results of consultation should be attached to the draft text when it is sent to Parliament in case of a law and government in case of a government resolution. Each ministry or other initiating body defines the process under its own standards.

There are no formal or informal central guidelines on consultation. The government has not published any document spelling out the process, its duration and the methodology on how to engage with stakeholders. It has not either set control or quality check on consultation procedures. The methodology on impact assessment states that public consultation can be conducted at different stages of the assessment, when defining the problem, formulating the objectives, defining alternatives to regulation. However it does not provide specific requirements or methodology. OECD countries like the United Kingdom have developed consultation guidelines that provide guidance and support to departments in undertaking consultations (Box 4.1).

Box 4.1. Consultation guidelines: the case of the United Kingdom

Increasing the level of transparency and increasing engagement with interested parties improves the quality of policy making by bringing to bear expertise and alternative perspectives, and identifying unintended effects and practical problems.

Prior to replacing it with the much shorter "Consultation Principles" in 2012 (updated in 2013), the United Kingdom had a detailed "Code of Practice on Consultation", which aimed to "help improve the transparency, responsiveness and accessibility of consultations, and help in reducing the burden of engaging in government policy development."

Box 4.1. **Consultation guidelines: the case of the United Kingdom** (*cont.*)

Although not legally binding and only applying to formal, written consultations, the Code of Practice constitutes a good example of how a government can provide its civil servants with a powerful tool to improve the consultation process. The 2012-13 Consultation Principles highlighted the need to pay specific attention to proportionality (adjusting the type and scale of consultation to the potential impacts of the proposals or decision being taken) and to achieve real engagement rather than merely following a bureaucratic process.

The 16-page Code of Practice issued in 2008 was divided into seven criteria, which were to be reproduced as shown below in every consultation.

- *Criterion 1: When to consult.* Formal consultation should take place at a stage when there is scope to influence the policy outcome.
- *Criterion 2: Duration of consultation exercises.* Consultations should normally last for at least 12 weeks with consideration given to longer timescales where feasible and sensible.
- *Criterion 3: Clarity of scope and impact.* Consultation documents should be clear about the consultation process, what is being proposed, the scope to influence and the expected costs and benefits of the proposals.
- *Criterion 4: Accessibility of consultation exercises.* Consultation exercises should be designed to be accessible to, and clearly targeted at, those people the exercise is intended to reach.
- *Criterion 5: The burden of consultation.* Keeping the burden of consultation to a minimum is essential if consultations are to be effective and if consultees' buy-in to the process is to be obtained.
- *Criterion 6: Responsiveness of consultation exercises.* Consultation responses should be analysed carefully and clear feedback should be provided to participants following the consultation.
- *Criterion 7: Capacity to consult.* Officials running consultations should seek guidance in how to run an effective consultation exercise and share what they have learned from the experience.

An example of a UK government response to consultation can be found at https://www.gov.uk/government/uploads/system/uploads/attachment_data/file/181637/dla-reform-response.pdf.

Source: www.bis.gov.uk/files/file47158.pdf for the 2008 Code of Practice on Consultation and www.gov.uk/government/uploads/system/uploads/attachment_data/file/255180/Consultation-Principles-Oct-2013.pdf for the updated Consultation Principles, which replaced the 2008 Code of Practice.

Implementation

As the consultation process is not formalised, each line ministry has developed its own practices. Ministries have a network of stakeholders to whom they send draft laws at the same time when the draft is sent out for inter-ministerial consultation. In some cases, ministries set up advisory councils to consult stakeholders. For example the Small and Medium Business Council is regularly consulted by the Ministry of Economy and other ministries, such as the Ministry of Social Security and Labour. Another example is the area of administrative simplification, where the government has established a so-called

Sunrise commission for consultation with stakeholders. Initially set up in 2009, this commission was transformed into the "Better Regulation Supervisory Commission" in 2014. It is composed of representatives of business associations, think-tanks, the Association of Lithuanian Municipalities, and government officials. It is charged with submitting proposals on administrative burden reduction for businesses (see Chapter 6 on the management and rationalisation of existing regulation).

Active participation in regulatory policy demands a significant amount of time. Not everyone has or is willing to invest the time in these processes. This may present a problem when trying to attract those who are not used to actively participate in public decision-making. At least, governments should allow sufficient time for those consulted to submit their comments. Some OECD governments have set up a minimum consultation period. In 16 countries this period ranges between 4 and 6 weeks (Figure 4.1).

Figure 4.1. **Minimum periods for consultations with the public**

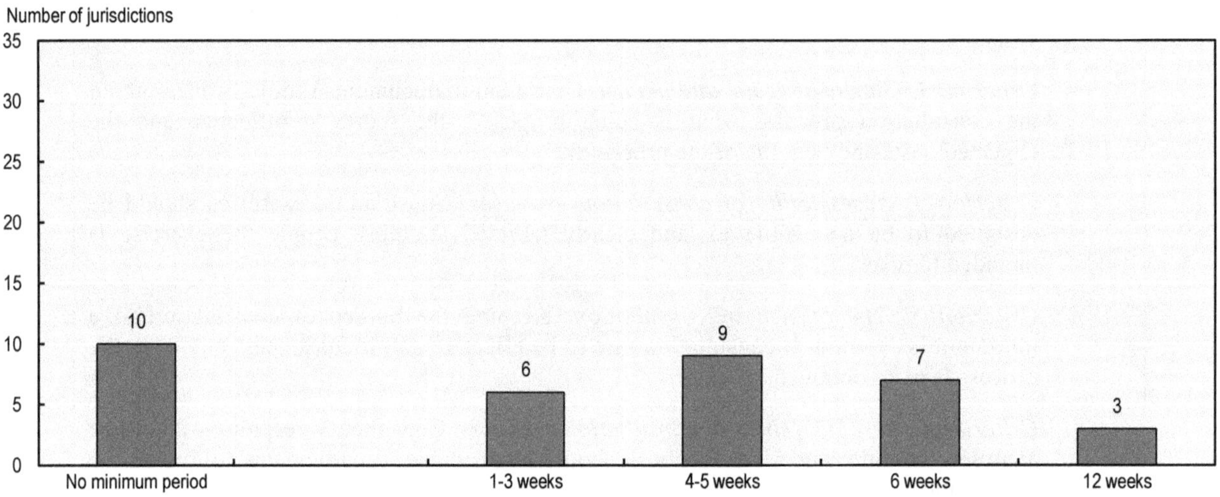

Note: Based on data from 34 OECD countries and the European Commission.

Source: OECD (2015), *Regulatory Policy Outlook*, forthcoming.

In Lithuania, when sending the text for comment to stakeholders, ministries are required to give a standard time of 10 working days for feedback. It is extended to 15 working days for draft laws that are over 10 pages, and it is reduced to 5 working days in the case of emergency legislation. In some cases consultation with stakeholders takes place at an earlier stage of the draft development. As required by law, feedback received by ministries is attached to draft laws. Comments by other ministries that are not taken into account by the drafting authority are presented as a table in the explanatory note of the draft, with the reason for their rejection. There is also a possibility of general consultation when the draft law is published on the central register and made open to comments.

In addition to consultation on specific draft laws, the government has organised public consultations on policy issues since 2010. For example the Government Office organised six public consultations:

- "How would you propose to curb smuggling and trafficking of illegal goods?"

- "What means could be implemented to reduce unemployment and create new jobs?"
- Public consultation on the Lithuanian progress Strategy "Lithuanian 2030"
- "What additional means would you propose on how to reduce youth unemployment?"
- "In which areas, in your opinion, corruption is the most widespread? Your proposals on how to eradicate the reasons for corruption."
- "Suggestions on the National Action Plan of the Open Government Partnership".

Public communication on regulations

All legal acts and draft legal acts are published in the Legal Act Register, which is an electronic register, held and managed by the Office of the *Seimas*. Publication in the Legal Act Register is set by the above-mentioned Article 3 of the Law on the Basics of Legislation, which states that law-making must be public. On 1 January 2014, the Legal Act Register entirely replaced the printed Official Gazette, which used to be published twice a week by the Publishing House of the *Seimas*. The Legal Act Register is accessible to all for free through its dedicated site (www.e-tar.lt) and through the portal of *Seimas* (www.lrs.lt). The Register gives access to the consolidated version of legal texts.

The publication of an act in the Legal Act Register is considered as an official publication. Normative legal acts come into force the day after publication, unless another date is stated in the act. The requirement for publication in the Legal Act Register extends to all kind of legal texts: the constitution and constitution laws, laws, presidential decrees and ordinances, government decisions and resolutions, international treaties, regulatory legal acts of ministers and heads of government agencies, other public institutions and agencies, statute and resolutions of the *Seimas*, rules of the constitutional court and municipal normative acts.

The Legal Act Register provides for a unified and easy access to legal texts, including in their consolidated version. However it in no way gives businesses or others time to understand the new law and make appropriate changes to be ready for the date it comes into force. An area for improvement is to include a notification system to be updated on selected topics and the publication of new laws sufficiently in advance before the entry into force to allow businesses and citizens to understand and prepare for the entry into force of new requirements. The review found that ministries seem unequally proactive in communicating and informing stakeholders on upcoming initiatives and legislation. In addition to the publication on the Legal Act Register, ministries and other public institutions usually publish information on main amendments on their official website, and provide newsfeed subscriptions. Some ministries also make an extended use of other media sources, including Facebook, web portals, radio, television and newspapers. OECD countries have developed interactive dedicated portals to facilitate transparency and access to information (Box 4.2).

Box 4.2. Consultation portal: The case of Denmark's *Høringsportalen*

In 2005, the Danish administration set up a dedicated portal to ensure greater transparency in the consultation process when preparing new regulations. The Consultation Portal (*Høringsportalen*) is hosted on the citizens' portal "borger.dk", which has a specific page on law making (www.borger.dk/forside/lovgivning/hoeringsportalen).

The Consultation Portal collects consultation documents, dating back to mid-2005, relating to the preparation of regulation by all ministries and agencies. Publication is mandatory for all draft bills and executive orders. Other documents are also published for consultation. They include policy or strategy papers, European Commission's draft regulations, draft technical standards, and guidelines.

Documentation includes the draft, the call for consultation (which specifies the deadline) and the list of institutions and people, which have been called for hearing. Once the consultation period is over, the government also publishes the written comments, which have been received. Comments to draft law must be published no later than when the bill is forwarded to the parliament.

Draft regulations can be searched by category of document, date, authority, as well as key words. The portal also includes the possibility to receive regular updates, electronic notices and a newsletter on consultation.

Denmark's Consultation Portal can now be found at https://hoeringsportalen.dk

Source: OECD (2010a), *Better Regulation in Europe: Denmark 2010*, OECD Publishing, Paris, http://dx.doi.org/10.1787/9789264084551-en.

Bibliography

OECD (2015), *Regulatory Policy Outlook*, forthcoming.

OECD (2012), "Recommendation of the Council on Regulatory Policy and Governance", www.oecd.org/gov/regulatory-policy/2012recommendation.htm.

OECD (2010a), *Better Regulation in Europe: Denmark 2010*, OECD Publishing, Paris, http://dx.doi.org/10.1787/9789264084551-en.

OECD (2010b), *Better Regulation in Europe: United Kingdom 2010*, OECD Publishing, Paris. http://dx.doi.org/10.1787/9789264084490-en.

UK Department for Work and Pensions (2011), "Government's response to the consultation on Disability Living Allowance reform", Presented to Parliament by the Secretary of State for Work and Pensions by Command of Her Majesty, April 2011, https://www.gov.uk/government/uploads/system/uploads/attachment_data/file/181637/dla-reform-response.pdf.

UK Government (2008), "Code of Practice on Consultation", https://www.gov.uk/government/uploads/system/uploads/attachment_data/file/100807/file47158.pdf.

Chapter 5

The development of new regulations in Lithuania

This chapter reviews the processes for the development of new regulations, with special attention for forward planning, administrative procedures and legal quality; the use of ex ante *impact assessment of new regulations; and the consideration of alternatives to regulation.*

The structure of regulations in Lithuania

Written laws passed by the legislature are the main source of regulation in Lithuania. Substantive parts of the law are codified in the Civil Code, Civil Procedure Code, Criminal Code, Criminal Procedure Code, Code of Administrative Offences and the Labour Code. Laws adopted by the *Seimas*, Lithuania's Parliament, apply to all state institutions, i.e. the executive, the legislature, agencies and municipalities. The executive can pass resolutions that are implemented by the executive and its agencies. In some cases, a recommendation can be given to sub-national levels to apply government resolutions. This is, for example, the case for burden reduction and the use of impact assessment at the sub-national level (Box 5.1).

Box 5.1. The structure of regulation in Lithuania

Lithuania's regulation stem from the following key sources:

- Constitution of the Republic of Lithuania;
- Constitutional laws;
- Ratified international treaties;
- Laws: they are initiated by parliament, the President and the executive and adopted by Parliament; they represent the primary legislative source;
- Resolutions of the *Seimas* and government: they are adopted either by the Parliament or the Cabinet of Ministers;
- Ministerial and agencies orders/resolutions: they are adopted by a ministry or agency and concern primarily the activity of that body; and
- Acts of local municipal authorities: they are adopted by municipal councils within their areas of competence; they cannot conflict with laws and resolutions.

Trends in the production of new regulation

The President of the Republic, the executive and members of Parliament have the right to initiate laws by submitting a draft to the *Seimas*.[1] On average, approximately 900 draft laws are submitted to the *Seimas* every year. Approximately a third are submitted by the executive and two-thirds by members of parliament. About half of them are adopted and become laws. Approximately two-third of the adopted laws stem from an executive draft and one-third from a parliamentary draft (Figure 5.1).

There was a slight increase in the production of laws in 2011 and 2012 (505 and 494 laws adopted, respectively) when compared to 2010 and 2013 (428 and 405 laws adopted, respectively). This upward trend could have been the consequence of the elections in October 2012 (and the desire to have legislation passed at the end of a government mandate) (Figure 5.1).

Figure 5.1. **Presented and adopted laws in Lithuania**

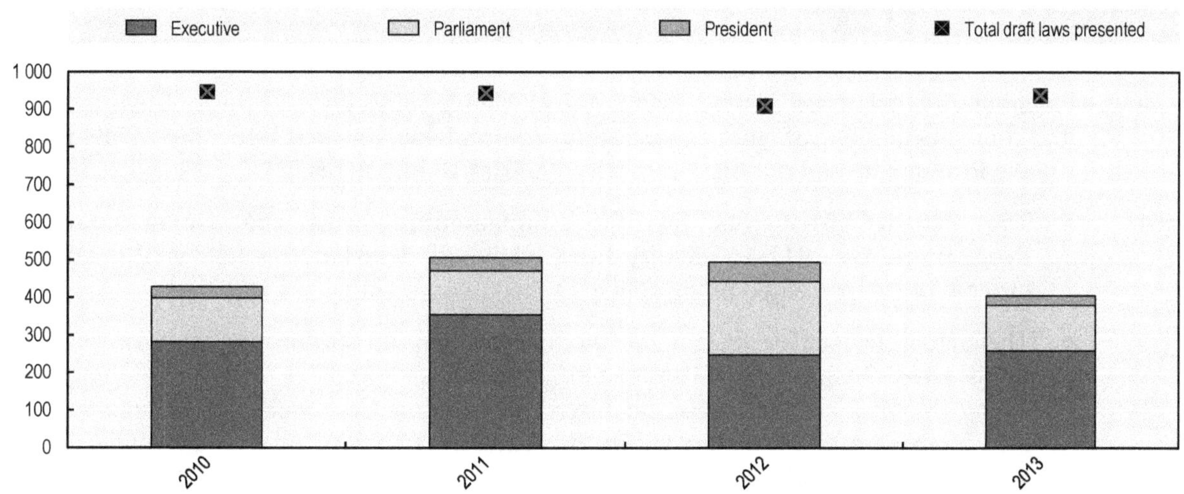

Note: Data covers registered laws (*Registruoti įstatymų projektai*) and adopted laws (*Priimti įstatymai*) in the annual parliamentary sessions of the *Seimas* (i.e. sessions IV-V in 2010; VI-VII in 2011; VIII-IX-I in 2012; II-III in 2013).

Source: *Seimas* statistics, www3.lrs.lt/pls/inter/w5_show?p_r=252&p_k=1.

It is difficult to determine whether a country passes too many or too few laws (or just about right). In addition to the challenge of determining an optimal legislative production in relation to the economic and social problems that public institutions need to address, the legal system as well as the administrative culture and the approach to decision making can determine a preference (or need) for legislating, rather than using other methods. Comparing countries of similar size, economic structure, legal culture and administrative tradition can, however, offer some reference point. Compared to neighbouring Estonia, Lithuania appears to adopt a significant number of laws. Between 2010 and 2013, Lithuania adopted on average 458 laws per year (compared to 115 laws adopted in Estonia). A number of these laws are amendments to existing legislation (Figure 5.2).

Figure 5.2. **Adopted laws in Lithuania and Estonia**

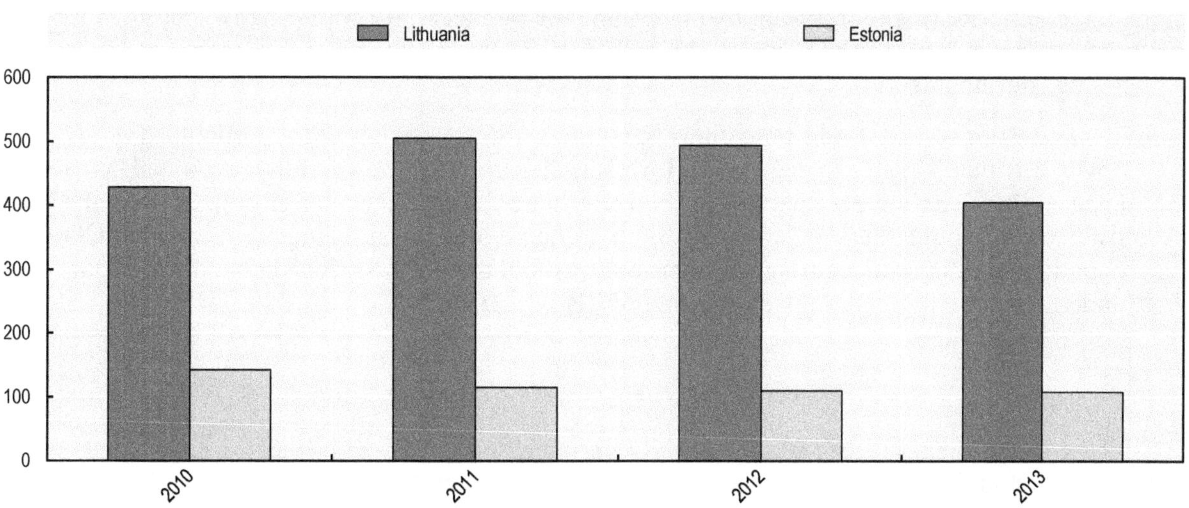

Note: Data covers adopted laws (*Priimti įstatymai*) in the annual parliamentary sessions of the *Seimas* (i.e. sessions IV-V in 2010; VI-VII in 2011; VIII-IX-I in 2012; II-III in 2013).

Source: *Seimas* statistics, http://www3.lrs.lt/pls/inter/w5_show?p_r=252&p_k=1; information provided by the Estonian Ministry of Justice.

Procedures for making new regulation

Forward planning

Planning of legislative initiatives within the executive relies on the Priority Measures for the Implementation of the Government Programme for 2012-16, the Annual Legislative Programme and the List of Priority Legislative Initiatives.

- The **Priority Measures for the Implementation of the Government Programme for 2012-16** identify some of the key legislative initiatives that are expected to be presented in the course of the government's term in office.
- The actual legislative agenda of the government is set through the **Annual Legislative Programme**. The Government Office prepares this Programme, taking into account proposals submitted by the ministries. Proposals include the title of the draft law or resolution, the objectives to be achieved by intended legislation, the timeframe for submission to the government and the Parliament. In addition, for draft laws that are still in the early stages, ministries have to submit information on the scope of the problem, intended changes and possible impacts. The Legislative Programme is approved by the government at the beginning of each year. Based on the annual Legislative Programme, the Government Office prepares a Semi-annual Legislative Programme that is submitted to the *Seimas* at the beginning of the spring and autumn parliamentary sessions.
- Since 2013, the Government Office has also prepared a **Priority List of Legislative Initiatives**. The Priority List includes legislative proposals whose impacts are expected to be assessed in greater depth. The List draws on proposals submitted by line ministries and proposals selected by the Government Office drawing in part on the 2012-2016 Priority Measures and to a large extent on the Annual Legislative Programme. In 2013, the Priority List included 14 proposals (all selected by the Government Office). In 2014, it included 26 proposals (2 submitted by ministries and 24 selected by the Government Office). The Priority List is approved by the Cabinet of Ministers. It is not usually submitted to the *Seimas* as the proposals included in the List are at an early stage of development.

The Priority List could potentially serve as a filter, offering an opportunity to slow down a certain "rush" to legislate. However, this role is not yet fully exploited as it appears that there are no clear and objective criteria for the inclusion of proposals on the list (which would then undertake a more in-depth impact assessment). Some OECD countries have introduced triage systems or threshold tests to filter legislative proposals to undertake more in-depth impact assessments (Box 5.2).

Box 5.2. Threshold tests to apply in-depth impact assessments

Canada applies RIA to all subordinate regulations, but employs a Triage System to decide the extent of the analysis. The development of a Triage Statement (low, medium, high impact) early in the development of the regulatory proposal determines whether the proposal will require a full or expedited RIA. Also, when there is an immediate and serious risk to the health and safety of Canadians, their security, the environment, or the economy, the Triage Statement may be omitted and an expedited RIA process may be allowed.

Box 5.2. **Threshold tests to apply in-depth impact assessments** (*cont.*)

Mexico operates a quantitative test to decide whether to require a RIA for draft primary and subordinate regulation. Regulators and line ministries must demonstrate zero compliance costs in order to be exempt of RIA. Otherwise, a RIA must be carried out. For ordinary RIAs comes a second test – qualitative and quantitative – what Mexico calls a "calculator for impact differentiation", where as a result of a 10 questions checklist, the regulation can be subject to a High Impact RIA or a Moderate Impact RIA, where the latter contains less details in the analysis.

The **USA** operates a quantitative test to decide to apply RIA for subordinate regulation. Executive Order 12866 requires a full RIA for economically significant regulations. The threshold for "economically significant" regulations (which are a subset of all "significant" regulations) is set out in Section 3(f)(1) of Executive Order 12866: "Have an annual effect on the economy of USD 100 million or more or adversely affect in a material way the economy, a sector of the economy, productivity, competition, jobs, the environment, public health or safety, or State, local, or tribal governments or communities".

Source: OECD (2015), *OECD Regulatory Policy Outlook*, forthcoming.

Administrative procedures

An administrative regulation, adopted in 2013, sets out the main procedures for drafting government legal acts and conducting quality checks before submitting proposals to the Cabinet of Ministers.[2] The regulation implements the provisions set out in the 2012 Law on the Basics of Legislation that identifies the guiding principles for preparing legislation (Box 5.3).

Box 5.3. **The 2012 Law on the Basics of Legislation**

Adopted on 18 September 2012, the Law No. XI-2220 on the Basics of Legislation establishes the principles and stages of legislation, rights and obligations of state and municipal institutions and other persons involved in the process of legislation. The law requires that all persons involved in the process of legislation must be guided by the following principles:

- necessity;
- proportionality and respect for rights and freedoms of an individual;
- openness and transparency;
- efficiency;
- clarity; and
- consistency.

Source: Art. 3, Sec. 2 of the Law on the Basics of Legislation, https://www.e-tar.lt/portal/lt/legalact/tar.b4fa4c56b8d5.

Legal quality

Specific technical requirements for legal drafting are set out in an order of the Ministry of Justice of December 2013.[3] These requirements apply to all institutions and agencies of the government (but not to independent entities like, for example, the

National Commission for Energy Control and Prices that regulates energy, drinking water supply and waste water treatment).

Draft laws and resolutions submitted to the government go through multiple legal checks:

- **The Ministry of Justice provides a legal opinion on all legislative proposals (law or resolutions) submitted to the government.** This opinion focuses on the legality of the proposals and the quality of legal drafting. The legal opinion does not assess in depth the 'appropriateness' of the regulatory choice and design, nor the 'effectiveness' in terms of costs and benefits.
- **Following the Ministry of Justice's legal opinion and any necessary modifications, the draft is submitted to the Legal Department of the Government Office for an additional checking on compliance with laws, government resolutions and technical legal requirements**. The draft is also examined on the subject matter by other units of the Government Office (Figure 5.3).
- Once the draft law is submitted to Parliament, **the Legal Department of the *Seimas* checks compliance of the draft with the laws which are already in effect and technical law-making requirements**.

Figure 5.3. **Government legal checks on draft legislation**

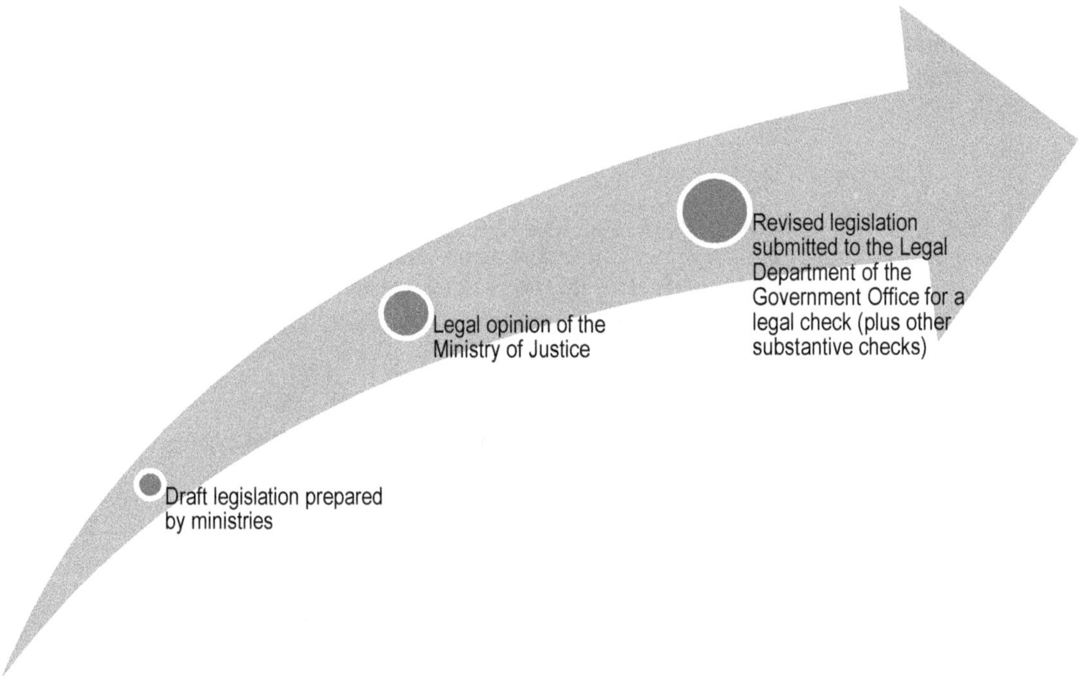

The role of the Ministry of Justice and the Government Office in checking legal quality changed over time. In 2009, the Legal Department of the Government Office was downsized and the main role in assessing the legality of draft legislation was assigned to the Ministry of Justice. In 2013, this decision was reversed and the role of the Government Office was restored.

Ex ante impact assessment of new regulation

Policy on regulatory impact assessment

Impact assessment was first introduced in 2003 as part of the reforms aimed at preparing Lithuania for EU accession (see Chapter 3 on regulatory reform and policies). A new impetus to support the use of impact assessment has come from the adoption of the Law on the Basics of Legislation in September 2012. Article 15 of the Law on the Basics of Legislation states that impact assessment must be conducted for all legislative initiatives that introduce new regulation or change legal regulation substantively. The provisions of the Law apply to all rule-making entities at all levels (national and sub-national).

The Law sets the following principles to guide the use of impact assessment:

- The extent and depth of impact assessment should be proportional to expected impacts: the decision to conduct the impact assessment will be taken by the sponsoring institution;
- Positive and negative impacts on the relevant sector as well as on individuals or groups of individuals affected by the draft regulation must be assessed.
- The assessment is expected to take into consideration impacts on:
  - the economy,
  - public finance;
  - social environment;
  - public administration;
  - legal system;
  - crime and corruption;
  - environment;
  - administrative burden;
  - regional development;
  - other relevant areas.

Any draft law, be it initiated by the government or the *Seimas*, has to be accompanied by an Explanatory Note that identifies, among other things, the objectives of the proposed legislation, its overall impacts, as well as impacts on the national and local budgets, business environment and corruption. Explanatory Notes also list the institutions and stakeholders consulted during the preparation of the draft. Explanation of impacts is mostly descriptive (Box 5.4).

Box 5.4. Explanatory note for draft legislation

A draft law submitted to the *Seimas*, with the exception of a draft law submitted by the citizens of the Republic of Lithuania implementing the right granted by the Constitution, shall be accompanied by an explanatory note which must indicate the following:

1. the reasons leading to the preparation of the draft, the objectives and goals of the prepared draft;
2. initiators of (institution, persons or representatives authorised by the citizens) and persons in charge of drafting a law;
3. the current legal framework regulating the issues considered in the draft law;
4. envisaged legal regulation provisions and expected positive results;
5. assessment results of the planned legal regulation impact (provided such an assessment must be carried out during the preparation of the draft law and its results are not presented in a separate document), potential negative consequences of the enacted law and the measures which should be taken to avoid these consequences;
6. effect of the enacted law on crime and corruption;
7. effect of the implementation of the law on business conditions and business development;
8. incorporation of the law into the legal system, the legal acts which must be adopted, the legal acts currently in force which must be amended or repealed upon adoption of the submitted draft;
9. the compliance of the draft law with the requirements of the Law on the State Language, the Law on Legislative Framework and the assessment of the definitions used in the draft and the terms referring to the definitions in accordance with the procedure laid down by the Law on the Term Bank and the legal acts implementing this Law;
10. the conformity of the draft law with the provisions of the European Convention for the Protection of Human Rights and Fundamental Freedoms and the European Union documents; and
11. those who should adopt secondary legislation, if necessary for the implementation of the law, and the time limits for adoption thereof.

Source: http://www3.lrs.lt/pls/inter3/dokpaieska.showdoc_l?p_id=492370.

Draft laws and resolutions prepared by ministries can also include a separate statement assessing regulatory impacts. This is not mandatory as impacts can be presented in the Explanatory Note. This statement is relatively short (a couple of pages even for relatively complex legislative proposals) and mostly descriptive. It covers overall impacts, fiscal impacts and administrative burden. There is no explicit requirement for the consideration of alternative options to the proposed legislation (Box 5.5).

Box 5.5. **Expected regulatory impact statement**

Title	
Responsible institution	
Objectives	
Impacts on relevant areas	
Public finance impacts	
Impacts on administrative burdens and other relevant areas	
Other information	

Source: https://www.e-tar.lt/portal/lt/legalact/tar.814f485eb18b/tais_474315.

Legislative proposals included in the Priority List of Legislative Initiatives – 14 in 2013 and 26 in 2014 – undergo a more in-depth Regulatory Impact Assessment (RIA). As of March 2015, 14 of them had been completed. These RIAs are more comprehensive: they include a wider range of impacts (e.g. social impacts and impacts on the public administration) and the consideration of alternative options (no action plus at least two options). The level and scope of quantification of the assessment can vary. An effort is made to use some data to back up the assessment of the problem and the proposed solutions. Nevertheless, the RIAs that have been conducted appear to include general descriptions of expected impacts with some quantification of administrative costs (but less developed analysis of other benefits and costs) (Box 5.6).

Box 5.6. **Regulatory impact assessment for priority legislative initiatives**

Priority item			
Institution			
Problem description			
Purpose		- Status quo - 1st Option - 2nd Option	
Impact on relevant sector		- Status quo - 1st Option - 2nd Option	
Impact on public finances		- Status quo - 1st Option - 2nd Option	
Impact on administrative burden			
Economic impact			
Other impacts	**Status quo**	**1st Option**	**2nd Option**
Social			
Public administration			
Regional development			
Legal system			
Crime			
Comparison of alternatives			
Proposed option and implementation			
Other information			

Source: https://www.e-tar.lt/portal/lt/legalact/tar.814f485eb18b/tais_474315.

Institutional framework

Policy

The Government Office is responsible for developing and co-ordinating impact assessment policy by:

- formulating the overall policy, requirements and methodologies;
- monitoring the quality of impact assessment of priority legislative initiatives;
- providing support and advice to public sector institutions conducting impact assessment.

Two staff members of the Strategic Planning and Monitoring Unit with background in law, economics and public management work full time on impact assessment. In addition, other sector units in the Government Office take part in the monitoring of the quality of impact assessments. The Strategic Planning and Monitoring Unit checks compliance with the policy and methodologies for impact assessment (e.g. consideration of alternatives, quality of evidence, etc.), whereas the sector units check policy content (e.g. alignment with government priorities, availability of alternatives, etc.) There is also a network of staff from other ministries who can be consulted and provide advice on the evaluation of impacts.[4]

The Ministry of Economy is responsible for developing methodologies for measuring the reduction of administrative burden on businesses and the Ministry of Interior is responsible for methodologies on measuring administrative burden on citizens.

Implementation

For legislative proposals that are not included in the priority list, the assessment of the impacts included in the Explanatory Note (or presented separately in a statement of expected regulatory impacts) is prepared by the ministry which drafts the proposed legislation. It is usually the ministry's department or unit in charge of the relevant policy area which is primarily responsible for the quality of the impact assessment. The ministry's legal department conducts a legal quality check of the draft legislation, including the explanatory note and the impact assessment, before the package – draft law or resolution, explanatory note and/or separate statement of expected regulatory impacts – is posted on the online legislative platform and other ministries and external stakeholders can provide comments. All ministries do not look at all draft legislation. The Rules of Procedure of the Government and other acts determines when a certain act must be sent to a specific ministry (in all other cases the drafting ministry decides with which ministry to consult). There is no specific check on the quality of these assessments of impact conducted by the Government Office beside the legal check conducted by the Legal Department. The absence of any specific control on the quality of the impacts included in the Explanatory Note appear to constitute a "missing opportunity" as it could help improve the quality of all legislation initiated by the government.

The process is different for the measures included in the Priority List. For these measures, responsible ministries prepare the RIA before the preparation of the draft legislation. Four institutions check the quality of the RIA:

- The Government Office for the overall quality of the impact assessment;
- The Ministry of Finance for the quality of assessment of fiscal impacts;

- The Ministry of Economy for the quality of impact assessment on the economy including competitiveness, SMEs and administrative burden on enterprises; and
- The Ministry of Interior for the quality of impact assessment on public management, administrative burden on citizens and central government and local government institutions and agencies.

Quality assurance institutions have 10 working days to review the impact assessment results and present their comments to the drafting institution. Final alternatives and impact assessment results are then presented to the government and discussed either in the Government Strategic Committee or the government (preparatory) meeting. Based on the decision of the government, the drafting institution prepares either a draft law or a non-regulatory measure. In practice, however, there is a tendency, even for these measures, to develop alternatives and a draft legal act at the same time, and to go for the regulatory measure. As of March 2015, all measures on the Priority list led to the preparation of a draft law and no one to the adoption of another measure.

Methodological guidance and training

Methodology and guidance

In 2012, the government approved the Methodology on Impact Assessment of Draft Legislative Acts, which serves as the main guide for government institutions preparing impact assessments. The Methodology includes questions to be considered when preparing impact assessment, covering:

- relevant area;
- public finance;
- administrative burden on citizens and central government and local government institutions and agencies;
- economy (including competitiveness, SMEs, administrative burden on enterprises);
- social environment;
- public management;
- environment;
- regional development;
- legal system;
- crime; and
- other areas where appropriate.

The Methodology recommends the use of Cost-Benefit Analysis (CBA) or Cost-Effectiveness Analysis (CEA), when possible. The Government Office developed specific guidance to help ministries apply CBA and CEA. In practice, CBA and CEA are rarely used when developing regulatory proposals, even for the more in-depth impact assessments for the proposals included in the Priority List, reflecting a general lack of analytical skills among civil servants.

The Ministry of Economy and the Ministry of Interior developed methodological guidance on how to calculate administrative burden on businesses and citizens, based on the Standard-Cost Model. Both methodologies were adopted by the government and define the formulas to be used to calculate administrative burden.

When conducting impact assessment, ministries can outsource advice and analyses when they do not possess the required expertise or skills or face time constraints. The service is usually acquired through a public procurement procedure. Ministries responsible for sectors such as energy, environment, social protection or transport tend to rely on external advice.

Training

The Government Office leads training on the overall approach to impact assessment. Between 2009 and 2011, about 120 civil servants – staff developing regulations and heads of strategic planning units – were trained in impact assessment. Training covered:

- process of *ex ante* impact assessment (steps and participants, principles, impact assessment aspects);
- main methods and cost-benefit analysis;
- *ex post* impact assessment (steps and methods, design of *ex post* impact assessment).

Upon request of the institution preparing the RIA, the Government Office can organise discussions with some quality assurance institutions (Ministry of Finance, Ministry of Economy, and Ministry of Interior). In addition, the institution preparing the RIA can collaborate separately with each quality assurance institution (it is, for example, common practice to discuss the RIA with the Government Office in the last stages of the preparation of the RIA).

The Ministry of Economy also organises special trainings/seminars on how to identify and measure administrative burdens for businesses. Training sessions have taken place at least once a year for state and municipality institutions. Further support is given to civil servants via telephone, e-mail or live consultations on concrete measurement issues and questions. In order to stimulate administrative burden reduction at municipal level, the Ministry of Economy will train officials from all municipalities in the course of 2015. The trainings are organised in the main Lithuanian cities in the centre of a region, inviting municipalities of that region.

Training on impact assessment is an optional module in the initial training for newly-recruited civil servants.

Public consultation and communication

The ministry responsible for drafting the legislation decides whether public consultation is necessary given the scope of the proposal. It also decides on the extent of consultation. Moreover, the Methodology on Impact Assessment stipulates that public consultation can be arranged at different stages of impact assessment: when defining the problem, formulating the goals or regulation alternatives, assessing the impact of alternatives, etc.

In practice, ministries tend to consult with stakeholders through formal and informal working groups and networks, sometimes also in the early stages of preparation of the draft legislation. However, feedback from stakeholders appears to be sought more to confirm a preferred option rather than to identify and evaluate different options. The Explanatory Note provides too little information and data to engage stakeholders in a constructive discussion on the impacts of the proposed legislation (with the view of improving its provisions).

Evaluation of progress

The Government Office is conducting a review of the impact assessment process in consultation with the other institutions, in order to take stock of the use of impact assessment. Results are expected to be presented to the government in mid-2015. As of March 2015, the Government Office was preparing a questionnaire to be circulated among the quality assurance institutions (the Ministries of Finance, Economy and Interior).

Alternatives to regulation

There is no explicit policy encouraging the use of alternative to regulation such as certification, covenants, general rules as an alternative to permits. The Methodology on Impact Assessment of Draft Legislative Acts requires providing several options to solve identified problems but does not provide any guidance on possible non-regulatory options.

Risk-based approaches

When checking the quality of impact assessment, the Government Office may ask institutions to assess the risks in implementing different options. However, risk assessment is not systematically used and legislation is generally not based on risk analysis or any systematic focus on activities relating to business and citizens with a high risk profile.

Notes

1. Under Article 68 of the Constitution, citizens also have the right to submit legislative proposals, provided that a draft is supported by at least 50 000 signatures. However, laws stemming from citizens' proposals are rare.
2. Government Resolution No. 337 "Regarding Adoption of the Rules of Procedure of the Government of the Republic of Lithuania", 17 April 2013.
3. Order of the Minister of Justice No. 1R-298 of 23 December 2013.
4. www.lrv.lt/lt/veikla/poveikio-vertinimas/kontaktiniai-asmenys/.

Bibliography

OECD (2015), *OECD Regulatory Policy Outlook*, forthcoming

OECD (2012), "Recommendation of the Council on Regulatory Policy and Governance", www.oecd.org/gov/regulatory-policy/2012recommendation.htm.

Chapter 6

The management and rationalisation of existing regulations in Lithuania

This chapter examines regulatory policies focused on the management of the "stock" of regulations, including initiatives to simplify the existing stock of regulations, and initiatives to reduce burdens which administrative requirements impose on businesses, citizens and the administration itself.

Reducing administrative burdens

Major part of the efforts of the Lithuanian government focuses, as in many OECD countries, on administrative burden reduction, mainly the ones on businesses. However, there are also projects on reviewing licences, improving enforcement and implementation, and some basic policies for more systematic *ex post* reviews of regulations. E-government plays an important role in administrative simplification, however, there is a need for better co-ordination with the simplification projects.

Reducing administrative burdens on businesses

The Lithuanian government adopted a Better Regulation Programme in 2008. Its main focus was on administrative burden reduction on businesses and prevention, as well as simplification of licences and permits, as it was launched in parallel with a similar programme at the EU level run by the European Commission. In the first phase of the programme, information obligations stemming from national legislation were mapped. The European Council imposed an obligation on EU Member States to set a national quantitative target to reduce administrative burdens on business in 2009. In reaction to this, the Lithuanian government set this target as a 30% reduction by the end of 2011, and identified the following priority areas for administrative burden on business reduction: *i)* tax administration; *ii)* employment relations; *iii)* statistics; *iv)* environmental protection; *v)* transport; *vi)* real estate transactions and *vii)* territorial planning and construction. The target is in fact 5% higher than in most of the EU Member States which usually adopted a 25% reduction target, similarly to the European Commission.

After mapping the information obligations stemming from regulations conducted in 2008-09, the measurement was conducted in 2010-11, with resources from the project "*Assessment of Administrative Burdens, Improvement of the Quality and Efficiency of Legal Regulation and Strengthening of Administrative Capacities in the Context of Better Regulation*" mostly financed through the European Social Fund. As in most EU Member States, a methodology, based on a modification of the internationally recognised Standard Cost Model, was used to measure administrative burdens in monetary terms.

The Ministry of Economy, based on the results of the measurement and in co-operation with other participating ministries, has prepared legislative proposals aiming at reducing administrative burdens in the seven priority areas in 2012. By adopting these measures, the 30% reduction target would have been achieved and administrative burdens for businesses would be reduced significantly in Lithuania. Unfortunately, the proposals have been mostly abandoned by the *Seimas*. This has led to a fact that so far, only 5% reduction of administrative burdens has been achieved.

The biggest issue among the aforementioned simplification proposals seems to be simplification of information obligations stemming from the Labour Code. Since the government decided to adopt a new Labour Code in the meantime, it has been decided not to amend it before a new draft is prepared.

Beside the fact that the *Seimas* did not adopt proposed legislative measures, insufficient horizontal co-ordination inside the government has also contributed to failing to achieve the ambitious burden reduction target. The project was co-ordinated by the Ministry of Economy. This decision was, however, not accompanied by strengthening competences of the Ministry in co-ordinating the project and putting pressure on other ministries to contribute to achieving this goal. Other line ministries did not feel an ownership of the project and were, especially in the beginning, reluctant to provide simplification proposals to the Ministry of Economy. In fact, in the first stages of the projects, when asked to come up with simplification proposals, line ministries suggested only minimal changes that would not lead to any meaningful reductions. Therefore, an external consultancy company had to be hired to come up with more valuable simplification proposals and communicate them with responsible ministries.

At the end, a consensus was achieved and proposals which would lead to meeting the 30% reduction target were developed and submitted to the government. This however started another round of negotiations, during which many proposals were refused or watered down. These rather disappointing results led to a frustration among those civil servants participating in the project as well as among stakeholders who might think that the government is not serious about its promises to reduce administrative burdens.

The programme on reducing administrative burdens has received a new boost from the new government through the adoption of a Law on Administrative Burden Reduction that came into force on 1st of July 2013 (with some amendments in January 2014). This law established a new Better Regulation Supervisory Commission consisting of 19 representatives of state administration (newly, the Association of Local Authorities is also represented) and stakeholders (Lithuanian Confederation of Industrialists, Public Policy and Management Institute, Lithuanian Business Confederation, Lithuanian Lawyers Association, The Council of Small and Medium-sized Business, Association "Investors forum", Lithuanian Free Market Institute, Lithuanian Tourism Association, Lithuanian Business Employer's Confederation, Lithuania Industry, Trade and Crafts Association). The Commission's institutional composition is approved by the Governmental resolution, concrete representatives are appointed by the Prime Minister's resolution. The Commission, established in 2014, is supposed to provide the government with proposals on administrative simplification based on its own ideas and evaluation of proposals received from other parties. The first batch of proposals has been incorporated into the Administrative burden reduction plan for 2014-15.

In theory, this Commission has also a right to evaluate legislative drafts submitted to the government from the point of view of potential administrative burdens. This right has not been used so far.

The new law also sets an obligation to prepare and submit to the government (and subsequently the parliament) the two-year Administrative Burden Reduction Plans. First of these plans for 2014-15 including 92 simplification measures was approved by the government on 22 July 2014.[1] The plan includes concrete measures such as simplification of the licensing regime in the area of gambling and lotteries, simplification of the application for a temporary residence permit when arriving to Lithuania for work related purpose, simplification of the process of declaring insolvency, etc. Each measure includes a specific deadline for implementation as well as a ministry responsible for implementation.

In addition, the law introduces an obligation for municipalities to reduce administrative burdens stemming from local regulation. It is, however, not clear how this obligation should be enforced, though government representatives in the regions are supposed to monitor the implementation of this obligation. Since municipal administrations are independent from the central administration, the government does not have any lever to put pressure on municipalities to comply with this obligation. In December 2014, the Ministry of Economy asked municipalities to submit information about administrative burden reduction in municipalities. The results show that 41 municipality out of 60 have administrative burden reduction plans or include reduction measures into municipality strategic plans. It is, however, not fully clear to what extent municipalities take this obligation seriously.

Administrative burdens are also assessed *ex ante* when developing new legislative drafts. As of July 2014, any change of the level of administrative burdens must be expressed in monetary terms every time the new draft law or resolution changes, eliminates or creates an information obligation for business. A burden evaluation report must accompany the draft as part of RIA and must be submitted to the Ministry of Economy for a review.

The Government Resolution of 22 July 2014 also introduced another very interesting measure. It has set an obligation to each individual ministry or state administration agency with regulatory powers not to increase the overall level of administrative burdens caused by regulation in the ministry's competence in any given calendar year. This, in fact, is a form of a "one-in one-out" approach, a measure that has been recently introduced in several OECD countries (see Box 6.1). Interestingly enough, this measure is not presented by the government as a "one-in one-out" approach but rather as a new reduction target (ministries each calendar year should not increase but are advised to reduce the level of administrative burdens).

Box 6.1. **One-for-One Rule in Canada**

In response to the Red Tape Reduction Commission's *Recommendations Report: Cutting Red Tape...Freeing Business to Grow*, the Canadian government introduced a bill to enshrine the One-for-One Rule into legislation on 29 January 2014 to control the administrative burden on business.

Through the One-for-One Rule, the government is reducing the administrative burden in two ways:

1. When a new or amended regulation increases the administrative burden on business, regulators are required to offset – from their existing regulations – an equal amount of administrative burden cost on business.
2. It requires regulators to remove a regulation each time they introduce a new regulation that imposes new administrative burden on business.
   - Regulators are required to provide offsets within two years of receiving final approval of regulatory changes that impose new administrative burden on business.
   - The value of the administrative burden cost savings or cost increases to business are made public in the Regulatory Impact Analysis Statement when the regulatory change is published in the Canada Gazette.

Canada was the first country to give such a rule the weight of legislation.

Box 6.1. **One-for-One Rule in Canada** (*cont.*)

Guidelines and tools are available to help departments and agencies implement these new requirements. To demonstrate results to business and to Canadians, an Annual Scorecard Report is published on the systemic regulatory reforms the government is putting in place, particularly on the implementation of the One-for-One Rule, the small business lens, and service standards for high volume regulatory authorisations. The Scorecard Report is posted on the Treasury Board of Canada Secretariat's website annually. The Scorecard is reviewed by the Regulatory Advisory Committee and then provided to the Auditor General. The Treasury Board of Canada Secretariat's Regulatory Affairs Sector is leading the implementation of this systemic reform.

Source: www.tbs-sct.gc.ca/rtrap-parfa/ofo-upu-eng.asp (accessed on 26 March 2015).

Implementation of this measure seems to be, however, rather weak. It is not clear how the government plans to enforce such cap on administrative burdens. The amendment to the Methodology for Determining the Administrative Burden of Business of 22 July 2014 stipulates that the Ministry of Economy is "responsible for the supervision of the change in overall level of administrative burden on businesses". It will also annually report to the government, based on evaluations submitted to the ministry by individual ministries/agencies. However, the ministry does not seem to have the necessary teeth to enforce it *vis-à-vis* other ministries. Given that the Ministry of Economy is "only" one of the line ministries, it might be difficult for it to put pressure on other line ministries or agencies not to increase administrative burdens stemming from regulations in their area of competence. It is also not clear what the government will do when a ministry decides to increase administrative burdens without offsetting. The competence for monitoring and enforcement of the cap should be given to an institution closer to the centre of government as it is the case in other countries using a similar approach to limiting the increase of administrative burdens. The government should also demonstrate its determination not to pass any new laws causing an increase of administrative burdens wherever the drafting ministry will not clearly state where and how these burdens would be off-set. A mechanism for an independent control of the quality of the evaluations of administrative burdens submitted by individual ministries should also be created.

Given the past negative experience with horizontal goals for reducing administrative burdens for the administration as such, the cap is now set for each ministry individually. Therefore, it is not possible that an increase of administrative burdens, if deemed necessary, caused by new regulation in the competence of one ministry can be off-set by a reduction of administrative burdens stemming from regulations in the competence of other ministry(ies). Although the reasons for such decision are understandable, this might cause problems in the future whenever there is a need to adopt important laws that might increase administrative burdens. It might be therefore useful to consider setting some situations (government priorities, when the off-set would be enabled.

Furthermore, there seem to be problems in communicating this measure across the administration. In fact, at the time of the review, many ministries interviewed were not aware of this cap and therefore were not able to provide the review team with a description of mechanisms to ensure compliance with it.

In January 2015, the Ministry of Economy presented the government with information on the evaluation of the change in the overall level of administrative burdens on business for 2014. The calculation involves legal acts that were adopted between

22 July 2014 and 31 December 2014. The results show that in 2014, the administrative burdens for businesses were reduced by EUR 1.85 million. Seven institutions reduced administrative burdens in their area of competence, in case of 6 institutions the overall level of administrative burdens did not change, but 4 institutions actually increased the level of administrative burdens. Eighteen institutions had not amended or adopted any legal acts, influencing administrative burdens.

Reducing administrative burdens on citizens

In parallel with reducing administrative burdens on businesses, the Lithuanian Ministry of Interior introduced several initiatives on reducing administrative burdens on citizens. The Methodology for measurement and reduction of administrative burden for citizens was developed based on the Standard Cost Model, providing guidelines for public institutions on how to measure administrative burden on citizens and indicating possibilities of qualitative evaluation of administrative burdens on citizens. The Ministry of the Interior organised trainings and seminars on practical use of the methodology for public institutions.

Ex post *reviews of regulations*

The large stock of regulations and administrative formalities accumulated over time needs regular review and updating to weed out obsolete or inefficient material. Approaches vary from consolidation, codification, recasting, repeal, guillotine rule (nullifying rules that are not centrally registered by a certain deadline, which can be triggered by governments finding out that they are unable to compile a list of regulations in force), ad hoc reviews of the regulations covering specific sectors, and sunsetting mechanisms for the automatic review or cancellation of regulations past a certain date. The concept of simplification can also be extended to the need to modernise existing rules in order to adapt regulatory frameworks to changing societal needs and technological developments. A typology of regulatory reviews is described in Box 6.2.

Box 6.2. **Approaches to regulatory reviews**

The Productivity Commission issued a Research Report that lists a number of good design features for each review approach which help ensure that they work effectively, drawn from Australian and international good practices. The Commission considered the following main approaches:

Stock management approaches (have an ongoing role that can be regarded as 'good housekeeping'):

- *Regulator-based strategies* refer to the way regulators interpret and administer the regulations for which they are responsible – for instance through monitoring performance indicators and complaints, with periodic reviews and consultation to test validity and develop strategies to address any problems. Ideally, the use of such mechanisms is part of a formal continuous improvement programme conducted by the regulator.
- *Stock-flow linkage rules* work on the interface between *ex ante* and *ex post* evaluation. They constrain the flow of new regulation through rules and procedures linking it to the existing stock. Although not widely adopted, examples of this sort are the "regulatory budget" and the "one-in one-out" approaches.

Box 6.2. Approaches to regulatory reviews (*cont.*)

- *Red tape reduction targets* require regulators to reduce existing compliance costs by a certain percentage or value within a specified period of time. Typically, they are applied to administrative burdens reduction programmes.

Programmed review mechanisms (examine the performance of specific regulations at a specified time, or when a well-defined situation arises):

- *Sunsetting* provides for an automatic annulment of a statutory act after a certain period (typically five to ten years), unless keeping the act in the books is explicitly justified. The logic can apply to specific regulations or to all regulations that are not specifically exempted. For sunsetting to be effective, exemptions and deferrals need to be contained and any regulations being re-made appropriately assessed first. This requires preparation and planning. For this reason, sunsetting is often made equivalent to introducing *review clauses*.
- *"Process failure" post implementation reviews (PIR)* (in Australia) rest on the principle that *ex post* evaluation should be performed on any regulation that would have required an *ex ante* impact assessment. The PIR was introduced with the intention of providing a 'fail-safe' mechanism to ensure that regulations made in haste or without sufficient assessment — and therefore having greater potential for adverse effects or unintended consequences — can be re-assessed before they have been in place too long.
- Through *ex post review requirements in new regulation*, regulators outline how the regulation in question will be subsequently evaluated. Typically, this exercise should be made at the stage of the preparation of the RIA. Such review requirements may not provide a full review of the regulation, but are particularly effective where there are significant uncertainties about certain potential impacts. They are also used where elements of the regulation are transitional in nature, and can provide reassurance where regulatory changes have been controversial.

Ad hoc and special purpose reviews (take place as a need arises):

- *"Stocktakes" of burdens on business* are prompted or rely on business' suggestions and complaints about regulation that imposes excessive compliance costs or other problems. This process can be highly effective in identifying improvements to regulations and identifying areas that warrant further examination, but their very complaint-based nature might limit the scope of the review.
- *"Principles-based" review strategies* apply a guiding principle being used to screen all regulation for reform – for instance removal of all statutory provisions impeding competition (unless duly justified), or the quest for policy integration. Principles-based approaches involve initial identification of candidates for reform, followed up by more detailed assessments where necessary. Approaches of this kind are accordingly more demanding and resource-intensive than general stocktakes. But if the filtering principle is robust and reviews are well conducted, they can be highly effective.
- *Benchmarking* can potentially provide useful information on comparative performance, leading practices and models for reform across jurisdictions and levels of government. Because it can be resource-intensive, it is crucial that topics for benchmarking are carefully selected. Benchmarking studies do not usually make recommendations for reform, but in providing information on leading practices they can assist in identifying reform options.

Box 6.2. **Approaches to regulatory reviews** (*cont.*)

- *"In-depth" reviews* are most effective when applied to evaluating major areas of regulation with wide-ranging effects. They seek to assess the appropriateness, effectiveness and efficiency of regulation – and to do so within a wider policy context, in which other forms of intervention may also be in the mix. In the Australian context, extensive consultation has been a crucial element of this approach, including through public submissions and, importantly, the release of a draft report for public scrutiny. When done well, in-depth reviews have not only identified beneficial regulatory changes, but have also built community support, facilitating their implementation by government.

Source: OECD (2015), *OECD Regulatory Policy Outlook*, forthcoming.

There are some general requirements set by the Law on the Basics of Legislation to conduct monitoring and reviews of existing regulations. The following should be taken into account when reviewing existing regulations: *i)* effectiveness of the measures set out in the legislation in achieving the objectives of the regulation; *ii)* positive impacts and adverse effects on the regulated area and other areas (economy, public finances, social environment, public administration, legal framework, scope of corruption, environment, administrative burdens, regional development etc.) as well as on the regulated subjects; *iii)* direct and indirect benefits stemming from regulations and the beneficiaries; *iv)* conformity of the regulatory impacts with the planned objectives; *v)* necessity for amending or abolishing the regulation. Monitoring and reviews of existing regulations should be conducted by central and municipal administration institutions in the areas of their competence.

There is a lack of evidence on to what extent such reviews are conducted systematically and regularly by line ministries. Based on the interviews conducted by the review team, these reviews take place rather occasionally, ad hoc and without any systemic approach (with the exception of the licensing review).

In addition, according to the Law on the Basics of Legislation, the Ministry of Justice issued the Description of Procedure for Conducting the Monitoring of Legal Regulation[2] on 8 May 2013 as a ministerial order. This document launched a programme of *ex post* reviews of regulations, setting out the objectives, terms and conditions for such reviews and identifying regulations to be reviewed. According to the order, the reviews are performed when it is necessary in the view of the government's programme; the priorities set by the government; strategic plans and annual action plans of ministries and other institutions; in the light of evaluation of emerging issues; following substantive changes in the regulated area or under other circumstances.

The Ministry of Justice plays a co-ordinating and methodological role but the line ministries are responsible for conducting the reviews. The respective law is rather vague on how the reviews should be conducted and which institutions are obliged to conduct such reviews and at which point of the lifecycle of regulation. The Ministry does not actively promote regulatory reviews in a sense of putting pressure on other ministries to review regulations in their area of competence. The ministry is only gathering information from other ministries on the number of reviews in particular areas. This information is then published in an annual report; however, this report does not contain any information on the results of the reviews. In 2014, 22 regulations were reviewed. This has lead so far to an amendment of one legal act, two amendments are currently pending in the *Seimas*. Ten more legal acts should be amended based on these reviews.

Individual pieces of legislation are usually reviewed, not whole regulatory frameworks or sets of regulations (e.g. regulations in the environmental sector). The review of licences or the administrative burden reduction efforts is an impressive exception.

According to the Description of Procedure for Conducting the Monitoring of Legal Regulation, ministries are allowed to create *ad hoc* working groups for *ex post* reviews of regulations in which other institutions and also NGOs, academics, think tanks, interest groups and other stakeholders would be represented. There are no strict requirements for stakeholder engagement in regulatory reviews and the composition of such working groups is a discretionary competence of the line ministries. Stakeholder input is heavily relied upon in case of administrative simplification and administrative burden reduction. In 2009-11, the Sunrise Commission, partly comprised of business association representatives, worked with the Ministry of Economy. This Commission helped to review nine economic sectors, looking for suggestions for simplification and burden reduction. The Better Regulation Supervisory Commission was created in 2014 to foster greater co-operation between main regulating institutions and stakeholder groups (business, academic and not-for profit entities) in an attempt to find further ways to reduce regulatory burdens.

The approach to *ex post* reviews of regulations should be made more systemic. There is a need for a whole-of-government programme with clearly set goals and a timeline. These efforts should be co-ordinated from one centre which should also be responsible for checking the quality of these reviews, adherence to the timeline and should be also providing methodological guidance and assistance to the involved ministries. The methodology should be preferable based on the Regulatory Impact Assessment methodology. In addition, to be able to assess performance, or "fitness" of regulations *ex post*, their goals need to be clearly set *ex ante*. Some examples of successful regulatory reviews are described in Box 6.3.

Box 6.3. Coping with the accumulation of regulatory impacts: The EC, Switzerland and the United States

Where evaluations are undertaken, the total impact of new regulations can be estimated on single regulation, on a sectoral level or in aggregate.

In the **United States**, the OMB's Office of Information and Regulatory Affairs (OIRA) must by law report annually to Congress on the expected costs and benefits of all new 'significant' regulation passed in the previous year.[1] To the extent possible, OMB commits to provide an estimate of the total annual benefits and costs (including quantifiable and non-quantifiable effects) of Federal rules and paperwork in the aggregate, by agency and agency programme, and by major law.

In 2012, OIRA the issued a two page Memorandum requiring agencies to engage in assessing the cumulative impact of their rules (US Government, 2012a). The memo follows EO 13563 of 2011. The goals of this effort should be to simplify requirements on the public and private sectors (especially SMEs); to ensure against unjustified, redundant, or excessive requirements; and ultimately to increase the net benefits of regulations.

To this end, the directive calls agencies to take nine steps, including engaging in early consultation; using Requests for Information and Advance Notices of Proposed Rulemaking to obtain public inputs; considering, in the analysis of costs and benefits, the relationship between

Box 6.3. **Coping with the accumulation of regulatory impacts: The EC, Switzerland and the United States** (*cont.*)

new regulations and regulations that are already in effect; and co-ordinating timing, content, and requirements of multiple rulemakings that are contemplated for a particular industry or sector.

The estimated annual benefits of major Federal regulations reviewed by OMB from 1 October, 2003 to 30 September 2013, for which agencies estimated and monetised both benefits and costs, are in the aggregate between USD 217 billion and USD 863 billion, while the estimated annual costs are in the aggregate between USD 57 billion and USD 84 billion (US Government, 2014, p. 1).

The **European Commission** has also embarked in a similar exercise when it launched its Regulatory Fitness and Performance programme (REFIT), with a view to make EU law simpler and to reduce regulatory costs.[2] The differences with the OMB review are nonetheless remarkable – REFIT it is not grounded in a legal base; the Commission has no obligation to report annually to the European Parliament; and the scope of the review focuses on regulatory burdens on business.

In June 2014, the Commission reported on the progress in implementing REFIT and proposed a number of new initiatives for simplification and burden reduction, repeals of existing legislation and withdrawals of proposals pending in legislative procedure (EU 2013; 2014). Among the achievements so far are the withdrawal of 53 pending proposals in 2014 alone (and about 300 since 2006); and a reduction in administrative burdens by 33% since 2006 in 13 priority areas, leading to savings of EUR 41billion.

Switzerland completed in 2013 a comprehensive review of the regulatory costs affecting business, which stem from federal legislation. The review was prompted by an initiative of the federal parliament and covered thirteen main sectors. In the exercise, the Federal Council pioneered a new methodology in Switzerland – the so-called "Regulatory check-Up" – heavily inspired by the German RCM.[3]

This methodology seeks to capture various direct compliance costs, including staff and equipment costs as well as investment and financial costs. A key stage in the assessment process is the identification of the "action obligations" which firms must face when complying with a given regulation or legal framework. Relevant regulatory costs are calculated from the difference between the overall gross costs and the "business-as-usual costs". This implies setting an alternative (counterfactual) scenario, which describes the activities that firms would have undertaken in the absence of the regulation under review.

The evaluation exercise enjoyed the active and steady involvement of the stakeholders most directly affected by the regulation. On the basis of the findings, the Federal Council has identified more than thirty simplification measure for the period 2014-15.

1. See www.whitehouse.gov/omb/inforeg_regpol_reports_congress. The legal obligation upon OMB is enshrined in the US Regulatory Right-to-Know Act of 2000.

2. See http://ec.europa.eu/smart-regulation/refit/index_en.htm.

3. See www.seco.admin.ch/aktuell/00277/01164/01980/index.html?lang=fr&msg-id=51395.

Licensing reform

A screening of all licences and permits needed to start a business activity was launched in 2012. The Ministry of Economy was responsible for conducting this screening. The main goal was to screen all licences/permits in order to assess their necessity and proportionality, and to abolish the ones which are unnecessary and/or disproportionate. Another goal was to identify licences that could be replaced by simple declarations and also to review administrative procedures to obtain a licence or permit and to simplify them where possible by abolishing unnecessary requirements that are overly burdensome for businesses. Last but not least, the goal was also to ensure the possibility for businesses to complete all administrative procedures for obtaining a licence or permit from a distance, using electronic means.

A methodology was adopted by the Lithuanian government in 2012 (and amended in 2013) setting up principles for cases of business activities where licensing should be used as a regulatory measure and in which cases a simple declaration could be used.

In 2012-13, the Ministry of Economy reviewed around 423 licences, including those in the competence of other ministries (Ministry of Environment, Energy, Finance, Culture, Social Security and Labour, Health, Education and Science, Transport and Communications, Interior, Justice, Economy, Agriculture) and the Bank of Lithuania. At the beginning of 2014, the Ministry presented its suggestions on abolishing licensing and/or replacing them with declarations. These suggestions were approved by the government. The responsible ministries were tasked to draft the amendments of legal acts in their competence, following these approved recommendations. The responsible ministries drafted most amendments of legal acts in their competence by the end of 2014, with the few remaining amendments expected to be ready by mid-2015. In total, 56 laws will need to be amended. As of June 2015, 7 laws had been amended by the *Seimas,* with 11 more under discussion. The government prepared 32 draft amended laws for the submission to the *Seimas*, while the remaining 24 drafts are expected to be ready in the nearest future.

According to the proposals, after amending respective legislation, 9 business activities would no longer need licensing at all and 45 business activities could be started by simple submission of a declaration. For nearly 160 activities the authorisation procedures would be simplified.

ICTs and administrative simplification

There is a central government portal in Lithuania that should serve as a single point accesses to all public and administrative services for the citizens and businesses – the E-Government Gateway (www.epaslaugos.lt). All services provided by central government institutions as well as municipalities are accessible via this portal. Users can take advantage of the service classification system, which can be found on the homepage of the portal. The classification of users of the portal into groups – citizens, businesses, service providers – facilitate users' searches for a specific service.

A number of electronic services comprising the streamlining of complicated public administrative procedures by turning them into a user-friendly process based on the one-stop shop principle have been developed in Lithuania and have been operating successfully through the E-Government Gateway. The Gateway provides access to 566 public services. New electronic services in such areas as taxes, state social insurance, reports to police, legal entities registration, traffic information, libraries, services for patients and others, are being actively developed and more and more of these new services are presented to their users. According to statistics, the most popular electronic services are those related to income tax declaration, job search, healthcare, social security, personal documents issuing; and in case of businesses, the most popular services are the ones related to declaration of social contributions, declarations of income tax and submission of VAT declarations. The uptake of the electronic services in Lithuania is also increasing: in 2014, 41.5% of Lithuania's residents, and 100% of businesses, were using electronic services.[3]

ICT has also been used to simplify access of businesses and citizens to information on the regulatory framework. The Point of Single Contact for Services and Products (PSC) introduced in 2009 serves as a single point of contact in compliance with the EU Services Directive. It serves the following purposes:

- simplification of procedures for obtaining permits and licences to service providers and provision of full information about the requirements applied to their activities;
- ensuring access to concrete national rules for business with respect to the products which are not regulated by the EU in order to supply such products to the Lithuanian market.

Any relevant information on providing services and trading in Lithuania can be accessed through the PSC's website Business Gateway (www.verslovartai.lt/en/) both in Lithuanian and English. The website has a safe message box which enables businesses and entrepreneurs to send on-line their requests for obtaining permits to perform their activities and communicate directly with the competent authorities. PSC responds to the queries about the requirements applied to products or about competent authorities through the distant communication means: the website's information system. The Business Gateway is however not interconnected with the E-Government Gateway. In many cases, the website just provides information on regulations and administrative procedures, in some cases it enables to request a licence through the message box (basically an enhanced email service) and only in few cases the process is fully automatic allowing electronic submission of documents and obtaining a licence or a permit also electronically. The State Enterprise Centre of Registers – a public entity responsible for administering the three main state registers (i.e. Real Property Register and Cadastre, the Register of Legal Entities and the Address Register) – is developing an electronic licensing registry in order to administer in one place the data and information on all licences that have been issued. All public institutions issuing licences and using licensing information systems will have to submit their information on licences that have been issued, revised or withdrawn to this registry automatically starting on 1 September 2015

An important technological solution designed in Lithuania significantly contributing to the successful development of electronic services, is the Lithuania's State Information Resources Interoperability Platform (SIRIP). The platform enables data exchange between major public data registers and information systems, which is necessary for the provision of the majority of electronic administrative services. The E-Government Gateway is based on the SIRIP infrastructure. Public authorities can use SIRIP functionalities without implementing their own solutions for: centralised data exchange among public authorities, national and cross-border identification of citizens, business entities and civil servants, payments, e-service design (including testing environment), e-service monitoring, auditing and administrating, digital content management and e-service descriptions placement, e-messaging and e-document delivery. SIRIP connects 159 government institutions.

There are, in addition, several examples of electronic services provided in particular areas of public service, such as the E-Service System for Insurers (persons obliged to pay the state social insurance contributions) called EDAS established in 2008. EDAS allows the insurers to submit social insurance statements and applications electronically as well as to get information from the database of the State Social Insurance Fund Board. The Ministry of Finance's State Tax Inspectorate operates "My STI" – an electronic service website where taxpayers can find relevant information, e.g. on tax debts and overpayments, reminders about tax payments, as well as to provide or receive electronic documents, etc.

Several public services are provided through electronic means; however, the approach to providing electronic public services suffers from a lack of co-ordination among these different services. Many information systems of individual ministries are not interoperable. In addition, there is a lack of co-ordination between the administrative simplification efforts and those focusing on using ICTs and e-government approaches. Some examples of good co-ordination of administrative simplification and e-government efforts are described in Box 6.4.

Box 6.4. Co-ordination of administrative simplification and e-government

In Japan, the department promoting e-government is the Administrative Management Bureau (AMB) in the Ministry of Internal Affairs and Communications. It also holds jurisdiction over streamlining administrative organisation and method of administrative affairs.

ICT is a key support tool for the Action Plan on Administrative Burden Reduction in Sweden, linked to the government's policy on ICT for the public sector. The Action Plan assumes an extensive deployment of ICT, for example electronic filing of documents, one-stop shops, and forms for downloading from agency homepages.

In Slovenia, mixed project teams consisting of lawyers and information technicians are created for the main e-government projects. The aim is that the content is prepared as much as possible and in co-operation with implementing institutions.

The online administrative service system, Government for Citizen (G4C) in Korea offers various Internet-based administrative services such as receiving 1 200 types of paper applications, issuing 188 kinds of certificates – such as the certificate of residence – and providing information on 71 types of registration, for example property registration. In its upgraded version, the service items will be significantly increased to 4 000, 2 000 and 300 types respectively. Through these and other measures, Korea expects to save up to KRW 600 billion in costs and public benefit effects as less time and money will be spent by citizens' agency visits, civil service fees, paper work and management and public servant labour costs.

In Finland, e-government is seen as a key way to reduce administrative burdens and, consequently, the development of e-government has been explicitly included in the national action plan to reduce administrative burdens on businesses, as a horizontal priority area. On the other hand, the reduction of administrative burdens, both on businesses and citizens, is one of the objectives of the government's recent e-government development measures.

Source: OECD (2006), *Cutting Red Tape: National Strategies for Administrative Simplification,* Cutting Red Tape, OECD Publishing, Paris, http://dx.doi.org/10.1787/9789264029798-en.

Common Commencement Dates

Lithuania is applying a similar approach to the so called Common Commencement Dates implemented in some OECD countries (e.g. the United Kingdom, the Netherlands). According to the Law on the Basics of Legislation, legal acts modifying or setting new legal requirements for economic entities should usually enter into force on 1 May or 1 November; however, never sooner than three months following their official publication. This provision is not applied where a regulation is created or modified to implement the EU legislation, international agreements, and where a more favourable legal regulation is established for economic entities. Similarly, tax laws that set down new taxes, new tax tariffs, tax exemptions, sanctions for breaching tax laws or that essentially change the procedure for taxation shall enter into force no sooner than following six months after their official publication. This provision is not applied to laws amending taxation laws related to the law on the approval of financial indicators of the State budget and municipal budgets of the appropriate year, and to legal acts that harmonise Lithuania's national legislation with the legislation of the European Union or international treaties or are in fact beneficial for businesses.

According to a ministerial order issued by the Ministry of Justice on 17 December 2013, the institution presenting a legislative draft must, when publishing the document on Lithuanian legal acts information system, mark the draft with a special status stating that the draft "*regulates business environment*". However, since the order was issued only by the Ministry of Justice, not all institutions comply with it (e.g. the *Seimas*), therefore it is difficult to estimate how many draft legal acts actually "escape" the rule.

Notes

1. https://www.e-tar.lt/portal/lt/legalAct/af2bf32005da11e4b836947d492f2f50
2. The legal act available in Lithuanian at: http://www3.lrs.lt/pls/inter3/dokpaieska.showdoc_l?p_id=448316&p_tr2=2.
3. According to the information provided by the Ministry of Transport (partially based on data from the Eurostat).

Bibliography

Confédération Suisse (2013), "Rapport sur les coûts de la réglementation : Estimation des coûts engendrés par les réglementations et identification des possibilités de simplification et de réduction des coûts", www.news.admin.ch/NSBSubscriber/message/attachments/35609.pdf.

EU (2014), "Regulatory Fitness and Performance Programme", COM(2014)368final, http://ec.europa.eu/smart-regulation/docs/com2014_368_en.pdf.

EU (2013), "Regulatory Fitness and Performance (REFIT): Results and Next Steps", COM(2013)685final, http://ec.europa.eu/archives/commission_2010-2014/president/news/archives/2013/10/pdf/20131002-refit_en.pdf.

OECD (2015), *OECD Regulatory Policy Outlook*, forthcoming.

OECD (2012), "Recommendation of the Council on Regulatory Policy and Governance", www.oecd.org/gov/regulatory-policy/2012recommendation.htm.

OECD (2006), *Cutting Red Tape: National Strategies for Administrative Simplification,* Cutting Red Tape, OECD Publishing, Paris, http://dx.doi.org/10.1787/9789264029798-en.

Treasury Board of Canada Secretariat (2015), "The 2013–14 Scorecard Report: Implementing the Red Tape Reduction Action Plan", www.tbs-sct.gc.ca/rtrap-parfa/report-rapport/2013-14/asr-fea-eng.pdf.

US Office of Management and Budget (2014), "2014 Draft Report to Congress on the Benefits and Costs of Federal Regulations and Unfunded Mandates on State, Local, and Tribal Entities", https://www.whitehouse.gov/sites/default/files/omb/inforeg/2014_cb/draft_2014_cost_benefit_report-updated.pdf.

Chapter 7

Compliance, inspections and enforcement in Lithuania

This chapter considers the processes for ensuring compliance and enforcement of regulations. It looks at tools, approaches and principles that have been used and implemented to strengthen compliance and enforcement.

The baseline for reviewing inspection and enforcement reform

This chapter uses as reference point for assessing Lithuania's inspection and enforcement reform the eleven best-practice principles that the OECD has compiled, based on international experience (Box 7.1).

Box 7.1. The OECD Best Practice Principles for Regulatory Policy: Regulatory Enforcement and Inspections

1. Evidence based enforcement. Regulatory enforcement and inspections should be evidence-based and measurement-based: deciding what to inspect and how should be grounded on data and evidence, and results should be evaluated regularly.
2. Selectivity. Promoting compliance and enforcing rules should be left to market forces, private sector and civil society actions wherever possible: inspections and enforcement cannot be everywhere and address everything, and there are many other ways to achieve regulations' objectives.
3. Risk focus and proportionality. Enforcement needs to be risk-based and proportionate: the frequency of inspections and the resources employed should be proportional to the level of risk and enforcement actions should be aiming at reducing the actual risk posed by infractions.
4. Responsive regulation. Enforcement should be based on "responsive regulation" principles: inspection enforcement actions should be modulated depending on the profile and behaviour of specific businesses.
5. Long term vision. Governments should adopt policies on regulatory enforcement and inspections: clear objectives should be set and institutional mechanisms set up with clear objectives and a long-term road-map.
6. Co-ordination and consolidation. Inspection functions should be co-ordinated and, where needed, consolidated: less duplication and overlaps will ensure better use of public resources, minimise burden on regulated subjects, and maximise effectiveness.
7. Transparent governance. Governance structures and human resources policies for regulatory enforcement should support transparency, professionalism, and results-oriented management. Execution of regulatory enforcement should be independent from political influence, and compliance promotion efforts should be rewarded.
8. Information integration. Information and communication technologies should be used to maximise risk-focus, co-ordination and information-sharing – as well as optimal use of resources.
9. Clear and fair process. Governments should ensure clarity of rules and process for enforcement and inspections: coherent legislation to organise inspections and enforcement needs to be adopted and published, and clearly articulate rights and obligations of officials and of businesses.
10. Compliance promotion. Transparency and compliance should be promoted through the use of appropriate instruments such as guidance, toolkits and checklists.
11. Professionalism. Inspectors should be trained and managed to ensure professionalism, integrity, consistency and transparency: this requires substantial training focusing not only on technical but also on generic inspection skills, and official guidelines for inspectors to help ensure consistency and fairness.

Source: OECD (2014), *Regulatory Enforcement and Inspections*, OECD Best Practice Principles for Regulatory Policy, OECD Publishing, Paris, http://dx.doi.org/10.1787/9789264208117-en.

History and overview of inspection reform in Lithuania

Compliance and market access issues: EU accession and beyond

Effective inspections and enforcement regimes foster reliable compliance, and compliance (if regulations are adequately designed and "fit for purpose") in turn leads to improved outcomes in crucial areas such as safety of products on the market (both food and non-food), or environmental protection. As such, over the past couple of decades, the European Union has put an increasing focus on improving the effectiveness of enforcement regimes in existing and aspiring member states. This is particularly true in goods that are traded fully freely in the Single Market and with a significant risk level, such as food (for which the EU Food and Veterinary Office has a supervisory and advisory role over national authorities), but also increasingly non-food products (with increasingly developed guidance on market surveillance, to be now further strengthened as part of the new Product Safety and Market Surveillance Package). The EU has also been gradually developing its guidance on environmental inspections (the environment being by nature a cross-border issue), and a new framework on this topic is under development.

In line with this, the first phase of reforms affecting inspections and enforcement in Lithuania was part of the EU accession process. This resulted in particular in the set up of the State Food and Veterinary Service (SFVS), which has developed into one of the strongest and most forward-looking inspection agencies in Lithuania, as well as in the reform of the product safety system and the creation of the State Non-Food Products Inspectorate. Thus, reform and improvement work in the inspection and enforcement sphere has been going on for well over 10 years already.

This EU involvement allows assessing results in terms of social welfare for some of these functions, in particular for food safety. Successive reports by the EU FVO (2011-14) and the EFSA (2012-13) shows that Lithuanian "official controls" (inspections and enforcement, monitoring etc.) are in line with EU guidelines, and effective at securing good levels of food safety in the country, at the production and consumer levels. In other regulatory areas, however, evaluating results may be more difficult (reliable data is often difficult, or costly, to obtain), or improvements may be less satisfactory. Improving impact (and measurement) remains one of the priorities of reform.

Overview of the reform process: origins, development, current status

Following the onset of the global financial crisis and the elections of 2008 that brought a new coalition to office, the government embarked on a regulatory reform agenda. This aimed at facilitating business creation and growth (essential in a time of sharp economic contraction), reducing costs for the state or at a minimum maximising efficiency so as to "achieve more with less state resources" (crucial given budgetary austerity), and transforming relations between authorities on the one hand, and businesses and citizens on the other. The new approach to regulation intended to emphasise trust and compliance promotion rather than distrust and bureaucratic control.

Given the importance of inspections and enforcement issues in terms of administrative burden, investors' confidence, relations between private persons and the state (inspections being the primary "interface" between economic operators and the public administration), as well as budgetary costs (considering the large number of employees of inspection bodies), reforming inspections was, logically, one of the key priorities of this reform effort (along with licensing). The reform was led in particular by the Ministries of Justice and Economy, with strong direct personal engagement of the ministers themselves in the first years.

Preparation of the reform and consideration of possible directions started in 2009. The legal foundation for the reform, as well as some of the most important directions, were set first by a Government Resolution in May 2010 (subsequently amended and strengthened in 2011 and 2012), and by the adoption of amendments to the Law on Public Administration at the end of 2010. A new Chapter IV was added to this Law (originally adopted in 1999), covering "Supervision of Activities of Economic Entities" (the term "supervision" was consciously preferred to "inspection" as being broader and putting less emphasis on inspection visits, and more on an integrated approach to compliance promotion).

The reform team got inspiration for many of the reform's aspects from the United Kingdom's *Hampton* principles (Box 7.2), and proceeded to implement them – in some ways more radically or consistently than in the United Kingdom (which the centralised system of inspections in Lithuania made easier). The government got some limited international assistance starting 2011 (mostly from World Bank Group experts – with lack of funding limiting the scope and depth of such input), but the reform in its original impulse and design was a home-grown initiative. The Lithuanian reform team looked at the problems of the country, at existing international experience, and these efforts resulted in the revised Law on Public Administration.

Box 7.2. **The Hampton Principles**

Sir Philip Hampton's 2005 review, "Reducing administrative burdens: effective inspection and enforcement" considered how to reduce unnecessary administration for businesses. The Hampton Review set out some key principles that should be consistently applied throughout the regulatory system:

- regulators, and the regulatory system as a whole, should use comprehensive risk assessment to concentrate resources on the areas that need them most;
- regulators should be accountable for the efficiency and effectiveness of their activities, while remaining independent in the decisions they take;
- no inspection should take place without a reason;
- businesses should not have to give unnecessary information, nor give the same piece of information twice;
- the few businesses that persistently break regulations should be identified quickly and face proportionate and meaningful sanctions;
- regulators should provide authoritative, accessible advice easily and cheaply;
- regulators should be of the right size and scope, and no new regulator should be created where an existing one can do the work; and
- regulators should recognise that a key element of their activity will be to allow, or even encourage, economic progress and only to intervene when there is a clear case for protection.

Source: "Assessing our Regulatory System – The Hampton Review", Department for Business Innovation and Skills (2005), http://webarchive.nationalarchives.gov.uk/20121212135622/http://www.bis.gov.uk/policies/better-regulation/improving-regulatory-delivery/assessing-our-regulatory-system.

The Law on Public Administration: Chapter on supervision

The provisions of the chapter on supervision included in the law are comprehensive as well as, in many ways, highly innovative in the emphasis they put on providing guidance and assured advice to economic entities. In spite of some shortcomings (mostly on the questions of "non-routine" inspections, as well as the lack of definition of, and emphasis on, risk), these provisions remain among the best internationally for primary legislation covering inspections. The ways in which the law's new provisions change the focus from "inspecting" to "promoting compliance" are, in particular, worth studying and imitating for other countries, including OECD member states with a longer history of regulatory reform.

In terms of scope, the law defines "supervision" as consisting of:

- Provision of consultations (put first on purpose)
- Inspection visits
- Analysis of available information
- Enforcement measures.

Noteworthy is thus the way in which inspections and enforcement are not anymore seen as the exclusive ways to implement legislation, but as complementary tools alongside advice (which comes first), and analytical work.

The principles set forth by the law include:

- Burden minimisation and strict proportionality of inspection and enforcement measures – in line with international best practice (and recently adopted OECD principles).
- Neutrality and Transparency (which align very well with procedural justice considerations, see previous section).
- Planning of inspections (this is the principle where the law is weakest because it does not clarify the basis for such planning, which in good practice should be the risk level).
- Functional separation of inspection and sanctions (a practice which limits the scope for abuses of discretion, and helps spread new approaches to enforcement – it has been recommended e.g. by the World Bank Group in many transition economies, and recently introduced in France for labour inspections).
- Requirement for supervising institutions to provide methodological assistance to economic entities – this particularly important principle is one of the crucial innovations of the law.
- Risk assessment and risk focus as foundations for inspections. The actions of supervision institutions should concentrate on establishments presenting the highest risk, defined as the combination of the likelihood and potential magnitude of harm. The definition of "harm" takes into account any harm to values of any kind protected by applicable legal norms. This is quite a broad definition and it will require practical guidance to avoid inspection institutions taking too vague an interpretation of it. It is worth considering narrowing the definition (through secondary legislation) so it focuses primarily on health, safety, the environment, and some fundamental public goods (including state revenue).

The most advanced and innovative part of the law, compared to other examples of primary or secondary legislation applying to inspections and enforcement, is the article dealing with consultations (guidance). First, because providing advice is squarely defined as a priority for supervision (inspection and enforcement) agencies (in line, again, with best practice and OECD principles) – whereas this is a role that, in many countries, is still debated. Second, because the law foresees that advice officially provided is to some extent "binding" on inspection agencies: if an economic entity acts in compliance with such advice (be it directly provided by an authorised inspectorate staff, or officially published), it cannot be subject to sanctions if later on this advice it is found to have been incorrect (which of course does not mean that the economic entity will not have to fix whichever problems exist – only that it will not be sanctioned for what is a good faith mistake, where it followed official advice). The law does provide a few (reasonable) exceptions, but this rule remains quite ground breaking. This type of "assured advice" is something that has been discussed in a few countries (including the United Kingdom), but has mostly been resisted by state administrations for fear of the liability it puts on them. Lithuania has made it a reality. This norm has also been the foundation for the development of inspectorates' call centres (see further in this chapter), in order to ensure that advice and guidance provided are of consistent quality (given the binding nature of this advice).

On inspections visits themselves, the law leaves some of the specifics to secondary legislation, in particular methods for planning and for inspection visits, which are to be developed by each inspectorate. While this is not unusual (and much has been done on this front, as evidenced in the next section), it remains a weakness that the law does not define very clearly the foundation on which both should be developed. There are important norms on inspections that are directly in the law, however: the requirement to announce "routine" inspections in advance (at least 10 days), as well as to have a methodology to define the frequency of planned inspections (even though, again, "risk" is missing). The list of admissible grounds for "non-routine" inspections is also limited, but in a way that is vague and fails to link it to risk considerations. This is one of the weakest aspects of the law. The recently adopted amendments (November 2014) have introduced risk assessment as a fundamental principle of inspections planning. This is a very welcome development. Logically, this should apply to all inspections and simultaneously provide greater clarity on how to target "non-routine" inspections, develop better checklists and planning methods etc. It remains to be seen how the amendments will be implemented. Secondary legislation clarifying and specifying how to understand and apply the provision of the law, which is worded very broadly (defining risk as the probability and magnitude of any type of harm to any kind of values protected by law), would be very useful.[1]

The law also introduces important changes regarding sanctions:

- During the first year of operations, sanctions that lead to operations of the economic entity being suspended should not be imposed (except in demonstrated emergencies)
- Sanctions (their volume, level etc.), or the number of identified violations, should in no way be used as performance indicators for inspectorates.
- On 1 January 2015 amendments to the Law on Public Administration entered into force, introducing and defining the term "minor legal violation". A minor violation is defined as one that causes only little harm to the protected goods and values. In the case of a minor violation an inspector issues only a verbal note if

the violation can be remedied immediately while he is present, or he issues a written note to remedy the violation within a reasonable period of time. A fine is not imposed. This is a welcome improvement, and in line with changes in practices that hitherto were only grounded in secondary legislation, and thus were relatively fragile and open to challenges.

Both points are perfectly in line with the efforts to make inspectorates more effective at promoting compliance, while also being more supportive of economic growth.

The law has a number of other positive and important norms. These include:

- Requirements for annual reporting on performance by inspectorates (which have to include details on their compliance-promotion work, on compliance levels, and on issues in legislation which they recommend to address, based on their "real life experience").
- The obligation for inspectorates to post information on their websites on their field of competence, norms to be respected by businesses etc.
- A "tell it only once" norm, giving the right to economic entities to refuse to submit information to an inspectorate if they have already submitted it to another state body (in which case they should indicate which one) – however, the norm is less strong than a comparable one in Italy which specifically makes it an offense for an official to ask for a certificate (official document) issued by the state, and thus puts the onus on public officials being banned from asking twice, rather than businesses having the right to opt out.

The rules are directly applicable to all inspectorates except for the rules on inspections (e.g. advance notification etc.) that are not directly applicable to those dealing with taxes, customs, supervision of financial services and supervision of competition (though they remain for them as "recommendations"). Overall, the legal framework is strong (and, in some cases, the law's provisions are being invoked directly in legal proceedings – thus it serves not only as a reform framework, but directly as giving new rights to economic entities). The rest of the reform process, the successes on the areas where the law was most innovative, as well as the limitations, demonstrates the effectiveness of this instrument – but also the need for an implementation mechanism.

Reform implementation: Mechanisms, key directions, monitoring

Adopting enabling legislation for reform is a fundamental step, but experience across the world indicates that this will have only very limited impact on inspection and enforcement practices if there are no active efforts to follow up on implementation. Indeed, such a reform requires profound changes that can only take place if the government shows constant attention and intervenes to overcome resistances within inspectorates.

Government Resolution No. 511 (2010) and the "implementation mechanism"

As indicated above, the original version of the Government Resolution on "Optimisation of Functions of Supervisory Authorities" was in fact adopted *before* the amendments to the Law on Public Administration – but it has lesser normative status compared to the law, and also more provisions pertaining to implementation. It was subsequently amended several times (2011 and 2012), but with only marginal changes. The Resolution not only sets forth the objectives of the reform, and of supervision, but also establishes a mechanism for implementation, and prescribes the use of a number of tools and methods.

Objectives:

- Reduce burden;
- Optimise the use of limited resources to manage risks;
- Fight corruption;
- Move towards a compliance promotion approach.

Mechanism:

- "Expert Group" gathering the key ministries and most important inspectorates;
- Co-ordination and guidance entrusted to Ministers of Economy and Justice;
- Regular reporting to the government.

Tools and methods:

- Checklists for inspections strongly recommended;
- Focus on consultations – and measures (e.g. FAQs, call-centres) to ensure their uniformity and reliability;
- Risk-assessment as basis for supervision;
- Special status for start-ups during first year of operation (no suspension of operation, one month to correct mistakes/violations before imposing sanctions etc.);
- Common Commencement Dates for new regulations (see Chapter 6 on the management and rationalisation of existing regulation); and
- A number of other measures (on information, reporting etc.), which were generally taken up in the Law on Public Administration.

"Supervision groups":

- In order to improve co-ordination and limit overlaps and duplication, the resolution introduced nine "supervision groups", gathering inspectorates in a related field.
- The grouping made sense, and was useful to some extent, for example, to share practices; but hopes to achieve better co-ordination of planning and data sharing did not fully live up to expectations. This proved difficult to achieve, and instead the focus was put on work within the Expert Group.

Overall, the resolution set very sound principles and a number of very important reform tools – most of which were also taken up in the law, but not all. In particular, the Resolution is the source of all the implementation work on risk-based inspections planning, and checklists. It also created the Expert Group, which was reported by key reform actors to have been a very good setting for focused and effective reform work. Indeed, the most successful inspectorates in terms of reform, and those that offer the best examples, all were part of this group (but some quite "unsuccessful" ones were also part of it). It also gave the ministers of justice and economy a clear task to give some guidance and steering to the reform.

It failed, however, to build a strong implementation mechanism – which could have included a more formal decision making mechanism and "vetting" mechanism on inspection methodologies, a time-specific and resource-specific action plan, and resources allocated to reform support and co-ordination. It also did not give specific guidance on how to build good checklists, or how to define risk and develop risk criteria. The newly adopted amendments to the Law on Public Administration, which put risk at the centre of inspections and supervision work, are a good opportunity to adopt new, stronger secondary legislation to ensure better reform implementation.

These two shortcomings were to some extent alleviated by the creation of a specific division within the Ministry of Economy, and the adoption of comprehensive and clear guidelines for checklists and risk criteria development (both based on best international practice), as a joint decision of the Ministers of Economy and Justice (both of these changes taking place in 2012). However, this joint decision only has a weak status and thus compliance with it remains mostly voluntary for inspectorates – and the "supervision optimisation" (inspection reform) division only has limited resources to deal with a vast number of tasks. The fact that the institutional mechanism was relatively informal has been one of the reasons why, over time, implementation has slowed down.

Key directions of reform and relative reform slowdown

Over the first years of reform, Lithuania managed to achieve impressive results in a number of reform directions, while essentially "postponing" others – conscious choices were made to prioritise the actions that were deemed most likely to produce significant impact quickly: checklists development, development of guidance and consultation activities, changes in enforcement, risk-based approaches. Improvements in performance management were also introduced (and work is currently ongoing to develop this further). Unfortunately, reform implementation has then slowed down. While work has been done on some key issues that were missing from the first phase of reform (development of IT systems, consolidation), little results have been achieved so far, and there are a number of concerns. Some important areas (reviewing inspectorates' mandates and goals, improving governance) have also been neglected.

Summarising the main reform outcomes from the first phase (until 2012-13) looks as follows:

- Development and adoption of checklists for all major inspectorates, covering the most widespread types of economic activity, particularly SMEs (over 65 checklists in 2012 – now 148 in total).
- Introduction/improvement of risk-based planning systems in major inspectorates where they were hitherto absent (e.g. labour, non-food products…) – and further consolidation in those where they already were in use (SFVS, tax).
- Set up of uniform consultation practices and call-centres in several major inspectorates (SFVS, Consumer Rights Protection, Labour, Non-Food Products, Territorial Planning…) – and further development of e-services in the Tax Inspectorate (which led the way on consultations, and had a call-centre operational since 2006).
- "First Year Declaration" whereby inspectorates voluntarily sign on better treatment for new businesses (including no sanctions on first visit in most cases) – signed first by 9 main inspectorates, then by several dozen others (now 50 out of 60).

- Clarification of enforcement practices in respect to "minor violations" (agreement on definition of some minor violations for at least some inspectorates). Amendments to the Law on Public Administration that entered into force in January 2015 have now given a legal basis to "minor violations" (defined as those that can only cause limited harm) and clearly indicated that inspectors should only issue warnings in such cases.
- Adoption of performance criteria for inspectorates – however too many indicators with too frequent reporting schedules, and further improvements needed to make the system more meaningful.

Since 2013, efforts to further develop these reform elements across all inspectorates have been limited, even though some numbers (e.g. number of checklists) have improved significantly. "Best performers" among inspectorates (notably tax, labour, the SFVS) have continued to work on improving their practices, processes, staff qualifications etc. – but little progress has been made in other institutions. While there have been some recent efforts to look again at the performance management system and push inspectorates to adopt indicators that more closely reflect their goals in terms of public welfare, this is still ongoing, and has not been part of a broader effort to review the goals and mandates of inspectorates. The main direction of reform work has been consolidation – and preparatory work has been done on the development of an information management system for inspections. These two streams of work can be summarised as follows:

- ***Information management systems***: as early as 2012, it was recognised that many inspectorates lacked a good information system that would allow them to properly plan inspections, record their results, and generally turn risk-based approaches into practices. Rather than build separate systems for each of them, introducing a unified or partly-unified system for several or even most inspectorates was found to be the most effective and efficient approach. However, the expertise procured in 2013 seems to have produced rather inconclusive findings and recommendations, and decisions and action on this issue are still pending. This means that real improvements in targeting and planning are still elusive in most inspectorates, and that also optimal risk assessment is impossible even for inspectorates which do have their own information system, since there is no data sharing with others.
- ***Consolidation***: in the first phase of reforms, some limited consolidation took place (a few mergers), resulting in a list of 60 inspecting institutions, which still was very large. Many of these inspectorates were small, but a considerable number of overlaps, duplications, unclear mandates etc. remained, as well as fragmentation that is not conducive to effectiveness and efficiency, and leads to confusion for businesses. The government decided to focus on consolidation, defined an action plan and a process. Working groups gathering state and non-state stakeholders in 11 areas reviewed the existing situation, proposals, possible options and submitted conclusions in September 2014. Ministries are now working on turning conclusions into proposals for legislation to change the institutional setup and significantly decrease the number of inspectorates. However, as far as can be observed, only limited attention is being paid to reviewing the mandates of inspectorates – many of them are problematic, and merging problematic entities will not solve the issues. Proposed mergers also do not always correspond to international best practice. These difficulties will be discussed below in the "shortcomings" and "recommendation" sections – but

clearly the consolidation process is still far from having delivered significant results.

Overall, the reform achievements are quite significant if one looks at these outcomes, even considering the slowdown in the past couple of years. If there is progress on IT and consolidation issues, this slowdown itself could easily be reversed. What is important, however, is to look at what impact these reforms have achieved.

The Lithuanian government has shown real attention to tracking reform implementation through regular surveys, four in total, covering 2011 (full year), and 2012, 2013, 2014 (first half year). During the earlier phase of reform, in addition, a shorter-term, "scorecard"-type tool was used to track compliance of inspectorates with reform requirements. This unfortunately seems to have been abandoned, but the survey results are what matters to assess the impact of reform – which we discuss in the next section.

Reform impact: Summary of main improvements and limits

Assessing reform impact is not always easy, considering the many aspects that are affected by inspections – administrative burden, investors' confidence, public interest outcomes (safety, health etc.). Reliable or recent measures are not always available for all of these. Impact may also vary significantly between different regulatory spheres and inspectorates, or even for different impact measures in a given inspectorate (burden may go down, but effectiveness not go up, or vice versa etc.). In order to reach a balanced assessment of reform impact we use here three complementary approaches: business survey data (directly reflecting administrative burden, and some essential features of reform implementation and inspectors-businesses relations)and consolidated insights from direct interviews and desk review (giving a comprehensive view of all aspects of the inspections and enforcement system) – and finally "focused" highlights presenting the situation in specific agencies (both strengths and weaknesses).

Survey data

A total of 4 representative business surveys have been conducted so far covering business inspection issues[2] – one end 2011 (covering 2011 data), and three in summer 2012, 2013 and 2014 covering the first half of each respective year. The first survey had a sample size of around 500, successive ones a sample of 1 000 – thus, data is adequately representative. Overall quality of survey work is good, and data can be used with a good degree of confidence. However, experience with these and many similar surveys (e.g. those conducted on the same topic by the World Bank Group over more than 10 years) leads to treating more "qualitative" answers with caution. When respondents are asked to comment on whether inspectors are helpful, professional etc., or whether the situation has improved, their statements are likely to be influenced by a number of factors (see World Bank Group, 2009). For this reason, we will focus on the data from more "objective" questions, on whether an inspection took place, and whether certain tools or practices (e.g. checklists, advance notification etc.) were used.

A few additional points of caution and clarification are required. First, the sample size in 2011 was smaller, and the published survey data is not fully complete, with the number of inspections per enterprise inspected in particular missing. An estimate had to be calculated from the published data, but there is room for error. Second, in the latest survey publication (2014), there is again a way to present inspection duration that leaves room for error, since the average duration was not given in the report, and has to be again calculated from incomplete data.

Finally, since 2012, surveys cover only half a year. While this allows having data during the year and thus evaluate reform progress and steer further actions, it is in fact not best practice for a number of reasons. First, inspection frequency, duration etc. may vary during the year, in particular for some agencies (SFVS, Tax etc.). Some may inspect more in summer (food, for instance), others towards the end of year (tax, in many countries). Capturing only a half-year leaves room for error. In addition, in order to compare annualised results, an extrapolation has to be done. Assuming that inspectorates have a constant volume of resources, the number of inspections should remain relatively stable from one half-year to the next. This means that the product of percentage of enterprises inspected, and of number of visits per inspected business, is constant. Thus, to extrapolate from half-year to full year, we have multiplied both by √2.[3]

The percentage of businesses inspected declined at the beginning of the reform process, but is rising again

After a strong decrease from 2011 to 2012, the percentage of businesses covered by inspections increased strongly in 2014 (Figure 7.1). Looking down at breakdown by agency, this appears to be mostly driven by an increase in Tax, SFVS and Labour inspections (Figure 7.2). It should be noted that the State Tax Inspectorate reports that its control actions during this time would have in fact gone down. However, since the data reported by the STI appears to be for a narrower type of inspection visits, this is not absolutely comparable. Experience elsewhere suggests that representative survey data is a reliable source to assess burden on businesses, and this clearly appears to have gone up. It may be driven by a variety of visits that may not always be registered as formal "inspections" or "tax audits", but is none less real.

Figure 7.1. **Percentage of all businesses inspected in a given year**

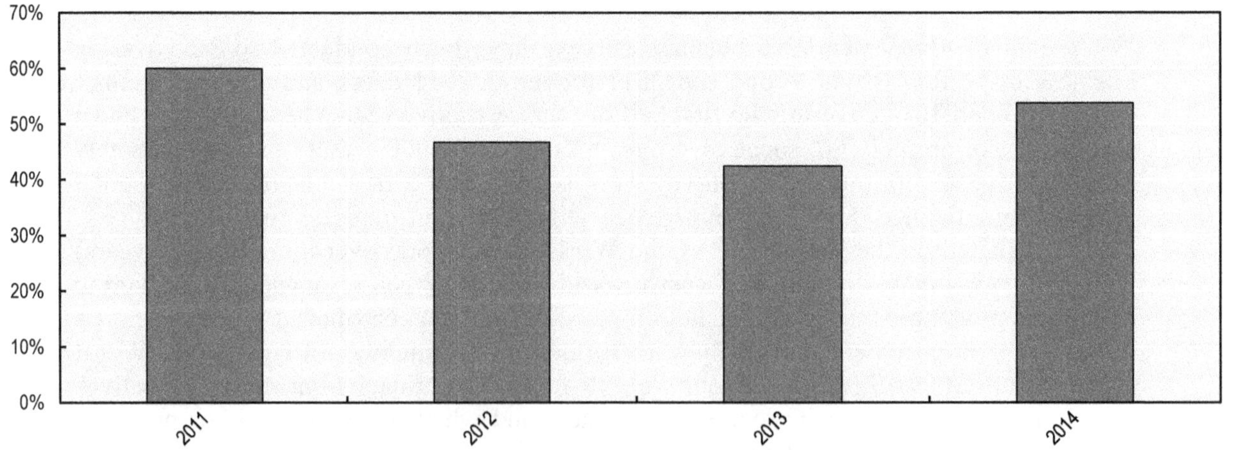

Source: 2011-14 business surveys commissioned by the Ministry of Economy, www.ukmin.lt/web/lt/verslo_aplinka/verslo-prieziura/ataskaitos.

Figure 7.2. **Percentage of businesses inspected in a given year, by agency**

(only most important ones listed)

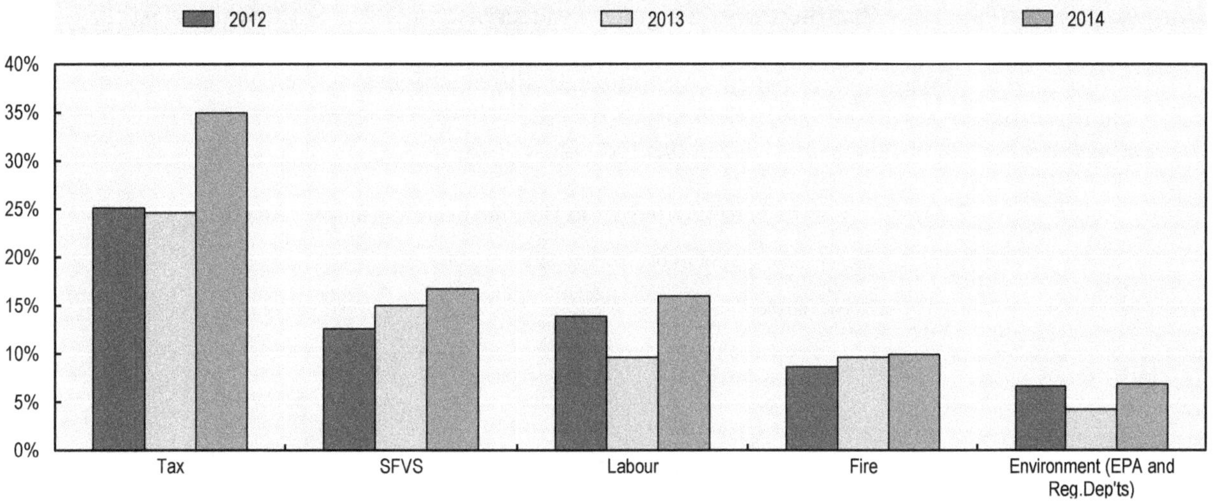

Source: 2011-14 business surveys commissioned by the Ministry of Economy, www.ukmin.lt/web/lt/verslo_aplinka/verslo-prieziura/ataskaitos.

The number of inspection visits per inspected business went down at first, but this has not been confirmed over time (Figure 7.3).

Figure 7.3. **Average number of inspection visits per inspected business, per year**

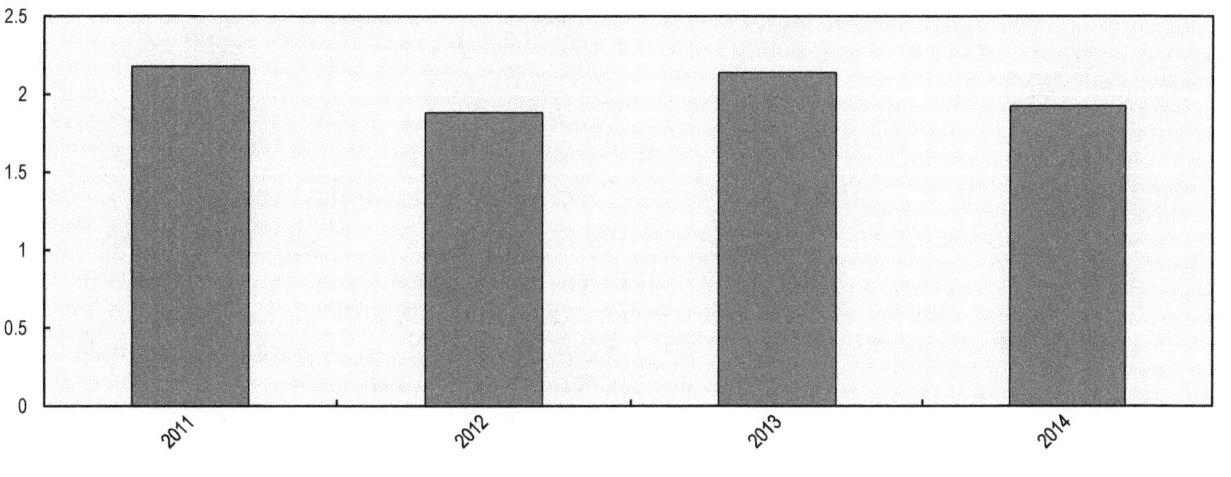

Note: For 2011, OECD estimates based on survey data.

Source: 2011-14 business surveys commissioned by the Ministry of Economy, www.ukmin.lt/web/lt/verslo_aplinka/verslo-prieziura/ataskaitos.

Duration has probably decreased a bit, but not very significantly

Data on duration is presented in survey reports in ways that make it difficult to calculate a reliable average. Figures for specific inspectorates suggest real improvements for some: tax inspections average went down from 4.6 hours to 2.9 hours between 2011 and 2014, labour: from 3.2 to 2.6 hours. But inspections by Regional Departments of Environment went up from 2.9 to 3.3 hours over the same period. The average duration for 2011 is estimated at somewhat above 3 hours, whereas in 2014, it may be slightly below 3 hours. Overall, the decrease (if confirmed) is not very substantial.

Evolution of administrative burden

Taking here the administrative burden in its narrow sense, i.e. only from inspections' duration,[4] it is visible that there was a significant decrease in 2012, but that this has been partly reversed in the meantime. The below figures are estimated assuming that the duration of inspections is constant. As indicated above, there may in fact have been a small decrease, so the overall decrease in burden may be somewhat stronger than suggested below, but the trend is as presented below (Figure 7.4).

Figure 7.4. **Changes in burden from time lost during inspections**

Compared to previous year and to 2011

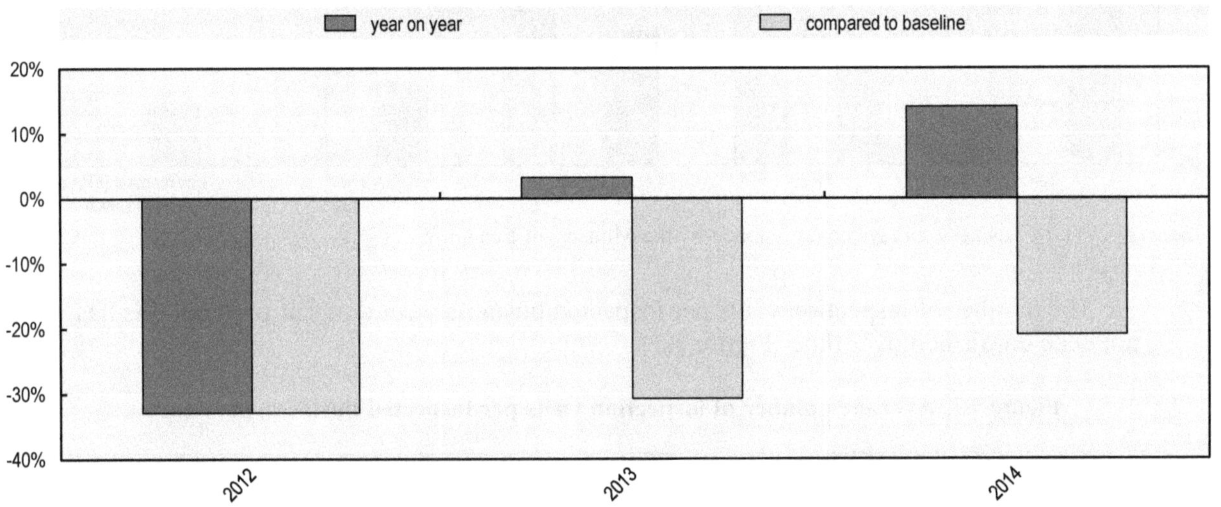

Source: 2011-14 business surveys commissioned by the Ministry of Economy, www.ukmin.lt/web/lt/verslo_aplinka/verslo-prieziura/ataskaitos.

Compliance with reformed procedures is overall good, and improving

Advance notification is complied with in 63% of cases in the latest survey, a number that has been roughly stable since 2012. The percentages vary, however, between inspectorates: 73% for Fire Safety inspections, 58% for Tax, 49% for Labour and only 33% for SFVS. It is known that the EU Food and Veterinary Office (FVO) strongly advises against advance notification in inspections, even though there is some evidence that, when used appropriately, it does not in any way harm the inspections' effectiveness – and this adverse guidance explains the low percentage for the SFVS. The relatively low figure for Labour is likely due to a lot of inspections based on complaints and/or trying to "catch" illegal employment.

Use of check lists has improved over time, in line both with the elaboration of more checklists (covering more agencies, and more economic activities), and with greater familiarity with the tool. In 2012, only 46% of respondents indicated that checklists had been used, in 2014 the figure is 58%. Some inspectorates have higher compliance: 63% for SFVS, 66% for Labour, 77% for the Environmental Protection Agency (EPA). Fire has only 51%, whereas this is a field where checklists are particularly applicable. There is clearly scope for improvement on this front. The State Labour Inspectorate (SLI) reports that its percentage may be even higher (close to 90% based on its own data) – the lower percentage reported by businesses may reflect discrepancies between practice "on the field" and inspectors' reports, or it may come (as suggested by the SLI) from the inclusion of visits to control illegal work, which do not necessarily rely on a checklist.

From 2012 to 2014, the percentage of respondents indicating that inspectors also checked points *not* included in checklists has increased strongly: from 40% to 49% in 2013 and 53% in 2014. The most frequent cases are in Tax, SFVS and Labour inspections (in declining order). This suggests that there may not be major cause for concern (but for remedial action): first, because checklists are relatively less important in Tax inspections (where they are more of a reminder of items to check, what matters being the overall compliance level – whereas in technical safety inspections, checklists are a clear guide to compliance "step-by-step"). Second, because it is in fact normal that checklists require regular improvements and revision, particularly when they are a new tool. If inspectors are finding the need to inspect a lot "outside", it means a review process is required. In any case, this points to the importance of sustained implementation efforts – to ensure that progress is not rolled back, but on the contrary further deepened. The fact that in more than 90% of cases (in every year) no sanctions were imposed for violations "outside the checklist" confirms this case for relative optimism. The "worst offender" (largest share of sanctions for items not included in checklists) is the Environmental Protection Agency – an institution where clearly further reform is needed (see below).

Finally, even though this should not be taken as an indicator either way, it is worth noting that the proportion of inspections where warnings or sanctions are imposed is remarkably stable between 2011 and 2014, with 75-80% of inspections not resulting in sanctions, and fines imposed in less than 10% of inspected enterprises.

Reform awareness: limited, but some improvements

Over time, the percentage of respondents aware of the inspections reform process as such has remained stable, and low, at around 25%. However, awareness of specific tools and features seems to be improving, with awareness of checklists the most notable, increasing from around 30% to 80% in 2014. This suggests that additional information and outreach efforts could be done, and may be beneficial to ensure that reform momentum is sustained, by building stronger support for what has been achieved, and for next steps.

Summary conclusion on data

The trends over successive years as suggested by survey results tend to confirm the picture described above of a reform process that went strong at first, but has since slowed down considerably, and with some reversals in specific areas. The strong increases in some inspectorates' coverage in recent years would have to be further investigated: what motivated them? Did they yield beneficial results in terms of impact? If not, then these increases should be reconsidered.

It is difficult to compare such data internationally because of the lack of comparable surveys in OECD countries. The percentage of enterprises inspected and the number of yearly visits compared favourably to many post-Soviet countries (where surveys have been conducted by the World Bank Group), but this is not the group with which Lithuania is trying to benchmark itself.

The United Kingdom does not have directly comparable data but estimates based on a combination of different surveys and reports suggest that the percentage of enterprises covered is definitely most probably around 35 to 40% – which suggests that there is room for improvement in Lithuania. In Italy, surveys conducted in 2012 by ISTAT showed that around 37% of all SMEs were inspected every year – the frequency of visits, however, was higher than in Lithuania (around 5 per inspected business). Thus, in terms of overall burden, Lithuania may already be in a somewhat better position.

This data is consistent with the overall perspective of a reform process that has been very strong at first, with some "world class" reforms in particular with respect to compliance promotion, and thus has already allowed Lithuania to "leapfrog" practices in many "old" EU and OECD members. There remains, however, considerable space for progress to reach "best practice", and the fact that reforms have slowed down has not allowed to bridge this gap, but rather has let it widen again.

Effectiveness

Assessing effectiveness of the inspections and enforcement system is complex. Data is often missing, or is not independently produced, i.e. inspectorates produce themselves the data against which they should be evaluated. This is particularly problematic when the data is primarily compliance rates: since compliance is checked by inspectorates, they may have incentives to major or minor it, depending on the policy of the government. Only independent monitoring, evaluation, measurement allows to have full confidence in results assessments.

In spite of this, there are a number of cases where data has sufficient reliability, either because it comes indeed from external sources (e.g. the EU), or because it relates to issues which are highly visible and where statistics are far more likely to reflect reality more-or-less fully (fires, deaths). The evidence coming from these suggests that effectiveness of regulatory delivery efforts in Lithuania is variable:

- Food safety: evaluations by the EU FVO and monitoring by the European Food Safety Agency (EFSA) both confirm that SFVS inspections and overall activities are effective and in line with good practices, and that the level of food safety in Lithuania is generally good (in line with EU norms and objectives). This does not mean there is no room for improvement, but clearly this is a field where efforts over the past ten years and more have borne fruit.
- Labour safety: whereas incidence of labour-related injuries and sick-leave are low, the incidence of *fatal* accidents is among the highest in the EU, and way above the EU average (Eurostat data). This is important because labour-related *fatalities* are mostly impossible to hide, and this means that the injuries and sickness data is certainly underreported. Compliance with occupational safety rules, and in particular the essential ones, is clearly still problematic, in spite of the Labour inspectorate's efforts – although it is well known that occupational fatalities incidence is linked also to other factors such as industrial structure.
- Fire safety: statistics compiled by the CTIF (International Association of Fire and Rescue Services) again show Lithuania with an incidence of fire-related deaths that is vastly higher than EU and OECD averages, and is in fact quite similar to neighbouring post-Soviet countries such as Russia or Ukraine. This is clearly a cause for concern, even though the numbers appear to be improving over the past 5 to 10 years.

Considering the *details* and *causes* of these gaps in effectiveness is, however, more important than just looking at the raw aggregate numbers.

In fire safety, there are in fact *no* fatalities and virtually no injuries in fires in manufacturing and business premises. Eighty five per cent of fire-related deaths occur in "residential buildings and hotels" – which are unfortunately not separated in official statistics, but anecdotal evidence suggests that in the past years there were no reported hotel fires, so the overwhelming majority of these deaths take place in residential buildings. The three leading causes of these fires (and deaths) are careless smoking, "other careless behaviour", and faulty electrical wiring or other electrical equipment. This all points to deeply engrained behaviours that are indeed (as the incidence of deaths) quite similar to those found in other post-Soviet countries, and to equipment and infrastructure that have aged, and were designed with far lower electrical usage levels. In short, what should be an absolute priority is education, aiming at changing private behaviours, and also programmes to support upgrading of electrical installations. The Fire and Rescue Service expends significant resources in inspecting businesses (with over 18% inspected per year) and, considering that there are no fatalities at all in business premises, this clearly looks like misallocated resources.

The statistics on occupational fatalities, in turn, may look quite disappointing considering that the labour inspectorate is one that has made considerable progress over the past years, both in targeting, methods, compliance promotion efforts etc. This comes, however, after many years when this was an institution that had made limited progress – hence a first issue is that impact of new methods has simply not yet had time to be visible (indeed statistics show some decrease after 2008, but still insufficient). This situation leads to at least four comments:

- The government should focus more on investigating areas where safety levels are low and "out of line" with EU and OECD averages, allocate resources for such investigations, and then direct relevant agencies to act on this basis;
- Resource allocation within the Labour inspectorate is based on a dual mandate: enforcing employment legislation, and occupational safety and health – thus, up to around half of the inspectorate is focused on employment law issues, and this leaves only limited resources to focus on Occupational Safety and Health (OSH);
- Risk focus of labour inspections could still be improved – in particular by *i)* further developing planning criteria (which, for now, take insufficiently into account the size of the business, and its prior compliance history) – *ii)* using systematic data sharing with other inspectorates, to better identify potentially problematic businesses (which again shows the importance of an integrated information system);
- Finally, as anecdotal evidence again suggests that much of this high incidence of fatalities is linked to reckless behaviour, the level of resources and efforts allocated to education probably needs to be increased.

These few examples show that, if the inspection and enforcement system in Lithuania is to significantly improve its effectiveness in terms of public welfare, more effort needs to be made in these directions; first, better data and more analysis; second; more government attention to this problem; third, better risk focus: and fourth, more "radical" rethinking of priorities, reallocation of resources, and even more attention to education and outreach.

Highlights on specific agencies

To conclude this assessment of the current level of development of the system and of the reform's impact, it is worth looking in more details at a few agency-level examples, focusing on some of the best practices, and some of the really problematic ones.

Good practices

- *Tax Inspectorate*

The State Tax Inspectorate (STI) has clearly defined its mission as supporting voluntary compliance with the maximum efficiency. It evaluates its performance in terms of compliance levels. It has a well-established practice of information and advice, with a centralised process. Its call-centre started operating in 2006 and served as model for others. It has also been one of the first inspectorates to plan inspections on the basis of risk (with an automated risk analysis and case selection system since 2007). A Tax Information Department was established in 2011. This enables better quality management.

Approximately 150 people work in this department. The department handles up to one million calls per year, and around 17 000 detailed inquiries. The staff relies on a database of 7 000 documents, Q&A etc., which is also accessible directly to the public. The STI also organises seminars, webinars etc. to conduct proactive outreach towards taxpayers. The Tax Information Department provides unified and coherent consultations, is organised to optimise the use of its resources and its efficiency, and to work as a "one stop shop" – taxpayers can get all advice either through the unique phone number (1882), or online via "My STI". The inspectorate also reported that providing advice, consultation and information was a key priority for its staff overall (not only in the Tax Information Department).

It was not possible to fully evaluate the risk analysis methodology, as the STI did not want to share details (many other tax services likewise prefer to keep their risk criteria confidential). It would however be useful to further examine these criteria, and in particular whether they include looking at variations, discrepancies vs. sector averages, etc. Most importantly, the practice of information sharing, already in place with Customs, should become more systematic with other inspectorates, in order to more effectively fight evasion (once again pointing to the need of a system to share information).

Overall, the STI still appears to have a high rate of inspections, as evidenced by business surveys – and one which has increased again in recent years. As suggested above, this increase should be evaluated – whether it was really justified, and whether it has brought gains in effectiveness. Depending on the answer to these questions, further course for the next years should be defined. While the STI clearly is one of the best inspection and enforcement institutions in Lithuania, and one that clearly also belongs to "international good practice", this should not be ground for complacency.

- *Food and Veterinary Service*

The State Food and Veterinary Service (SFVS), like the STI, has been one of the "trailblazers" in Lithuania in terms of risk management and of modern enforcement methods. This is of course partly due to the significant efforts expended by the EU to ensure that food safety services in new Member States are up to standard – but it is worth noting that the SFVS is clearly "above average" also within new Member States, both in terms of its level of integration, and its practices. On the integration side, the SFVS is really responsible for the whole food chain, and integrates not only inspection but also risk management and laboratory functions.

The SFVS clearly defines its mandate in terms of protecting the food chain and minimising contamination. Indicators include the level of food borne diseases and food poisoning outbreaks, as well as animal diseases incidence. It has been focusing increasingly over the past years on education, including not only towards businesses but citizens/consumers, to decrease food poisonings originating at home (it also co-operates with business associations). Information and consultation for food business operators are a key aspect of its work.

A "restaurant sticker scheme" is now starting, so far voluntary, along the lines of existing models in the United Kingdom and Denmark. It will allow to "leverage the power of the market" to drive higher compliance, since consumers will be able to know the food hygiene rating of the restaurant they plan to visit. Experience and evaluations have shown that such schemes are generally effective at increasing compliance without adding administrative burden on businesses.

Staff training is an area where further development would be useful. While specialised training on technical issues exists, most "on the job" training is relatively informal (mentoring by more experience inspector), and more formal programmes are mostly EU-driven. Developing a professional vision, competency model and formal training curriculum, as well as continuous evaluation and improvement, would be important for the further development of the service.

- *Labour Inspectorate*

The State Labour Inspectorate (SLI) has considerably transformed its approach over the past few years, since the start of the reform process. In this sense, it is a good example of what the reform process can achieve, since the STI and SFVS had started their development process earlier already. It now puts a square priority on reduction of accidents at work as a key goal, even though results (as indicated above) are still not really satisfactory.

Consulting and advice now makes up the majority of activities – through different channels: call-centre, online, on-site advice etc. In the call-centre over 40 inspectors are involved on a rotation basis (on average 7 inspectors each day). Each inspector provides approximately over 50 consultations per day. The SLI's vision is to engage with employers and support their compliance – attempting to show the advantages of good practices from other companies or countries. Its 142 inspectors spend a large share of their time on advice, and a team of approximately 15 consultants (2/3 on legal issues, 1/3 on OSH) works in the call centre. They get approximately 15 questions per day per consultant, with the majority on legal issues.

A limitation on efficiency is that there are always two inspectors per visit – one for OSH, and another focusing on employment law. While this means the businesses have only one visit, and each staff can have adequate skills, it is a drain on limited resources, and it should be investigated whether in many simple cases one inspector could not cover both areas. The SLI reports that this is already possible for very simple cases, but is rarely used because of corruption risks, and because working in teams allows for mentoring from more experience inspectors. These are reasons that may be valid, but are not fully convincing at first glance. A closer look at the practice would still be warranted to ensure that resources are used as efficiently as possible.

Planning of inspection visits is now done on the basis of risk, and relies on a new information system that was introduced in the past couple of years. Risk criteria include sector considerations, turnover of staff in the businesses, and records of earlier accidents. They do not differentiate by size of business and may insufficiently incorporate prior records – further development of the risk methodology may be useful. The SLI already shares information with the Tax Inspectorate to fight "informal" work (and the two conduct joint inspections) – sharing data with other inspectorates may help to increase effectiveness further.

Post-reform, the SLI has a "responsive" approach to violations, deciding on actions based on the overall picture in the business, the level of severity and risk of violations, the history of the company, the intent or lack thereof of violations etc. Each business can ask labour inspectors for advice and receive recommendations (although the responsibility for decisions rest with the business). However it was reported that inspectors were a bit reluctant to provide very firm and specific recommendations on improvement, not necessarily for lack of technical knowledge (though this may be an issue), but for fear of liability. Given the still high level of OSH problems, this is an area for improvement: inspectors should have full confidence and ability to be able to guide businesses in a clear and specific way. Generally, an even greater focus on OSH-related information, education and guidance is needed – including towards workers and the general public.

Finally, training is once again primarily informal and based on mentoring from experienced inspectors, but a form of "practical test" before confirmation. This is another area where further development would be beneficial.

Problematic practices

- *Territorial Planning*

The State Territorial Planning and Construction Inspectorate (STPCI) is a prime example of the considerable potential for further simplification and streamlining of the system, and in particular of the possible efficiency gains. While the inspectorate reports having changed its work principles, and put the emphasis on consultation, what is still unclear after several years of reform is what *purpose* this institution has. Of course, the institution has an official mandate ("carrying out state supervision of territorial planning and construction"), and activities (ensuring that territorial planning, construction works are carried out in conformity with the law) – but it is far from clear what is the *goal* of these in terms of public welfare, and what risk to the public these activities aim at mitigating.

In fact, the inspectorate appears as an inheritance from an era when the state was expected to drive and control every activity. When asked to define its mandate in terms of risks to the public that it would be addressing, it is practically impossible. The inspectorate checks that building and planning are done "in accordance with the law", but the goals of these controls are not well defined. Indeed, the inspectorate does not verify, for instance, whether construction complies with safety norms (which would address the construction safety risk), or with environmental norms, but rather that the buildings correspond to what has been planned originally. This is a kind of circular check that adds little value, and could very well be performed by the developer/owner. It is also far from being the only institution involved in the whole planning and construction permit, and building supervision (see Chapter 9 on territorial planning and construction permits). Its added value (on top of a system that is already too complex) is far from clear. While the inspectorate used, among other tasks, to check whether local authorities had issued construction permits and planning documents "in conformity to the law", it now reports to have set its main focus for this year and the next on verifying whether renovation of high occupancy residential buildings has been done in conformity with the approved building project. In neither case is it really clear what public interest the inspectorate is pursuing, why a specific state agency is required for this purpose, what risks it is addressing, and in which ways this is a rational use of public resources.

As far as could be assessed by the mission, and as was explained by STPCI representatives during meetings, it is only verifying formal compliance, i.e. whether a building was indeed built according to the plans that were agreed upon, for instance. This point was repeatedly confirmed by STPCI representatives, and is also consistent with earlier fact-finding work done by the authors of this review in Lithuania in previous years. Thus, the STPCI does not appear to have a strong role in ensuring safety of the buildings, protection of the environment, and other essential purposes of the planning and construction regulatory system. It chairs the commission that approves start of exploitation of new (or renovated) buildings, but this is part of a construction permit system that is in any case in great need of reform.

Supervision of other institutions involved in planning and construction approval does not, based on evidence from international practice, require a full-time inspectorate, and can be part of other internal audit functions of the state – and also can, and should, rely more on litigation. Compliance for its own sake should not be the goal, but mitigation of risks and harm – if there is no harm done to anyone, it is unclear what this double checking will provide. As to checking whether contractors have done renovation works according to contract, there is very little (if any) justification for having a state body do this. There are many private providers of such service, and there is no serious public interest involved. The fundamental principle of state regulation and regulatory enforcement should be that intervention is warranted only when there is evidence of market failure. In the absence of such market failure, maintaining an entire institution is questionable. With 265 staff, with roughly 2/3 to ¾ focusing on construction and the remainder on planning, the inspectorate is no small institution. At a time when there are so many demands on limited state resources, the inspectorate appears to be an institution that may have outlived its usefulness, regardless of the quality and qualifications of its staff (who could certainly be reallocated to higher priorities). The STPCI has indicated that it is increasingly moving towards more of a "consulting" than an "enforcement" role. While commendable, this still raises the question of what goals (in terms of public welfare, interest) these consultations aim to achieve. Chapter 9 provides further details on some aspects of the role of the STPCI and the questions it raises. The recommendation is to very seriously reconsider, as part of both inspections reform and construction permits reform, what the purpose of the STPCI is, what is effectively needed, and whether this institutional set-up is still relevant.

This case underlines a considerable weakness of the ongoing consolidation system: that it does not challenge the necessity of existing institutions, and does not seriously consider the relevance and adequacy of their mandates. It looks more as functional and sectoral proximity, and seeks to consolidate what looks roughly similar or related. Rather, consolidation should start from thinking through what functions are *actually needed*, and from there go to how they should be structured and organised.

- *Environment*

The situation with environmental inspections in Lithuania is quite confused, and there is general agreement among most experts that this is one of the priority areas for reform. It was difficult to obtain all the necessary information to have a precise view of the system, hence these remarks will be limited to a few, key salient features.

First, the institutional set up is highly problematic, with parallel supervision (including inspection) functions hitherto exercised by the Environmental Protection Agency (EPA) and Regional Departments of Environment (reporting to the Ministry). A new Environmental Protection Service has now been created in addition, and the respective roles and interactions of the three are still to be clarified. Survey results show a certain number of problems with their inspections – that they are the longest on average, have the largest share of sanctions imposed outside of checklists, etc.

Criteria for planning and targeting work also seem problematic. Regional departments appear to follow closely ministerial instructions, which is in contradiction with OECD *Principles* which state that political decisions should intervene at the strategy level, but not in operational decisions.

It appears difficult to believe that the environmental sphere can be in such a poor shape, in contrast with areas like occupational safety and food safety. It seems clearly that consolidating *all* supervisory functions related to the environment (those of the three institutions listed above, and any other as well) in one body should be a priority – along with the development of a sound mission statement, clear risk methodology, and professional methods.

- *Non-Food Products Inspectorate*

The State Non-Food Products Inspectorate (SNFPI) is an agency that is under the Ministry of Economy, which is leading the inspections reform – as such, it is a disappointment that there remain serious issues with this institution, and that the planned consolidation risks making these problems far worse.

Even though the SNFPI is not one of the largest institutions (at least 10 times smaller than the SFVS in terms of staff and number of inspections), it is an important one to ensure the safety of consumer goods. It is the main market surveillance institution in Lithuania. Over recent years, it has improved its methodology, developing checklists (but with a "laundry list" approach, including all kinds of requirements without real consideration for risk), implementing the "First Year Declaration" etc.

It also has a risk-based approach, but its criteria for risk are rather insufficient, since they consider mostly the amounts of "dangerous products", Rapid Alert System for dangerous non-food products (RAPEX) alerts, previous controls, complaints – but not really any analysis of actual health and safety effects in previous years. The inspectorate indicates that it is practically impossible at present to obtain data on causes of death and injury from the health care system, which makes better risk-based targeting extremely difficult. Clearly, this is an area where systematic information sharing, standardised reporting forms, etc. would help – and this has to come from the centre of government. Information sharing with institutions such as the Fire Safety service would also be crucial.

Beyond this, however, the main problem is that the inspectorate still shows *i)* a very confused approach to its own mission and *ii)* a far too large share of complaints-based work as opposed to pro-active targeting – and these two problems are at least partially linked. The inspectorate still considers as its mission to broadly ensure the "quality" of products, and to respond to consumer complaints about quality – and it considers that every product on the market should conform to a "standard". This looks like a clear leftover of early post-Soviet approaches, and is similar to what one could see e.g. in Ukraine, and requires changes in guidelines and practice.

The Law on Product Safety is one of the key pieces of legislation that were adopted or amended as part of the approximation process with the EU *"acquis communautaire"*. As such, many of its provisions are directly translated from the EU's General Product Safety Directive (GPSD) (2001/95/EC). The problems arise from the facts that several important sections of the GPSD were omitted, and other highly inadequate points added. The GPSD states that products on the market have to be safe, and a product shall be deemed safe when it conforms to either European standards, other voluntary national standards, EC recommendations, "product safety codes of good practice", "state of the art" or "reasonable consumer expectations concerning safety". In other words, the GPSD leaves considerable flexibility to put on the market new products that do not correspond to any particular existing standard, particularly for types of goods that are low risk and thus not covered by specific EU Directives or Regulations. Many inspectors, however, remain convinced that they need to find standards for everything, and that in the absence of standards they cannot evaluate safety. First, this is fully mistaken, since standards are only one of the instruments that can be used (compliance with standards gives what the EU calls a "presumption of conformity"), but never the only one. Second, this also means that the SNFPI tries and control far too many products, including many with a very low level of risk. Good practice market surveillance institutions in the EU, on the contrary, start from hazards and risk levels, define methods and tools to check product compliance, and plan their work on this basis, rather than starting from standards.

On complaints, the problems are far deeper, and can be traced back to the approach to consumer protection that was widespread in post-Soviet countries in the 1990s, and is still (unfortunately) in place in many of them to date. Since the Law on Consumer Protection (originally adopted in 1994) was less central to EU approximation and accession, it was not thoroughly revised as part of this process (though some amendments were adopted in 2007). In its Article 21 it foresees the following (emphasis ours):

- If the seller, service supplier fails to satisfy a consumer's request regarding the acquired unsafe and **(or) inadequate quality** goods or services, he shall have the right to appeal to the (…) Inspectorate (…) with respect to return of the goods, elimination of the deficiencies, reduction of the price, replacement and (or) provision of information. These institutions must examine the consumer's application not later than within 20 working days (…)
- After having examined the consumer's application, the (…) Inspectorate (…) shall **write out an inspection report** specifying whether or not the consumer's request is valid and **if it is valid, shall propose to the seller, service supplier to satisfy the consumer's request** within a set time limit. (...)
- If the seller, service supplier fails to meet the proposal of the Service, Inspectorate or the State Public Health Service to satisfy the consumer's request, these institutions shall submit a copy of the inspection report to the State Consumer

Rights Protection Authority which shall solve an issue regarding the defence of consumer rights.

These clauses are extremely problematic, in more ways than one. First, they put the inspectorate (and the state) in charge of solving "quality" issues (and conflicts), whereas there is no legal definition of quality, nor normative basis to assess it (as opposed from safety, for which the Law on Product Safety applies). Second, for every one of these complaints the inspectorate *has to conduct an inspection.* The English translation varies between "examination" and "inspection" – there is a similar back and forth in the original Lithuanian version, but it is clearer in its point 2 that this is an "inspection". In the end, the inspectorate does not have direct enforcement powers – it can make a recommendation, but if it is not followed, it can only refer the matter to the Consumer Rights authority (or the matter can go to the courts).

Data provided by the SNFPI shows that in 2014 over a period of just 9 months the SNFPI had to respond to over 2 000 complaints; 1 900 of these complaints were for "bad quality", a category which is not defined in law nor has clear assessment criteria. Following inspections, the inspectorate rated 2/3 of the complaints as "grounded" – and in most of these cases the seller agreed to a refund (half of these cases) or another arrangement. Only 6 to 7% of these cases were unresolved and forwarded to the Consumer Rights Authority. The other third of the complaints were considered "ungrounded". These cases concerned either extremely minor issues or, for example, products that the inspectorate actually deemed "conform". Over 25% of the complaints concerned shoes (a product category for which there is no harmonised EU standard or applicable regulation, given its low risk), nearly 8% textiles (mostly similarly unregulated, except specific cases like textiles for children), many complaints also concerned services (again, mostly unregulated ones). Some complaints cover deregulated goods (for instance, goods covered by some of the EU "New Approach" directives) such as electrical goods (main category with 37% of complaints), but again for these nearly all complaints concerned "quality" (and nearly none safety), and nearly half of the complaints were found to be "not grounded".

This practice, driven by completely outdated legislation, which contradicts basic principles of the market economy and of the EU Single Market, distracts the inspectorate from its real, core work (ensuring safety of non-food products), and from adopting best practices. With less than 100 staff (74 inspectors), the inspections following complaints make up more than 50% of the total, making any risk-based planning somewhat marginal. It means the inspectorate wastes around half of its already scarce resources on conflicts of a purely private nature, where there is no safety issue involved and no reason for the state to act. The lack of good statistics on product safety and injuries or deaths caused by unsafe products in Lithuania means that the negative impact of this misallocation of resources is difficult to estimate, but the serious situation with fire safety (see above) suggests that it may, in fact, be significant. The staff and management of the SNFPI to some extent understand the problem, but do not see a solution to it and see it as their duty to comply with the Law (which, indeed, gives them no choice).

Lithuania urgently needs a market surveillance institution that is up to international standards and best EU practice – with proper training of inspectors (another lagging area), real risk analysis and focus, prioritisation and sound methods. Legislation that prevents this development should be amended without delay, and consolidation plans that add to the confusion reconsidered.

- *State Health Care Accreditation Agency and State Medicines Control Agency*

Inspections of health care institutions and providers are essentially complaints-based. There are also some planned inspections and the institution reports using checklists, but the level of development of risk criteria is really insufficient. As reported by the State Medicines Control Agency (SHCAA), risk scores are determined entirely by the results of previous inspections, and whether violations were found (as well as the seriousness of these violations). Not having been inspected for a long time also increases the risk score. There appear to be no real criteria for rating objects in function of their *inherent* risk (type of facility, care processes practised there, type of public etc.), and of their *scope* (number of patients), whereas these are very well established criteria internationally. This also suggests that it may be worth looking at the quality of checklists, to see if they are more in line with international best practice than risk criteria. This is of concern, particularly in an area (health care supervision) where risk-based approaches are very well developed and classification on the basis of risk is easy (based on types of care provided, size, publics served and prior history), and where the use of checklists is also as developed as it is fundamental. As reported by SHCCA, draft primary and subordinate legislation has been prepared to regulate the evaluation of health care services (including requirements for medical devices and health care specialists). The draft legislation is expected to provide a more precise regulation of the quality of health care services and more objectively measurable risk criteria for inspections.

The State Medicines Control Agency appears to have risk criteria for its planning, which are essentially based on EU-wide guidance, but little analytical capacity and fine-tuning of its planning based on the Lithuanian situation in terms of health, medicines-related problems or accidents etc. It defines its mission in terms of fulfilling its inspection plan, and not in terms of achieving outcomes. There also appears to be no communication or outreach to the public, whereas this is known to be absolutely crucial to improving medicines safety.

Reform and system performance checklist

In order to allow for an overview of the state of progress with the reform, and of the overall quality of the inspections and enforcement regime, Table 7.1 presents a brief assessment of performance of Lithuania's inspections and enforcement regime against a set of criteria that draw on the OECD *Principles.* The checklist provides a basis for further analysis and an overview of the main priorities for further reform. The assessment reflects the findings presented in this chapter.

Table 7.1. **Inspections and enforcement reform and system performance checklist**

Evidence-based enforcement	
Clear, outcomes-focused mandates	
Effectiveness indicators linked to public goods	*While much of this is present for the "best" agencies, it is nearly fully missing for many others*
Regular effectiveness evaluation	
Allocation of resources based on risks and outcomes	
Science based risk assessments	

Table 7.1. **Inspections and enforcement reform and system performance checklist** (*cont.*)

Criteria	Assessment
Selectivity	*Too many agencies controlling too many issues where inspections are not appropriate*
REI agencies mandated on when really needed and cost-efficient	
Mechanisms in place to enforce regulation through civil action	
Resources allocated to support non-gov't regulatory enforcement	
Effectiveness and credibility of "co-regulation" schemes guaranteed	
Official recognition of the need for selectivity in REI	
Risk-focus and proportionality	*In some agencies, very advanced – but many inspectorates are lagging far behind*
Common approach or general practice of risk assessment	
Data on risks effectively collected, complaints managed as part of it	
Information systems to plan on risk basis, "unplanned" inspections limited	
Risk analysis and proportionality at all stages of inspection process	
Regular update of risk analysis, and transparent communication	
Responsive regulation	*Very good general guidelines and overall good implementation*
Enforcement differentiated based on regulatee's behaviour	
Gradation of available sanctions allowing credible deterrence	
Businesses with first violations, new bus., supported rather than punished	
Appropriate discretion given to REI agencies, with accountability	
Regular evaluation and adjustments of responsive regulation approach	
Information integration	*Some inspectorates have good systems but many do not – and no integration for now*
Communication of issues, risk data etc. easy and effective	
Interconnection with other databases (complete, up to date data)	
Unified index reference across REI agencies for all objects	
Joint database or regular data interchange for all REI agencies	
Information systems include all relevant risk data for planning	
Long-term vision	*The vision exists but it has some gaps and the mechanism is weak*
Official vision of REI, objectives, principles	
Institutional mechanism in place to drive progress	
Clear targets for REI agencies and regular assessment	
"Risk Regulation Reflex" avoided	
Co-ordination and consolidation	*Efforts are underway but for now fragmentation and multiplicity of agencies is still the rule, with co-operation only "ad hoc" and mostly informal*
Duplication of functions avoided	
One regulatory sphere = one REI agency (or mechanism to ensure coherence)	
Allocation of resources made considering all relevant agencies	
Act as "eyes and ears" for each other	
Sharing of records or main findings of prior inspections	
Limitation of re-inspection of same object in short time	
Joint planning or other practice to ensure co-ordination	

Table 7.1. **Inspections and enforcement reform and system performance checklist** (*cont.*)

Transparent governance	
Collegial governance, stakeholders represented	*Governance has not been a focus of reform. A few "good" cases raise the overall rating*
REI agencies have stable structure – and no conflict of interest/missions	
Management based on professionalism, open recruitment process	
Performance indicators for staff aligned with REI agency's objectives	
Clear guidance to staff on how to interpret rules, consistency, transparency	
Clear and fair process	
Overall process rules ensure balance of rights and powers in REI process	*Good general rules but there is room for further improvements*
Clear and comprehensive list of REI agencies and their functions	
Adequate possibilities to appeal, trusted by regulatees	
Requests for REI action effectively handled and in proportion to risk	
Powers of inspectors sufficient, checks and balances as well	
Compliance promotion	
Clear guidance documents to assist compliance	*Strongest point of reform so far – can be further strengthened and extended to all agencies*
Regular analysis of barriers to compliance	
Active outreach campaigns to businesses	
"Assured advice" practice	
Goal of REI agencies=maximise compliance, not # of sanctions	
Professionalism	
Recruitment and on-the-job training ensure appropriate qualification	*System for training and professional qualifications is too informal and lacks consistency*
Core skills defined for all inspectors, training to build these skills	
Competency of staff members assessed and developed regularly	
Overall capacity of REI agencies regularly assessed in same perspective	
Professionalism allows appropriate discretion, based on risk	

Notes

1. When the review was drafted, the full text of the amendments was not yet available. The content of the amendments has thus been reported here as presented by the Government, and was not directly verified. The amendments are now available in Lithuanian at: http://www3.lrs.lt/pls/inter3/dokpaieska.showdoc_l?p_id=487546&p_tr2=2. The full version of the law can be accessed at https://www.e-tar.lt/portal/lt/legalact/tar.0bdffd850a66/qqvlfpltmn.

2. All the survey reports are available (in Lithuanian) here: www.ukmin.lt/web/lt/verslo_aplinka/verslo-prieziura/ataskaitos. Unfortunately they are not available in the English version of the Ministry of Economy website – and are only released in Lithuanian. Publishing summaries in English would be useful. The 2011 survey was conducted by RAIT, 2012-13 surveys by *Socialinės informacijos centras* and the 2014 one by *Rinkos tyrimų centras*, all upon request of the Ministry of Economy.

3. Extrapolating survey data from half a year to a full year requires to understand the logic of the process studied, and the workload involved. In this case, both "percentage inspected" and "number of visits" are variables that are linked and, together, make up the 'total inspection visits per year in the country'. Since this last number is constrained by inspectorates' total staffing and workload, which is roughly constant across the year, it is impossible for *both* 'percentage' and 'number' to be multiplied by two to annualize the data, otherwise the resulting variable 'total visits' would be multiplied by 4 (implying a doubling of workload). We assume that the ratio of 'additional businesses visited' (percentage inspected) and of 'additional visits in same businesses' (number of businesses) is roughly constant. Thus, the equation writes itself as follows:

   P = percentage inspected, N = number of inspection visits, H = half year, Y = year.

   PY x NY = 2 x PH x YH – which is equivalent to: PY x NY = (√2 x PH) x (√2 x YH).

   Hence: PY = √2 x PH and NY = √2 x NH.

4. The administrative burden is defined here as: Percentage inspected x Number of inspection visits x Duration of inspection (average). The baseline is the value for 2011. What matters to assess the reform is more the variation than absolute numbers.

Bibliography

Blanc, F. (2012), “Inspection Reforms: Why, How, With What Results?”, OECD, Paris.

EU (2013), “More Product Safety and better Market Surveillance in the Single Market for Products”, COM(2013)74final, http://eur-lex.europa.eu/legal-content/en/txt/pdf/?uri=celex:52013dc0074&from=en.

OECD (2014), *Regulatory Enforcement and Inspections*, OECD Best Practice Principles for Regulatory Policy, OECD Publishing, Paris, http://dx.doi.org/10.1787/9789264208117-en.

OECD (2012), “Recommendation of the Council on Regulatory Policy and Governance”, www.oecd.org/gov/regulatory-policy/2012recommendation.htm.

World Bank (2009), *Doing Business 2010: Reforming through Difficult Times*, World Bank Group, Washington, D.C.

Chapter 8

The interface between supra-national, sub-national and national levels of government in Lithuania

This chapter examines the multi-level dimension of regulatory policy at the sub-national and supranational levels. It looks at the allocation of regulatory responsibilities at the different levels of government, the capacities of local governments to produce quality regulation, and co-ordination mechanisms between the different levels of government. It also details the processes that are in place to manage the negotiation of EU regulations, and their transposition into national regulations, as well as the interface of national regulatory policy and governance with Better Regulation policies implemented at EU level.

Structures, responsibilities and funding of local governments

Structure of local governments

Lithuania is a unitary state. According to the Constitution, the right of self-government is guaranteed through 60 municipalities and elected municipal councils and mayors.[1] The local council is the municipality's legislative and decision-making body and is composed of members elected by direct universal suffrage for four years along with the mayor, who is also a member of the council. The local council adopts the budget, enacts local legislation, and has the power to establish smaller territorial units.

By local council decision, each municipality can be administratively divided into smaller territorial units (*seniunija*). These units are generally responsible for the provision of daily local services to citizens in a given municipal area. The territorial unit is headed by a civil servant (*seniūnas*) appointed by the director of the municipal administration.[2]

The size of municipalities varies significantly in terms of population. More than a third of the Lithuanian population live in five municipalities (Vilnius, Kaunas, Klaipėda, Šiauliai, and Panevėžys), which have the highest population density in Lithuania. These differences entail significant variations in the resources at the disposal of municipalities and, consequently, in the administrative capacity of municipalities.

Administratively, the country was divided in 10 counties with centrally-appointed governors and county administration. The county administrations were abolished in 2010. Counties still exist as territorial units. Ten central government representatives conduct legal checks over municipal acts.

Responsibilities and powers of local governments

Municipalities have **independent and delegated responsibilities or functions**.[3]

- Municipalities exercise their **independent functions according to the Constitution and the relevant legislation**. They have freedom of initiative, can adopt decisions and are directly responsible for the fulfilment of these functions.
- **State functions are delegated by the central government to municipalities**. Municipalities are free to take decisions, within the boundaries set by central government institutions. In some cases, delegated functions can be fulfilled through formal contracts between the central government and municipalities. Contracts usually apply to short-term and/or seasonal activities.

Municipalities cover a wide range of functions and provide basic public services such as pre-school, primary and secondary education; primary and secondary health care and public health services; culture, sports and tourism; environment, transport, sanitation and housing; promotion of entrepreneurship; and spatial planning and local development. Most of these functions are independent, which implies a certain degree of autonomy of municipalities (Table 8.1).

Table 8.1. **Municipalities' functions**

Independent functions	Delegated functions
Budgeting	Administration and registration of agriculture
Local fees and charges	Participation in local labour market measures
Management of municipal property	Management of local archives
Municipal establishments	Public registry services
Social maintenance	Social benefits
Territorial planning	Protection of children's rights
Local development	Administration of rural development measures
Spatial planning	State property management
Environmental protection	Participation in organisation of elections
Housing	Provision of state guaranteed primary legal assistance
Culture	Civil protection
Local public transport	Fire protection
Sanitation	Organisation of secondary health care according the law
Household waste	
Cemeteries	
Maintenance of local roads and public areas	
Education (pre-school, primary and secondary)	
Adult education (vocational training)	
Primary health care and public health services	
Libraries	
Local cultural centres and museums	
Social welfare	
Public safety and security	

Source: Art. 6 and 7, Law on Local Self Government, www3.lrs.lt/pls/inter3/dokpaieska.showdoc_l?p_id=474224; EU Committee of the Regions, http://extranet.cor.europa.eu/divisionpowers/countries/MembersNLP/Lithuania/Pages/default.aspx.

Lithuania's municipalities account for 28% of central and local government expenditures. This share is slightly above the share for the other OECD and EU peers (which are also unitary states) (Figure 8.1).

Figure 8.1. **Central and local government expenditures, 2013**

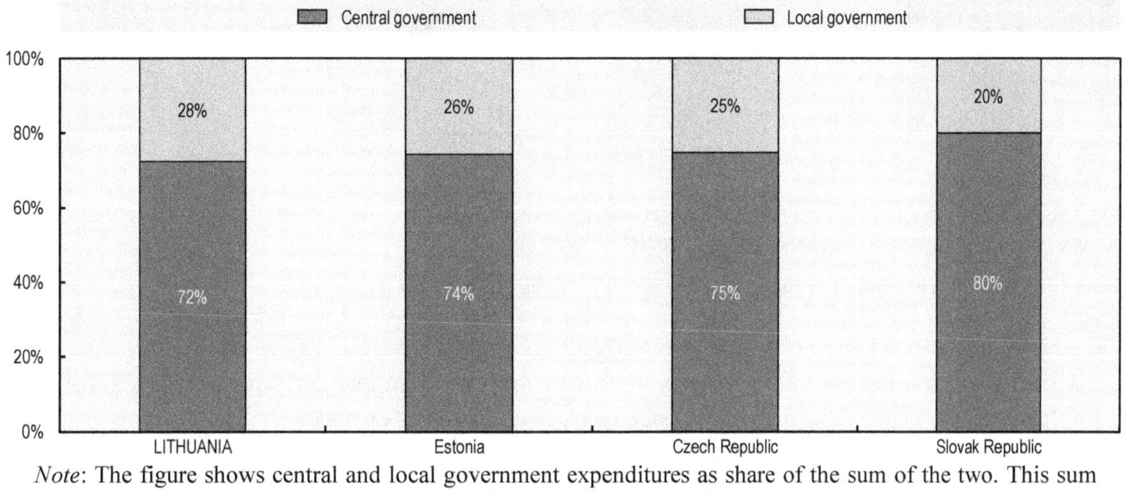

Note: The figure shows central and local government expenditures as share of the sum of the two. This sum represents general government expenditures minus spending of social security funds.

Source: Eurostat database, http://appsso.eurostat.ec.europa.eu/nui/show.do?dataset=gov_10a_main.

Notwithstanding the wide range of areas over which municipalities exercise some responsibilities, municipalities carry out primarily a service delivery and implementation role and have relatively limited regulatory powers. Regulations are set at the central level. Municipalities, however, do issue licences and permits, including, for example, construction permits, advertising licences or taxi licences.

To carry out their responsibilities, municipalities set their own executive institutions. They provide certain public services directly or through contracts with private service providers. For example, Vilnius municipality provides water services through a contract with a service provider. However, municipalities cannot regulate prices (which are regulated by the national regulator).

The central government exercises some legal oversight over the activities of municipalities. The ten representatives of the central government check whether draft or approved legal acts of municipal institutions are consistent with national laws and regulations and can request the repeal or the amendment of municipal legal acts. Municipalities can appeal these requests in courts.

Funding of local governments

Municipalities account for 28% of central and local revenues, slightly above Lithuania's EU and OECD peers (Figure 8.2).

Figure 8.2. **Central and local government revenues**

2013

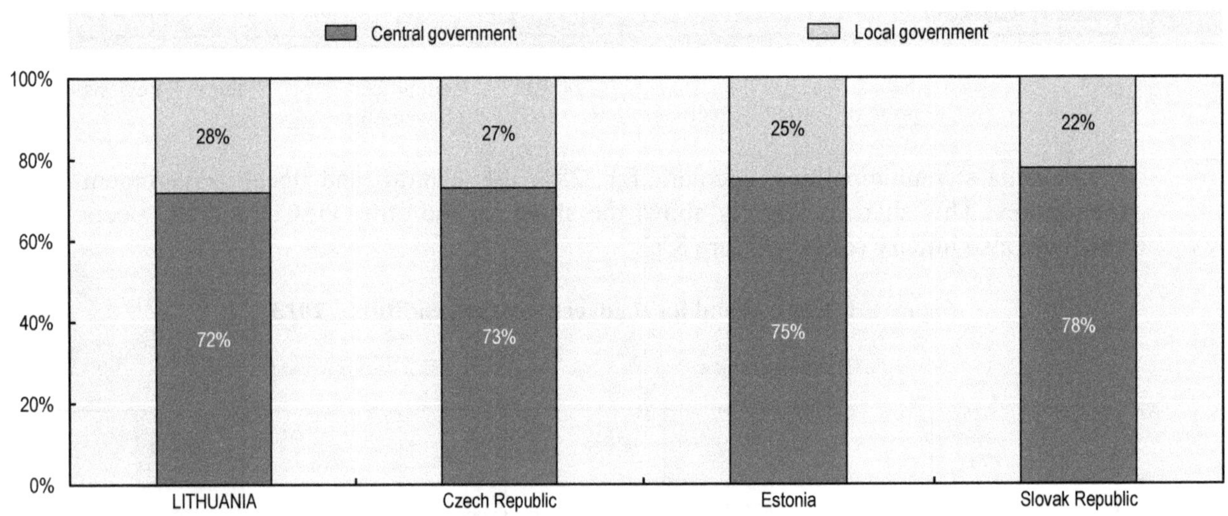

Note: The figure shows central and local government revenues as share of the sum of the two. This sum represents general government revenues minus revenues of social security funds.

Source: Eurostat database, http://appsso.eurostat.ec.europa.eu/nui/show.do?dataset=gov_10a_main.

Municipalities' revenues come mostly from central government's grants and a share of the general income tax. Property incomes and local taxes, on which municipalities have some leeway, account for only 6% of municipalities' revenues (Figure 8.3).

Figure 8.3. **Municipalities' main revenue sources**

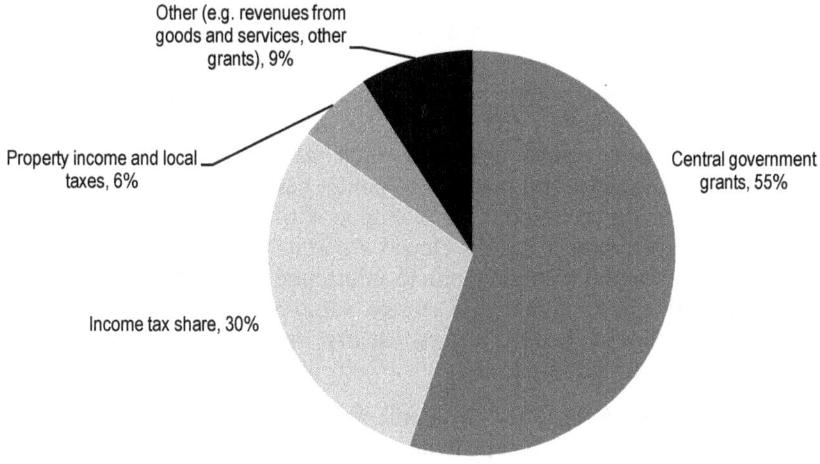

Source: EU Committee of the Regions, http://extranet.cor.europa.eu/divisionpowers/countries/membersnlp/lithuania/pages/default.aspx.

Better Regulation policies deployed at the local level

Central-local government agreements

The provisions of the Law on the Basics of Legislation apply to all rule-making entities at all levels, including municipalities. However, there is no central mechanism to ensure that municipalities comply with the law. The legal check on municipal acts conducted by the ten central government representatives posted across the country tends to focus on sensitive areas like public procurement as central government representatives have few staff to review municipalities' acts. Limited attention is devoted to legal quality or the consideration of possible burdens created by municipalities' administrative decisions.

The Better Regulation Supervisory Commission that was established in 2014 includes a representative of the Association of Local Authorities. There is relatively little support provided from the central government to municipalities to develop better regulation tools. In December 2014, the Ministry of Economy asked municipalities to produce information about initiatives on administrative burden reduction. The results show that 41 municipalities (out of 60) have administrative burden reduction plans or include reduction measures into municipal strategic plans. There seems to be limited co-ordination and follow-up on the implementation of these plans and measures.

The relatively high degree of autonomy of municipalities makes it difficult for the central government to influence decision making at the local level. This is a challenge that OECD members also face. Some of them have facilitated a direct involvement of the association of local governments in initiatives that are seen as serving also the purposes and objectives of local governments. For example, in Sweden, local governments have participated in the measurement of administrative burdens and the Swedish Local Government Association promotes standardisation and common administrative procedures across municipalities. In Denmark, local government associations actively participate in the design of simplification programmes that bring tangible results to local citizens like one-stop shops (Box 8.1).

Box 8.1. Co-ordination between central and local governments in Denmark and Sweden

In **Denmark**, the local association of municipalities (LGDK) participates in a Steering Group for Cross-national Initiatives (STS). This has actively involved municipalities in the discussion of methods and results in areas such as e-government initiatives and the De-bureaucratisation Programme. An example of policy based on co-operation between central and local government is the creation of a common citizens' portal. Following an annual agreement of 2007, the government has developed a portal, in co-operation with municipalities and regions. The portal provides a single guide to information regarding the public sector, and a common access for citizens to digital self-service solutions and access to own data across authority structures and levels. LGDK is also usually involved at a very early stage in the process of making rules, in an informal way.

In **Sweden**, the Swedish Agency for Economic and Regional Development – *Tillväxtverket*, a central government agency, has mapped the problems experienced by enterprises in their contacts with regional authorities and municipalities and possible solutions, in close co-operation with the Swedish Association of Local Government (SALAR). SALAR has also been active in identifying dysfunctional or unnecessary regulations created at the national level which impact on the local level. SALAR has also encouraged the standardisation of often diverging municipal approaches to the interpretation and enforcement of regulations.

Source: OECD (2010a), *Better Regulation in Europe: Denmark 2010*, OECD Publishing, Paris; http://dx.doi.org/10.1787/9789264084551-en; OECD (2010b), *Better Regulation in Europe: Sweden 2010*, OECD Publishing, Paris. http://dx.doi.org/10.1787/9789264087828-en.

In Portugal, the government has developed a simplification programme specifically addressed to municipalities. The *Simplex Autárquico* Programme (Simplex for Municipalities) was launched in 2008 to involve municipalities in simplifying administrative procedures in areas where both the central government and municipalities are involved (licences, certificates, and inspections). In keeping with their autonomous status, the Simplex *Autárquico* Programme is based on a voluntary participation of municipalities. It started with initiatives proposed by nine municipalities, to grow to more than 120 municipalities (out of the 308 municipalities that exist in Portugal).[4] The programme covers both specific action and sharing of experiences and peer-learning across municipalities (Box 8.2).

Box 8.2. Examples of Simplex *Autárquico* measures

Licences, prior authorisations and other similar administrative procedures (inter-sectoral measure)

- Gradually integrate into a single nationwide catalogue all licences and prior authorisations which affect the activities of citizens and companies and require interaction with municipalities. The catalogue will identify the types of licences, the procedures, the time and cost for obtaining the licence. It will provide a single point of access to all licensing procedures.
- Prepare technical guides and create a common set of indicators for monitoring the impact on municipalities of new licensing requirements in the field of urban planning and construction, industrial, commercial and touristic activities (such as the number of requests by type or procedure, response times).

Box 8.2. **Examples of Simplex *Autárquico* measures** (*cont.*)

- Dematerialise the procedures for obtaining licences and permits and allow for interaction with municipalities.

Consolidation of municipal regulations through exchanges of best practices (inter-municipal measure)

- To disseminate experience of participating municipalities in the area of consolidation of municipal regulations (rules and methods); and
- To implement legal techniques and tools to allow for permanent updating of regulations and make it available on line.

Source: OECD (2010c), *Better Regulation in Europe: Portugal 2010*, OECD Publishing, Paris, http://dx.doi.org/10.1787/9789264084575-en.

Initiatives developed by municipalities

Municipalities' size, capacity and, accordingly, impact on the local business environment vary as, understandably, initiatives to strengthen regulatory policy. Large municipalities like Vilnius tend to be more proactive in improving regulations, for example by proactively reaching out to stakeholders. Impact assessment is generally not conducted on municipal acts.

Consultation and communication

Recently, municipalities have developed e-tools for increasing e-democracy in their communities, for example, enabling people to find information of all decisions that are being drafted by the municipalities, to provide their comments and suggestions, to view municipalities' councils' meeting on-line, to discuss and share opinions on-line. However, municipal acts are still posted on local websites and not yet systematically put on the central legislative portal (www.e-Tar.lt).

Co-ordination mechanisms

The Association of Local Authorities (ALA) in Lithuania represents the interests of all municipalities vis-à-vis the executive, other state institutions and international organisations. The ALA is governed through a Board composed of 20 mayors that meets monthly.

ALA representatives participate in the meetings of ministries' representatives (vice-ministers, chancellors of the ministries) chaired by the Government Chancellor (held every Tuesday), as well as the government meetings chaired by the Prime minister (held every Monday and Wednesday).

Draft legislation is consulted with the ALA, which shares it with municipalities and collects inputs. However, consultations tend to be largely formal and have limited impact on the development of the legislation. This result might also reflect the search for a common position across the 60 municipalities, which however have different interests and priorities. In particular, large municipalities are underrepresented within the ALA and are setting up networks and alternative co-ordination mechanisms.

The interface between the national level and the EU

Negotiation

The process for co-ordinating the position of Lithuania in the negotiation process is standard and similar to many OECD countries which are members of the EU. It is described in a resolution of the government from 2014.[5] Individual line ministries are responsible for drafting positions in their areas of competence. It is the responsibility of the ministry to consult the position with other ministries and/or socio-economic partners. Working groups might be set up if needed and in case the issue discussed falls under the competence of two or more ministries or agencies

The Ministry of Foreign Affairs is in charge of co-ordinating the preparation of Lithuanian positions with regard to the legislative proposals within the European Union. A draft position, which falls under the competence of two or more state institutions and on which the state institutions concerned fail to reach an agreement, is then brought to a special inter-agency meeting, co-ordinated by the Ministry of Foreign Affairs. If no compromise is reached, the matter is brought before the Governmental Commission on the EU Affairs. If still no decision is possible, the issue is referred to the meeting of the Government of the Republic of Lithuania.

Draft positions for the European Council and the Council of EU meetings are adopted by the Governmental Commission on the EU Affairs and endorsed by the government. The ministry in charge is also responsible for receiving the approval of the draft position by the relevant Committee of the Parliament.

A special information system called LINESIS has been designed to enable automatic distribution of documents received from the EU institutions. It enables online co-operation among state institutions involved in the negotiation process in real time. Even selected NGOs and social partners have access to this system which enables them to submit their views and comments before the official position is prepared and to monitor the process of implementation.

A typical position should contain an impact assessment of the legislative draft. This is something which is rather rare even among OECD countries, however, the quality of the assessments elaborated by responsible institutions varies and is rarely sufficient. Strengthened control of the quality of these impact assessments in co-operation with the body responsible for checking the quality of ‘standard’ impact assessments (those accompanying draft laws submitted to the government) could lead to improvements in the quality of impact assessments and therefore better background documents used in the negotiation process.

In Germany, it is the *Normenkontrollrat* that co-operates with some ministries but also the European Commission in elaborating “national” impact assessments on the Commission’s legislative proposals. The UK Government’s *Guiding Principles for EU legislation* state that “Departments will endeavour to seek clearance for their proposed UK negotiating position promptly. Departments should analyse the order of magnitude of likely impacts of different negotiating options to help Ministers make evidence-based decisions. The analysis should be proportionate to the proposal and time available and be presented succinctly.”[6]

Transposition

The process of transposition and implementation of the EU law in Lithuania is highly centralised and well regulated. The Constitution provides for the main principle that the norms of *acquis communautaire* shall be an integral part of the legal order of the Republic of Lithuania. A detailed system of allocation of institutional responsibilities and procedural aspects of co-ordination and monitoring of the implementation process is set by the Law on the Government and the Government Resolution No. 21.

The European Law Department of the Ministry of Justice is the main body co-ordinating and monitoring the transposition of the *acquis communautaire* in Lithuania. When a piece of legislation is published in the Official Journal of EU, the EU Law Department registers the draft in LINESIS and assigns the draft to the competent ministry or other institution. One institution is always chosen as the responsible one even though several institutions might be later involved in the process. The responsible institution then prepares a *Plan for transposition and implementation of the EU law* which is then updated in real time.

Within 3 weeks after the assignment, the responsible institution has to come up with a description of concrete measures needed to implement the draft (e.g. drafting a new law, amending an existing one, administrative measures) and the deadlines for their preparation and adoption. The European Law Department supervises how the institutions are following the plan and the deadlines. The progress in implementing EU laws is discussed monthly at the meetings of the Government's EU Affairs Commission and sometimes, if necessary, presented to the government or the parliament. Co-ordination meetings are organised by the European Law Department in case of disputes and conflicts among institutions. These might be then discussed at the level of the EU Affairs Commission or even at the level of the government.

A correlation table has to be prepared and attached to every single draft legal act which is implementing the EU legal act. The European Law Department then reviews the table with its EU law legal experts. All the correlation tables must be uploaded to LINESIS. The European Law Department also reviews draft laws prepared by the Parliament for their consistency with EU legislation. In addition, the Department has a right to conduct *ex post* reviews of the existing legislation for their consistency with EU legislation, however, this right is used rather scarcely.

The *ex post* evaluation of regulations on the consistency with EU legislation takes place in the following cases: *i)* The European Law Department receives a draft law which is amending one of the existing legal acts that are transposing or implementing EU legislation; *ii)* The European Law Department receives an opinion from the public or private bodies that an EU law was implemented incorrectly; *iii)* The European Law Department by its own initiative identifies the need to ensure consistency; *iv)* The European Law Department receives a judgement from European Court of Justice and decides that national implementing measures must be re-evaluated and laws need to be amended.

The transposition process is described in Figure 8.4.

Figure 8.4. **The process of transposition of EU legislation in Lithuania**

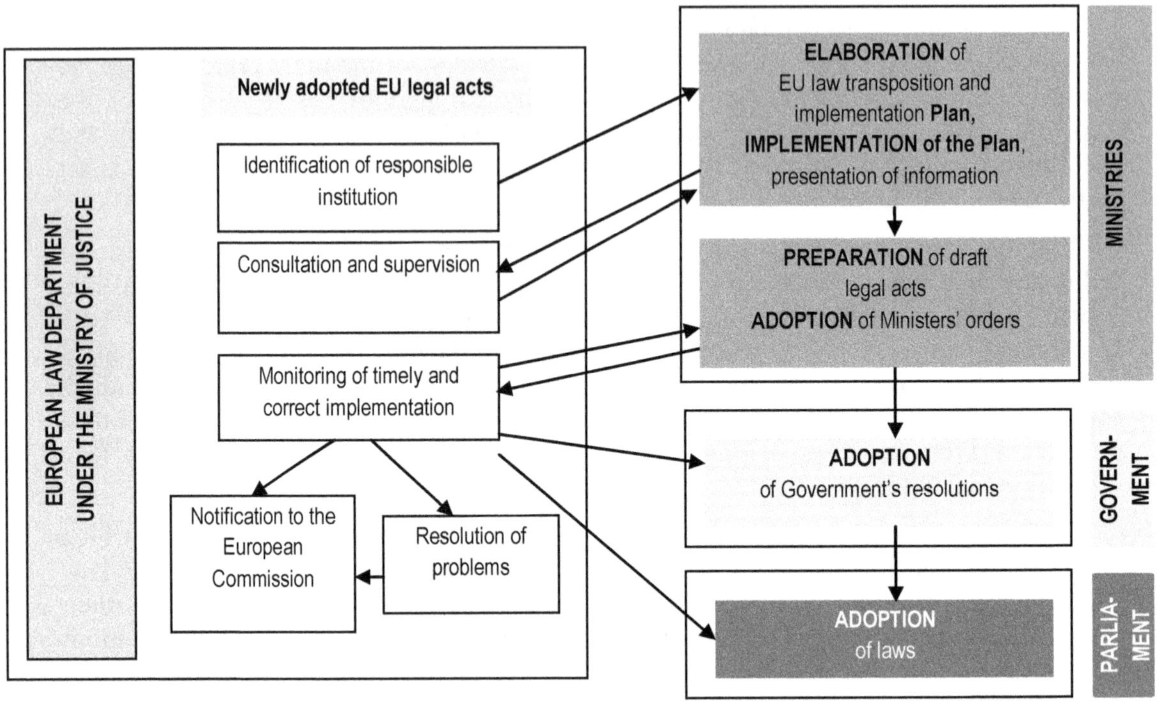

Source: The response of the Lithuanian government to the OECD questionnaire.

One of the issues of the transposition process is the fact that the civil servant(s) that was/were participating in a negotiating process on a particular piece of legislation at the EU level is not involved in its transposition. Therefore, the institutional memory the person might have is not fully used.

The issue of gold-plating

Special attention is paid to the issue of gold-plating. Despite the fact that there are no official statistics on the extent of the problem, the officials interviewed confirmed to the review team that gold-plating presents a big issue in Lithuania. The European Law Department is formally responsible for reducing administrative burdens during the process of EU law transposition. According to the Statute on functions of the European Law Department it has a power to evaluate compliance of draft laws or draft resolutions implementing EU laws with better regulation principles, especially regarding administrative burden reduction. At the moment the identification and evaluation of "gold-plating" cases is organised on ad hoc basis. There are no concrete recommendations or instructions on how to avoid gold-plating.

To better formalise the process of preventing gold-plating, the European Law Department is carrying out an EU funded project "*The assessment and reduction of administrative burden imposed on business during the implementation of EU law*". Its main aim is to create a set of recommendations for public institutions and a concrete methodology for preventing creation of unnecessary administrative burdens in the process of EU law implementation. The set of recommendations is going to be used in the future as a basis for *ex ante* control of draft laws. The main recommendations are described in Box 8.3.

Box 8.3. **Recommendations for preventing gold-plating in Lithuania**

During the pre-transposition stage (during negotiations at the EU level), the responsible national institutions should:

- Clarify the objectives of the draft EU legislation; evaluate subsidiarity of the initiative; conduct impact assessment and describe the data provided to the European Commission for the EU level impact assessment; compare the data of the EU level and national level impact assessments; identify potential issues and raise these issues during the negotiation process.
- Start preparations for the transposition stage; identify necessary measures for the transposition of the draft EU legislation and consult on them with relevant stakeholders.

During the transposition stage responsible national institutions should:

- Always start from the position that over-implementation must be avoided; evaluate the stock of existing regulations first, to avoid the flow of new regulations wherever possible; use derogations or alternative 'lighter regimes' wherever possible; conduct comparative linguistic analysis of the EU law; use technology based measures; use better regulations principles to choose smart and least burdensome implementing solution;
- If necessary perform additional impact assessment to complement the existing one. Consult with end-users of the legislation.

At the post-transposition stage, the responsible institutions should:

- Include a statutory duty/clause for an *ex post* review or enter the duty into the legislation review plan.

Source: Information provided by the European Law Department of the Ministry of Justice.

Notes

1. Chapter X of the Constitution of the Republic of Lithuania, www.lrkt.lt/documents2_e.html.
2. Council of European Municipalities and Regions (CEMR), www.ccre.org/en/pays/view/26.
3. Chapter 2, Law on Local Self-Government, http://www3.lrs.lt/pls/inter3/dokpaieska.showdoc_l?p_id=474224.
4. *Simplex Autárquico* website, www.simplex.pt/autarquico/00_index.html (accessed on 26 March 2015).
5. Government Resolution No. 21 "Regarding Preparation, Scrutiny and Presentation of the Position of the Republic of Lithuania on the Issues Discussed in European Union Institutions, and European Union Law (Acquis Communautaire) Transposition into National Law of the Republic of Lithuania and Its Implementation", https://www.e-tar.lt/portal/en/legalact/tar.db68bca9e3a0db68bca9e3a0db68bca9e3a0db68bca9e3a0db68bca9e3a0legalact/tar.db68bca9e3a0.
6. https://www.gov.uk/government/uploads/system/uploads/attachment_data/file/185626/bis-13-774-guiding-principles-for-eu-legislation.pdf (accessed on March 2015).

Bibliography

Government of Portugal (2011), "Relatório do Simplex autárquico 2010/2011", www.simplex.pt/downloads/relatorio%20simplex%20autárquico%202010_11.pdf.

OECD (2012), "Recommendation of the Council on Regulatory Policy and Governance", www.oecd.org/gov/regulatory-policy/2012recommendation.htm.

OECD (2010a), *Better Regulation in Europe: Denmark 2010*, OECD Publishing, Paris. http://dx.doi.org/10.1787/9789264084551-en.

OECD (2010b), *Better Regulation in Europe: Sweden 2010*, OECD Publishing, Paris. http://dx.doi.org/10.1787/9789264087828-en.

OECD (2010c), *Better Regulation in Europe: Portugal 2010*, OECD Publishing, Paris. http://dx.doi.org/10.1787/9789264084575-en.

Chapter 9

Territorial planning and construction permits in Lithuania

This chapter examines the reform aimed at simplifying construction permits and the extent to which this reform fits the overall regulatory policy and administrative simplification agenda.

The importance of efficient territorial planning, urban zoning and construction permits

What is a construction permit and what is it there for?

A construction permit implements an administrative decision to protect minimum safety and health standards and property rights. As a rule, the permit is granted by public authorities upon an explicit application, following publicly announced administrative procedures, and on the basis of both the presentation of a specific building plan and the existence of preliminary zoning document.[1] The permit grants legal permission to start construction of that specific building project. They are typically required for new buildings; structural additions; renovations; demolitions; temporary buildings; electrical, plumbing, heating, ventilating systems, etc. Hence, the permit is the final administrative authorisation to start work on a concrete building project, and one of the last steps before actual construction work starts.

Works for which no permit is required will generally be rather limited. For this reason, the governance of construction permit is likely to impact the overall economic development of a given territory. At the same time, building permits usually allow municipalities or relevant local authorities to enforce a building code that has been adopted as part of a broader construction law.

The regulatory purpose of a building permit is primarily to enforce important policy objectives enshrined in construction law, mainly focusing on maintaining minimum safety and health standards, and ensuring that construction does not adversely affect third parties. Building permits are also used by local authorities to verify that a new construction fulfils broader urban planning and zoning requirements (IFC, 2009, p. 13).

Territorial planning and construction permit procedures are integral part of urban governance. They have become a critical factor for leveraging a city's comparative advantages. This has become particularly relevant in modern economic globalisation and the subsequent intensification of inter-city competition for domestic and foreign investments. On the one hand, linkages must be ensured between issuing construction permits and planning territorial development, or achieving energy saving targets through more efficient buildings, for instance. On the other hand, construction permits often also constitute a significant source of revenue for local authorities – both directly and indirectly, which needs to be rationalised and made proportionate. Many entrepreneurs attach particular weight to the type and quality of construction regulation before taking investment decisions – both in transition and advanced economies. If designed well, construction permit reforms stimulate construction work, whose benefits extend beyond the sheer increase in number of workers employed in the sector. Construction related materials and services are purchased, often from local suppliers, local jobs are created, generating thereby greater spending and purchasing on the territory. It has been estimated that for every 10 jobs directly related to a construction project, another 8 jobs are created in the local economy (PriceWaterhouseCoopers, 2005).

Construction and territorial planning in a dynamic context

The 2008 financial crisis and consequent recession in many OECD countries have forced regional, metropolitan and local entities to re-adjust to the new economic conditions. Cities in particular are focusing on the best ways to attract corporate and institutional investment anew.

Most of the sub-national public investment goes to areas of critical importance for future economic growth, sustainable development and citizens' well-being. In terms of total investment by sub-national governments across the OECD, 37% is allocated to economic affairs, including construction (besides transport, communications, economic development, energy, etc.) (Figure 9.1).

Figure 9.1. **Share of direct public investment by economic function undertaken by sub-national governments, 2011**

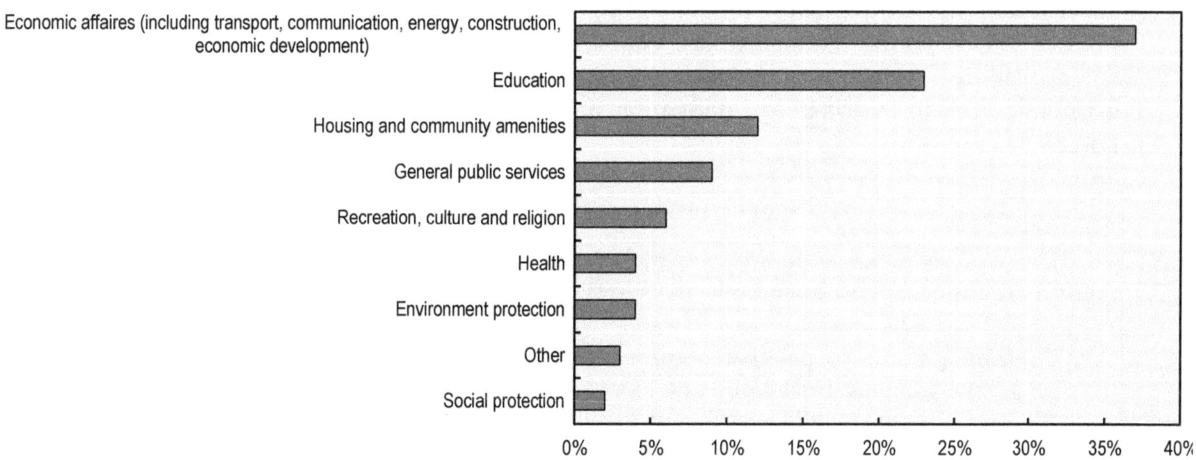

Source: OECD (2014), "Recommendation on Effective Public Investment across Levels of Government", p. 5, www.oecd.org/gov/regional-policy/recommendation-effective-public-investment-across-levels-of-government.htm,

The impact of the 2008 crisis has however had a dramatic repercussion on the allocation of direct sub-national public investment (Figure 9.2).

Figure 9.2. **Change in sub-national government expenditure in the EU (2000-2013)**

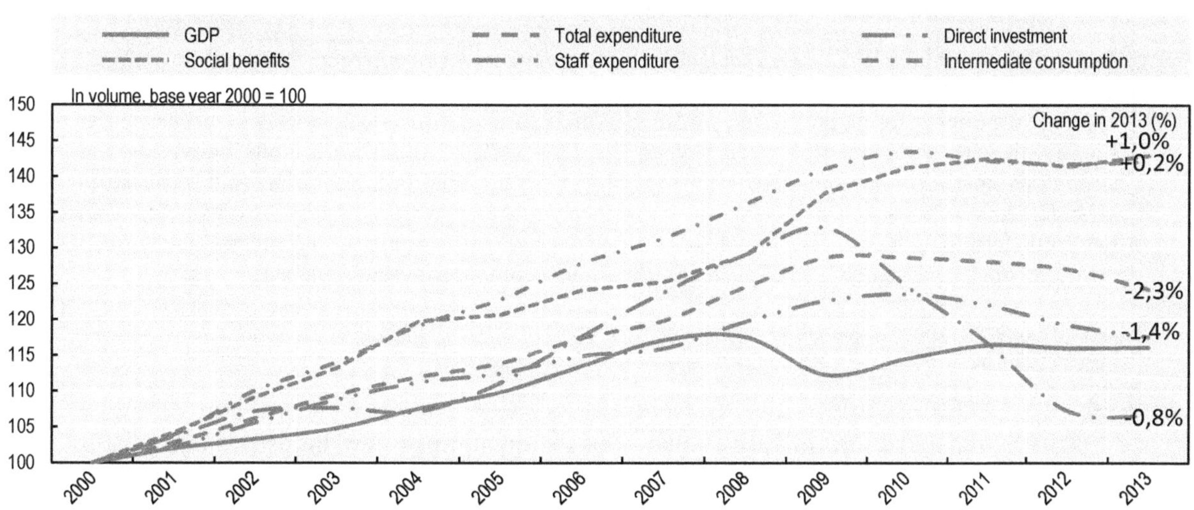

Source: OECD calculations based on Eurostat National Accounts data, http://appsso.eurostat.ec.europa.eu/nui/show.do?dataset=gov_10a_main.

The quality of the "business and investment climate" becomes a precondition in such a quest for new investments and plays a fundamental role in economic development, new job creation and capital attraction. A change in policy formulation and strategies is necessary, also and especially because grand state aid, transfer payments, tax revenues or debt re-financing are no longer channels of investment in the same scale – if at all (OECD, 2013a). Cities have recognised that they need to "become more focused on the conditions that will attract investment and secure business expansion and growth. They have to become both more investment-ready and more business-friendly and, if they can do so, then they can learn to use these new flows of investment to achieve wider social and other goals." (Clark, 2014, p. 3)

A paradigmatic shift is required – from "managerialism" to "entrepreneurialism". There is evidence that although national frameworks remain significant enablers and disablers of business activity, the majority of attributes required for business-friendliness success can and are regularly influenced by the action of local leaders at the city level (Clark, 2014). Public authorities are called upon to go beyond the sheer provision of social welfare services to citizens and embrace strategic and pro-active approaches to economic growth, risk-taking, innovation and an orientation toward the private-sector (Box 9.1).

Box 9.1. Main elements of the "urban entrepreneurialism"

The new approaches in urban spatial development, commonly referred to as "urban entrepreneurialism", have some distinctive characteristics:

- **from passive to positive planning** – because it ultimately aims at fostering and encouraging local economic development, it is intrinsically initiatory and pro-economic growth, trying to initiate economic growth rather than control and manage it;
- **from public-based to private-oriented and marked-driven** – while the previous approaches were basically led by the public sector, the new approaches aim at making full use of market mechanisms to achieve public goals with less public intervention. This triggers also forms of collaboration combining private resources and expertise; and
- **from traditional to corporate business values** – entrepreneurial planning tends to embrace characteristics once distinctive to private businesses, such as risk-taking, inventiveness, promotional and profit motivation.

Initial common areas where such urban entrepreneurialism emerged pertained to cultural policy and event hosting initiatives. Progressively, the potential of the new approaches has been applied to policies for building and housing, which form the physical fabrics of urban space. Finally, the full paradigm shift occurs when the new mode to stimulate private innovation and strengthen market functioning affects regulatory design and organisational and procedural arrangements. This implies relying on a variety of actors within formal governments, and between formal governments and the economy and civil society. Territorial and urban development "governance" replaces the notion of government for managing space.

Source: OECD (2007), *Competitive Cities: A New Entrepreneurial Paradigm in Spatial Development*, OECD Publishing, Paris, http://dx.doi.org/10.1787/9789264022591-en.

This is translated into initiatives that seek the creation of new industries and jobs by attracting investment and an economically active population instead of targeting more and more public resources to meet "special" or "additional" needs. There is increasing awareness of the fact that direct and indirect costs of doing business, the efficiency of the local and national frameworks, and the ways that regulations are designed and enforced, together make an important difference to how territorial development is achieved. Such entrepreneurial approach towards urban zoning has been dominant in former industrial cities that were struggling to restructure their economic base and it becomes particularly relevant also for transition economies (OECD, 2007).

In OECD countries, territorial development over the past decades has tended to emerge in metropolitan regions. There is a positive correlation between metro-regions' size and income, especially when they concentrate over 20% of national GDP. However, the growth capacity of metro-regions should not be overestimated as metro-regions are not always synonymous with success. An OECD study provided evidence that this correlation becomes negative at around 6-7 million – although this thresholds varies from country to country, suggesting diseconomies of agglomeration due to congestion and other related costs (OECD, 2006). The combination of economic advantages and difficulties posed by the rise of metro-regions presents a number of strategic choices or dilemmas that confront policy makers (Box 9.2).

Box 9.2. **Challenges in designing and developing metro-regions**

In OECD countries, territorial development policies are increasingly intertwined with urban – and in particular, metropolitan – governance. This presents a number of trade-off and challenges, including:

- **Positive or negative spill-overs?** Are metro-regions the cause of economic growth or its consequence? If the former, they need to be encouraged; if the latter, does their tendency to attract resources away from other regions do more overall harm than good?
- **Which public strategic vision in a market context?** A strategic vision is required to pursue the competitiveness of metro-regions. But can public authorities do this without attempting direct substantive economic planning which cannot work in a dynamic, changing economy?
- **Economic dynamism or liveable city?** Concentration of population, which partly account for metro-region's dynamism, causes also congestion, poor environment, housing shortages and the formation of ghettos. Is there a choice between economic dynamism and having a liveable city?
- **Appropriate scale or closeness to citizens?** The need for strategic visions and overall infrastructural planning in metro-regions, suggests some need for a relatively autonomous public authority at the appropriate geographical level. But this level will be remote from many citizens' local concerns. How can these tensions be balanced?
- **Metro-regions versus central/state government?** Autonomous public authority at the metro-regional level may seek devolved powers priorities whilst the higher levels of government (central or state government in federal countries) still want to maintain control on large cities. Where is the balance between these to be found?
- **Participation of private sector actors in metro-regions' governance?** Public authorities must involve the private sector in constructing regional partnerships for economic development. But can this avoid improper lobbying and a squeezing out of small and medium-sized enterprises by large corporations?
- **Unequal burdens or distorting subsidies?** The large spending needs of metro-regions create major fiscal challenges. At the same time, national goals – such as a demand for regional equity – might force metro-regions to contribute financially to the rest of the country. How can the right balance be found?

Source: OECD (2006), *Competitive Cities in the Global Economy*, OECD Publishing, Paris, http://dx.doi.org/10.1787/9789264027091-en.

The impact of public investment thus depends to a significant extent on how governments manage it. Both policy makers and economic operators are increasingly aware of the fact that the business and investment climate is likely to be successful only if it is tackled as it is – a complex and multi-dimensional phenomenon. To that end, a more refined, strategic and targeted approach at both national and local level is required, which accounts of the disparate needs, demands and supplies that a varied private sector expresses. This very much applies also to investment in territorial development, through policy instruments such as territorial planning, infrastructural design, urban zoning and construction permit procedures.

OECD evidence suggests that systemic challenges to the multi-level governance of public investment can hinder the achievement of best possible outcomes (OECD, 2013b). Challenges are to be faced in terms of:

- **Co-ordination** – while there is mutual dependence across levels of government, cross-sector, cross-jurisdictional and inter-governmental co-ordination are difficult in practice. The constellation of actors involved in policy design, public investment allocation, management and audit is large and their interests need to be aligned;
- **Capacity** – empirical evidence suggests that public investment and growth outcomes are correlated to the quality of government, notably at the local level. Recurring capacity bottlenecks particularly affect strategic planning, co-operation with private actors, long-term impact and risk assessment, capabilities for public procurement, etc.; and
- **Framework conditions** – these refer to the recurrent mismatch between budgetary frameworks, procurement requirements, regulatory and fiscal systems across jurisdictions.

To tackle these challenges and avoid dis-functionalities, the OECD (2014) has issued a *Recommendation on Effective Public Investment across Levels of Government*.[2] In this context, "administrative burden reduction is important at all levels of government. In some cases this can require the revision and simplification of formalities such as licences, permits and authorisations that are required for the development of public investment projects at the different levels of government (i.e. construction licences, transit permits, expropriations, among others)." (OECD, 2014, p. 24)

Against this background, the legal, organisational and procedural framework related to construction permits constitutes an important governance element. Over the years, the World Bank's Doing Business reports have consistently emphasised the extent to which building permits continue to be a significant obstacle to investment and business formalisation across economies. While one first, noticeable concern relates to informality, a further factor of inefficiency refers to what has been defined as the "gate-keeping function" of construction permits (see Box 9.3).

Box 9.3. The consequences of poor construction permit governance: Informality and the "gate-keeping factor"

There is general evidence that complex, costly, bureaucratic, and discretionary building procedures are associated with higher levels of informality. Corruptive practices can nest beyond these procedures and take massive proportions within issuing and enforcement agencies, adding risks to the community in terms of safety as well as significant costs to investors. Analysis of

Box 9.3. The consequences of poor construction permit governance: Informality and the "gate-keeping factor" (*cont.*)

World Bank Enterprise Survey data shows that the share of firms expecting to give gifts in exchange for construction approvals is correlated with the level of complexity and cost of dealing with construction permits (World Bank, 2009).

Besides "cow-boy building" and the related potential loss in human lives, informality generates costs because officially granted permits enable the formal registration of assets in public registries as property assets. Such registration leads to greater access to finance, and greater opportunity to invest in the formal sector.

Other challenges are triggered by a second type of governance problems – the so-called "gate-keeping function" of many authorities intervening in the construction permit procedure. In many countries, building laws include provisions requiring compliance with other requirements before construction can begin. In fact, pre-approvals from authorities other than those granting the building permit are always needed. These other approvals are often referred to by the generic term "applicable law," which is to say another law that is potentially applicable to building construction projects.[1]

For building permitting authorities, the withholding of a building permit is therefore the way to ensure compliance with such laws; hence building permits play a gate-keeper role to preserve a range of other public goods. In addition, "pre-approvals" generally include the obligation for investors and developers to confirm that they have legal title to the land, and that the proposed development is within the boundaries of the same property.

In short, multiple public agencies use the building permit process as one of their regulatory tools (or a "hook") to enforce their own public good. While this is a widespread practice in building permitting systems across the world, it creates the danger of building an insurmountable bureaucracy that is likely to discourage investment.

1. Concretely, "applicable laws" include laws, regulations, and bylaws which would prohibit construction unless complied. For example, an 'applicable law' could include provisions that: prohibit high-rise buildings in certain locations near runways and airports; a law that regulates construction in floodplains or agricultural areas; or a law that prevents the construction of commercial buildings, factories, or hotels near national heritage areas. For an investor or developer to meet these requirements, it is usually a precondition of applying for a building permit. The process of complying with relevant applicable laws involves obtaining 'pre-approval clearances' typically from agencies operating in land use planning; utilities; national or world heritage issues; environment; civil aviation; etc. [and] ministry of agriculture (in some cases) (IFC, 2009, p. 14).

Source: World Bank (2009), *Doing Business 2010: Reforming through Difficult Times*, World Bank Group, Washington, D.C.; IFC (2009), "Reforming Building Permits: Why Is It Important And What Can IFC Really Do?", The World Bank Group, Washington DC., pp. 14-15.

If excessively complex or burdensome, the procedure inverts what is the actual main objective of building permits – to ensure the health and safety of the community. This has important implications for policy-makers who need to strike the right balance between the cost imposed on private operators and the real benefits in safety and health standards.

Construction permits thus form part of those public services that are delivered by public authorities on the territory, and which have direct impact on both the actual efficiency of the procedural arrangements and the perception that economic operators have thereof. It is hence fundamental that any reform of the construction permit legal and procedural framework be linked to overarching public service and policy considerations.

As it was also noted (IFC, 2009, p. 15): "For reformers showing a strong interest in process simplification and streamlining, the "gate-keeper" role of the building permit process is often at the heart of the reform effort. While it can be relatively easy to reform the building permit process within a single municipality, it is always more complex to succeed in consolidating and simplifying multiple *ex ante* requirements from different public agencies."

The construction and real estate sectors in Lithuania

The economic size of the construction and real estate sectors in Lithuania is considerable. According to a recent study, the construction industry accounts on average for 6.5% of GDP in OECD economies (OECD, 2010, pp. 156-157). In Lithuania, that percentage (including connected sectors) approaches 10-13% of the national GDP for the construction sector and 5-6% of GDP for the real estate sector, according to data from related business associations.

In 2013,[3] investment in tangible fixed assets amounted to 16.6 LTL billion, registering a 12.3% growth compared to 2012. Almost 55% of all investments in 2013 were made in the construction of buildings and civil engineering structures (+8.5% compared to 2012). In terms of construction volume, domestic construction equalled LTL 7.3 billion (+11.3% compared to 2012) while investment abroad amounted to LTL 505 million (+11.1). The share of civil engineering infrastructures (mainly road and street construction) was 52.8% in 2013 (+8% compared to 2012).

In the second quarter of 2014, the volume of construction work carried out increased by 16.8% compared to the same period of 2013, amounting to LTL 2.2 billion (EUR 637 million). The share of construction of civil engineering structures accounted for 52% of total construction work carried out within the country and amounted to LTL 1.1 billion (EUR 318.6 million), i.e. 13.9% more than in the second quarter of 2013. The share of construction of non-residential buildings accounted for 36% of total construction work carried out within the country (a 12.5% increase against the same 2013 period), while residential buildings accounted for 12% of total construction work (some 70.2% more than in the second quarter of 2013.[4]

Statistics indicate that the great majority of the building activity and related investments are concentrated in the three main cities. In 2013, Vilnius accounted for 33.7% of the total annual construction work, followed by Kaunas (17.5%) and Klaipeda (14.1%). Even higher percentages are registered for dwellings: almost 58% of them were completed in the Vilnius county (41% on the City of Vilnius alone), 17% in Kaunas and 14% in Klaipeda. In the third quarter of 2014, 59.9% of all dwellings completed were located in the Vilnius county; 19.6% in the Kaunas county; and 9.5% in the Klaipeda county. When it comes to non-residential building, the largest proportion of those completed in the third quarter of 2014 fell within the Vilnius county (34.3%), with the Kaunas and Klaipeda counties following at 14.1% each.[5] This confirms the driving role that urban centres nowadays play in the economic development of the territory. Most construction work in Lithuania is related to new buildings (44%), with the rest almost equally shared between reconstructions (30%) and repairs and other interventions (26%).

Over the past months, nonetheless, the number of dwelling building construction permits issued has constantly decreased. On the basis of data from Infostatyba, the overall number decreased by 4.7% in the third quarter of 2014 compared to the same period of 2013. The construction of individual houses will remain predominant in the country as it accounts for 99% of all the dwelling building construction permits issued. In the third quarter of 2014, 561 building permits were issued for the construction of non-residential buildings, which is by 6.7% less than in the third quarter of 2013. Over the first three quarters of 2014, the number of non-residential building construction permits issued decreased by 16.9% compared to the same period of 2013, while the number of non-residential buildings whose construction was authorised decreased by 11.4%.[6]

Modernising construction permit and territorial planning procedures in Lithuania

Drivers for change

The reform of the construction and territorial planning procedures is firmly grounded in the government programmatic priorities. The improvement of the framework conditions for doing business in Lithuania have been a constant priority of the government. The government programme outlining the strategic objectives for the mandate 2012-16, adopted in December 2012,[7] pledges for job creation, industrial development and higher foreign investment. To achieve these goals, the government commits to, among other:

- investing State resources into infrastructure projects;
- renovating and modernisation public and residential buildings; and, notably in the "Improvement of the business conditions" chapter, to
- restoring trust between the authorities and business entities; reducing administrative and regulatory burdens in particular in relation to issuing licences and permits; and improving, accelerating and promoting territorial planning processes.

The government announced upfront the intention to "extend the list of cases where detailed plans are not necessary and simplify the procedures for the amendment of a detailed plan. We will reduce the abuse of the protection of the public interest. We will improve the procedures of land acquisition, alteration of the purpose of land, registration of construction, redemption of land for the purposes of the state and others."[8]

Not only were the objectives of the reform explicitly mentioned. Also the participatory approach to designing and implementing the reform was defined, calling for co-operation with "associated business organisations and other social partners in addressing issues relevant to the state and business as well as in drafting new laws and discussing them." A paradigm shift was furthermore announced with regard to the supervisory institutions, which "should, first of all, become business consultants and only in cases of deliberate abuse – punishers."[9]

Such a strong political commitment mirrors government external concern and evidence. Stakeholders' feedback and international comparisons are the main sources for action. From a business perspective, regulatory bottlenecks negatively affect investment decisions. Evidence from several investment consulting organisations indicate the relative weight that challenges linked to the regulatory and administrative framework in general, and the construction permit procedures in particular, plays in the private developers' decisions to invest in Lithuania and the overall region.

The relative importance of the regulatory environment as a factor for investment decisions has been highlighted by a survey carried out by a private consulting firm (Table 9.1).

Table 9.1. **Key criteria for building new manufacturing facilities in the CEE region**

Category	Weight	Sub-category	Weight
A Labour pool	25%	A1 Overall level of competencies	25%
		A2 Availability of labour force	25%
		A3 Experience with specific products	15%
		A4 Productivity	15%
		A5 Flexibility	15%
		A6 English language skills	5%
B Labour market regulation	15%	B1 Level of inclusion in trade unions	40%
		B2 Number of work councils	30%
		B3 Regulation of hiring/firing workers	30%
C Risk	15%	C1 Political risk	33%
		C2 Economical risk	33%
		C3 Financial risk	33%
D Proximity	15%	D1 Proximity of markets	35%
		D2 Proximity of resources	35%
		D3 Proximity of infrastructure (roads/railways/shipping lanes)	30%
E Infrastructure/building	15%	E1 Available buildings	60%
		E2 Regulatory environment	40%
F Easiness of implementation	15%	F1 Easiness of business functioning	60%
		F2 Easiness to get permits	40%

Source: Buck Consultants International (2011).

On the other hand, the attractiveness of the region suffers from the current quality of regulation and governance. Data related to companies investing in eleven manufacturing sectors between January 2010 and November 2014 indicate that regulatory or business climate related considerations ranked only fifth among the motivations for business to invest in the Central and Eastern European (CEE) region (Table 9.2).

Table 9.2. **Motives for investing in CEE countries (2010-14)**

Motive	Projects	% of FDI Projects	Companies	% of companies
Skilled workforce availability	37	47.4	34	45.9
Infrastructure and logistics	25	32.0	25	33.8
Lower costs	16	20.5	15	20.3
Proximity to markets or customers	15	19.2	15	20.3
Regulations or business climate	14	17.9	14	18.9
Domestic market growth potential	11	14.1	10	13.5
IPA or government support	10	12.8	10	13.5
Industry cluster/critical mass	4	5.1	4	5.4
Presence of suppliers or JV partners	3	3.8	3	4.0
Universities or researchers	2	2.6	2	2.7
Other motive	7	9.0	7	9.4

Source: fDi Markets, a service from The Financial Times Limited 2015. All Rights Reserved.

On the basis of this evidence, a number of complaints were reportedly conveyed to the attention of the government by various Lithuanian trade and professional business organisations. Concern was expressed especially in relation to the excessive length and complexity of the permit procedures. The cumbersome interplay of several authorities across various levels of government allegedly contributed to the perception of disproportionate transaction costs. In addition, the business community's distress also referred to complications in the process of verifying decisions by the public administration related to issuing the permits. Sub-optimal accountability arrangements and emergence of politicisation in interpreting and abiding with the procedures were mentioned as further elements of concern. Finally, the provisions regulating Environmental Impact Assessment (EIA) were pointed out as specific challenging areas.[10]

The Investors' Forum, Lithuania's association reuniting the largest investing organisations in the country,[11] for instance, identified land and territorial planning as the first of its "key proposals" to the government in 2013. Their specific demands (Investors' Forum, 2013, p. 14) were:

- "ensure existing legal instruments would not allow manipulating with public interests;
- improve territorial planning and construction procedures and increase transparency;
- develop industrial areas; and
- revise the proposed Environmental Impact Assessment Act and other legislation governing EIA and Strategic Environmental Assessment (SEA) procedures."

Another one-stop shop organisation promoting (foreign) investment in the country, InvestLithuania,[12] provided the OECD review team with anecdotal own evidence that issues linked to territorial planning and infrastructure are mentioned as problematic by up to 90% of the respondents (foreign investors) to internal questionnaires.

The OECD review team was reported that these and similar other statements have been consistently voiced by various private sector stakeholders. While no structured initiatives were launched to collect such complaints, informal and ad hoc meetings have contributed to set the reform's agenda.

Table 9.3. **Lithuania's Doing Business construction permit index (2006-2013)**

Year	DTF	Procedures (number)	Time (days)	Cost (% of warehouse value)
DB2006	79.38	11	148.5	0.5
DB2007	79.48	11	148.5	0.4
DB2008	79.51	11	148.5	0.4
DB2009	79.73	11	147.5	0.4
DB2010	79.77	11	147.5	0.3
DB2011	79.71	11	147.5	0.4
DB2012	81.83	11	125.5	0.4
DB2013	83.28	11	111	0.3

Note: No Doing Business ranking is reported for the country's performance before 2014.

Source: www.doingbusiness.org/Custom-Query/lithuania (consulted 23 March 2015).

Besides the complaint channel, the World Bank's Doing Business index has been explicitly and directly used by the government to prioritise reforms. Until 2011, the eleven procedures that had to be followed when dealing with construction permits required up to 147.5 days on average – a value which was initially reduced to 125.5 days in 2012. On average, such procedures caused an administrative cost fluctuating between

0.5% and 0.4% of a warehouse value. According to the Doing Business calculations, this performance positioned Lithuania at 79.71 "distance to frontier" (DTF) points (Table 9.3).[13]

By definition, Doing Business indexes are comparative and it is hence critical to appraise one economy's performance both in absolute and in relative terms. Compared to 13 neighbouring economies, in 2013 Lithuania equalled Finland as fifth-sixth best performing country, lagging some ten points behind leading Denmark and almost six points behind Germany, which is just behind Denmark (Table 9.4). Such a situation was considered by the government as relevant to trigger simplification initiatives in the sector.

Table 9.4. **Doing Business construction permit index 2012 (Lithuania and 13 neighbouring countries)**

Economy Name	DTF	Procedures (number)	Time (days)	Cost (% of warehouse value)
Denmark	91.59	7	64	1.3
Germany	87.27	8	96	1.2
Sweden	84.29	7	117	2.6
Estonia	84.04	11	103	0.3
Lithuania	**81.83**	**11**	**125.5**	**0.4**
Finland	81.53	15	64	0.9
Belarus	76.06	15	123	0.8
Latvia	70.14	15	191	0.4
Hungary	69.46	23	91	0.2
Slovak Republic	68.18	10	286	0.1
Czech Republic	63.15	24	143	0.2
Poland	60.64	20	213	0.8
Russian Federation	26.20	…	…	…
Ukraine	21.18	18	374	16.9

Source: Doing Business data, www.doingbusiness.org/ (consulted 23 March 2015).

Design and objectives of the construction permit framework reform

The government spelled out action points through which it intended to implement its regulatory quality and simplification commitments through a number of resolutions and other legal acts.[14] With regard to the construction permit simplification, the following sources are relevant:

- Government Resolution No. 4 of January 2012[15] details the methodology to identify and measure administrative burdens on businesses;
- Law (XI-2386) of November 2012[16] sets out the general concept of reducing administrative burdens at all levels of government and establishes the Better Regulation Supervisory Commission;
- Government Resolution No. 228 of March 2013[17] allocates main responsibility for the permit reform to the Ministry of Environment (Action 47);
- Government Resolution No. 931 of October 2013[18] stresses among other also the importance of improving energy saving and efficiency standards in residential buildings; it also sets the explicit target to increase the percentage of remote construction permit applications via the official information system Infostatyba from 36% (value in 2013) to at least 47% in 2014; and
- Government Resolution No. 964 of October 2013[19] establishes the main principles pertaining to evaluating the justification of a licensing system referring

to any economic activity; to preparing draft laws that regulate licensing of specific economic activities and draft licensing rules, models of issuing licences; and to the definition of terms and criteria for evaluating legal regulation efficiency. The Ministry of Economy is made responsible for the screening process of the licensing framework.

These legal acts intervened within the framework of the Construction Law as this was progressively amended since 2010.[20]

- Reduction in the number of cases for which it is mandatorily required to prepare the full-scale design of the structure (Article 20, 1 January 2014);
- Integration under the Infostatyba system (and digitalisation) of the procedures for document presentation and performance verification (Article 12, part 1, par. 12, and Article 23, p. 31, 1 January 2014);
- Introduction of the right for the builder (client) to choose the service provider, engineering networks and communications owner or operator (Article 20, part 4, 1 January 2014);
- Simplification of the procedure for legal recognition of the right to carry out activities by non-resident persons (Article 18, 1 January 2012); and
- Introduction of the right for architects and construction engineers to manage the design, construction, project supervision, engineering supervision of a simple and ordinary (not exceptional) structure without certification. Their qualification requirements are established by the government authorised institution (Article 10, p. 9, 1 January 2010).

The government focused on incremental administrative improvements rather than radical change. It did not deem necessary to modify the overall allocation of responsibility among the actors participating in the various stages of the construction permit procedures. The government hence embarked in the reform with the following main objectives:

- Reducing the number of institutions issuing and verifying specific requirements;
- Reducing the quantity of mandatory documentation necessary to obtain a permit;
- Shortening the length of administrative decision-making;
- Clarifying the overall process and the individual underpinning criterial and requirements; and
- Enhancing transparency, accessibility of documents and accountability.

Simplification of procedures to obtain construction permits

To achieve the objectives, the reform was conceived to unfold along several strands of action, which are partly still under consideration and partly already accomplished. The latter were mainly centred around:

- Reducing the maximum number of days allowed to public administrations to complete the procedures;
- Clarifying the building categorisation and reducing the number of authorities required to issue certifications; and

- Promoting the digitalisation of the procedures, notably through an upgraded version of the portal of the information system Infostatyba.

Discussions are by contrast still ongoing about intervening on other fronts, including a reform of the liability and insurance regime; the rationalisation of the inspection policy; and the possibility to revising dispute settlement mechanisms.

A first regulatory intervention sought to reduce the length of the construction permit procedures. Reportedly upon consultation with municipalities and stakeholders, the Ministry of Environment set the new deadlines for the overall construction permit procedure by reducing the number of procedural steps from seven to five and setting the maximum period for the verification of the design and the preparation of the construction permit to 30 working days for a permit to construct or reconstruct a specific structure and 25 days for a permit in all other cases (Figure 9.3).

Figure 9.3. **The simplified construction permit procedure in Lithuania**

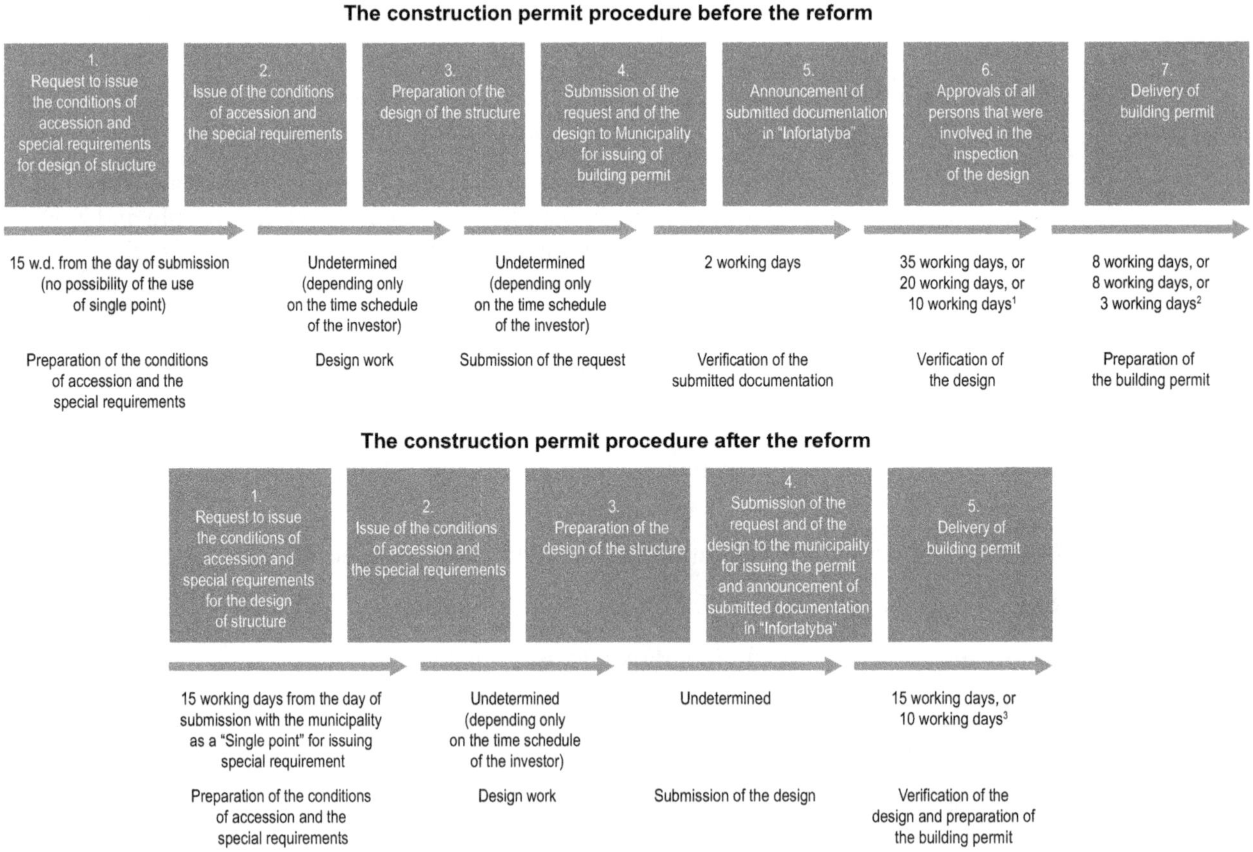

Notes:

1) 35 working days for a permit to construct or reconstruct a specific structure; 20 working days for a permit to construct or reconstruct a new ordinary structure; 10 working days for other cases.

2) 8 working days for a permit to construct or reconstruct a specific structure; 8 working days for a permit to construct or reconstruct a new ordinary structure; 3 working days for other cases;.

3) 15 working days for a permit to construct or reconstruct a specific structure; 10 working days for other cases.

Source: Information provided by the Ministry of Environment, January 2015.

Lithuania strengthened these simplification measures by introducing the "silence-is-consent" principle, according to which a permit is considered automatically granted if the public authorities do not provide a (negative) response by the expiration of the deadlines set in the law. Disagreement with the authorisation to grant a permit must be provided explicitly.[21]

A second strand of interventions referred to streamlining the risk-based approach to certification and control. Specific emphasis was put on clarifying the criteria for assigning a building project to exceptional categories that require dedicated certifications either because of specific preservation purposes or determined levels of risk. Such categories were allegedly excessively wide and prone to various interpretation and discretion. Not only were the definitions spelled out better. Also the number of such categories has been reduced from 15 to only seven. The reform also reduced the number of cases that require the involvement of all possible certifying authorities foreseen by the law (Box 9.4).

Box 9.4. Lithuania's new building categorisation

Further to the reform, all structures are divided into structures of exceptional, non-exceptional significance and simple.

The list of exceptional significance structures is reduced and includes buildings as laid down in the Law on Construction (Article 2, paragraph 3). Those are structures:

- in which hazardous materials are used or stored (according to their set limits);
- in which there is potentially dangerous equipment or potentially hazardous work is carried out;
- for which a public use of the building is foreseen with more than 100 people;
- that constitute high rise (more than 5 floors) apartment houses;
- that are registered as cultural heritage buildings; or
- that are characterised by complex design and sophisticated technology structures (according the consequences of the application classes of structural failure).

Source: Government of Lithuania (2015), January; and http://www3.lrs.lt/pls/inter3/dokpaieska.showdoc_l?p_id=468095&p_tr2=2.

Such clarification efforts clearly reflect good international practice (Box 9.5).

Box 9.5. Classifying buildings to rationalise control: Australia and France

Facing increasingly tight resource constraints, many government have embarked on so-called risk-based approaches to regulation. Such approaches seek to allocate resources rationally and efficiently, often there where the risk of infringements is higher or the magnitude of adverse impacts is greater.

Providing clearly defined categories of buildings for which various levels of screening are required is one application of such risk-based approaches. Often, countries have linked the classification of the buildings with the organisation (frequency and stringency) of the subsequent inspection policies.

Box 9.5. **Classifying buildings to rationalise control: Australia and France** (*cont.*)

Australia has developed a rather detailed classification system with up to nine building categories. Each category is linked to the use of the building and a level of risk associated to it. This allows for refinements. For instance, if an office building has one floor with residential apartments, that floor will be classified differently and different scrutiny and inspection criteria apply.

In France, the building classification is primarily based on occupancy and use, though height also plays a role. Accordingly, only non-residential buildings that receive visitors (such as malls, office buildings or movie theatres) and residential buildings up to 50 meters tall are categorised. Mandatory inspections are required for those buildings that host 300 people or more, and inspections may in turn relate to the whole building structure or to a specific part of the building such as framing, roofing or thermal performance.

At European level, a system of ten European Standards (EN 1990-EN 1999) provides a common approach for the design of buildings and other civil engineering works and construction products. They contribute to an integrated approach of European policies for the construction sector and ensure uniform levels of safety. As such, they are mandatory for Member States, although a margin for applying innovative risk-management policies is allowed and indeed incentivised (according to Article 9 of the Law on Construction).

Source: World Bank (2014), "What role should risk-based inspections play in construction?", in *Doing Business 2014*, The World Bank Group, Washington DC, pp. 46-51; http://eurocodes.jrc.ec.europa.eu/showpage.php?id=1; http://eurocodes.jrc.ec.europa.eu/.

A further measure sought to improve the performance of the Infostatyba, the digital support to the official information system governing the construction permit and State supervision procedures. Formally introduced in November 2003,[22] Infostatyba started being operational several years later after a series of tests and upgrades. The system is managed by the State Territorial Planning and Construction Inspectorate (STPCI) under the Ministry of Environment, which is responsible also for its further development and maintenance. The modernisation process of Infostatyba was carried out by external contractors. The government is considering the opportunity to further expand over the next months the operation of Infostatyba to also safety standard procedures.

Infostatyba works as both a front-desk and back-office interface with the support of the STPCI. While managed centrally, it is operated mostly by the staff of individual municipalities and it connects in real time all the public authorities that are to be involved in each permit application case. Training to operate the upgraded system has been provided by the STPCI to municipal staff. The STPCI also issued a system user manual which was circulated among municipalities with a description of the main functions step by step. Finally, the STPCI serves as a help desk office for any sort of questions and open issues related to Infostatyba. In 2014, the STPCI's IT department carried out about 4 500 consultations on the tool, mainly through phone assistance. The consultations were given for various users groups, ranging from public authorities dealing with remote procedures to designers, builders, inspectors etc. In addition, the Strategy and Analysis department of the STPCI provides legal advice – some 13 300 in 2014 alone.

Besides upgrading the application and validation software, changes to the Infostatyba web portal concerned also enhanced information to the publication at large. Statistics and accounting pages are regularly updated and individual citizens can now get information on the status of permits online.[23]

Leveraging on digital one-stop shops is considered to be international good practice and as such it was particularly welcomed by stakeholders. OECD countries widely recognise that the implementation of ICT and e-government forms to the construction permit framework brings several benefits (Box 9.6). It significantly contributes to meeting set deadlines and signalling possible delays or mistakes. This enhances the overall transparency and accountability of the regime, providing at the same time higher legal certainty to the applicant. For the public administration, the full digitalisation of the procedure allows precise performance tracking, which can yield more accurate feedback statistical data on where procedural or organisational bottlenecks nest.

Box 9.6. **Digitalising the construction permit procedures**

Building Information Modelling (BIM) technologies can play a decisive role in improving building code compliance strategies, significantly contributing to streamlining the design process, reducing time and costs. BIM systems manage essential building design, construction, maintenance, and overall project data in digital format throughout the building life cycle. This digital information, in its simplest form, is a three-dimensional representation of the building and its hidden specification details.

The *DesignCheck* programme is a case in point. Developed in Australia as a BIM providing an automated code-checking tool, designers can use this programme to check the code requirements at different stages of project design. Compliance consultants and building authorities can get automated data from architects, and basic checking and building-code compliance tests can be done rapidly and automatically, allowing those responsible for building compliance to focus on higher-risk features (World Bank, 2013, p. 19).

A further important contribution that ICT can make to administrative simplification relates to the creation of efficient one-stop shops. While the advantages are well documented, at present only 37 economies around the world have some kind of one-stop shop for construction permits. Since 2009, 17 economies have successfully implemented one-stop shops for permit applications (World Bank Group, 2014).

Source: World Bank (2013), *Good Practices for Construction Regulation and Enforcement Reform. Guidelines for Reformers*, Investment Climate / The World Bank Group, Washington D.C., p.19; World Bank Group (2014), Doing Business: Measuring Business Regulations, "Dealing with construction permits – Using one-stop shops to improve co-ordination", www.doingbusiness.org/data/exploretopics/dealing-with-construction-permits/good-practices#using.

Against the clear progress achieved so far, the digitalisation and modernisation of Infostatyba as a fully-fledged, well-performing one-stop shop still presents some margins for technical improvement and capacity-building. Issues that deserve further attention in the near future are mainly of technical nature. They include the overall limited size of the files that can be uploaded to the system; the impossibility to use the certified electronic signature; as well as the fact that the applicant has to restart the application anew if s/he made a mistake or wants to upload modified information. Limited funding is reported to be one main cause for postponing further technical upgrading.

A second category of challenges limiting the full exploitation of the one-stop shop refer to capacity-building in the public administrations. The actual application of Infostatyba is reported to be satisfactory, with some municipalities for instance reporting not to have needed extensive new training and staff re-conversion because an equivalent IT system was already in place. Some other municipalities, however, still face challenges in both re-organising staff in accordance with the new procedures and getting familiar with the latest ICT components. Two practices de facto have tended to coexist in the first reform months, with the formal procedures formally kicked off by the Infostatyba interface with the applicant but the actual back-office administrative interplay remaining largely paper-based. Both the STPCIand the business representatives interviewed by the OECD review team acknowledged this and attributed it to the natural transition that each reform of this type implies for public administrators.

The construction permit reform is not fully achieved and discussion is ongoing on various issues. One of those relates to the merit to revisit the insurance requirements for the sector, with in particular the idea of introducing mandatory insurance. The current regime in Lithuania foresees only the voluntary stipulation of insurance contracts between builders and owners of buildings. While the idea of generalising the principle and making it mandatory found initial resistance by some circles in the insurance industry, such stance no longer appears to reflect majority. A debate is currently ongoing in Lithuania on the opportunity to introduce mandatory insurance requirements.

Box 9.7. Generalising insurance and liability throughout the construction chain: France

In France, the principle of liability and insurance in the construction sector was enshrined in the Napoleonic Civil Code in 1804 already. It was nonetheless only through the so-called *Spinetta Law* of 1978 that all actors participating in the construction industry chain – not only architects and builders, but also owners (or contracting authorities) – have to hold insurance against potential faults in construction. The core of the system is indeed to rely on insurance companies to settle claims between themselves (avoiding litigation as much as possible) and to enforce some "discipline" on construction professionals in the form of higher premiums for those with a poor track record.

By so doing, the logic of the reform process has been to transfer responsibilities for compliance on private actors. This has not meant de-regulation, though; and the State has the power to enforce them through the court system. However, day-to-day control is carried out by mandatory technical control, performed by third parties (not the State). Construction permits require only basic plans and no detailed technical specifications. The liability of private contractors, the mandatory insurance and technical controllers are the three elements which ensure compliance. The progressive reform of the construction sector along these axes has allowed France to reconcile the two fundamental objectives of the reform – simplifying the procedures and ensuring quality and safety.

Source: Le coin du droit de l'urbanisme, "Évolution historique du permis de construire", www.coin-urbanisme.org/autorisations/permis/introduction/historique.html (consulted 23 March 2015).

International experience suggests that such a principle is particularly effective to avoid market and regulatory failures related to liability enforcement. Typical problematic instances are those where owners or developers are left with no recourse in case of building faults if builders/contractors went bankrupt in the meantime, or simply had insufficient resources to cover the damage. In other cases, even when builders were adequately insured, owners often have a difficult time getting the insurance to pay up, requiring lengthy and costly court cases to succeed. A formal and binding general requirement for liability and insurance for all actors involved in the construction process is likely to address similar situations (Box 9.7).

Rationalising the inspection regime is a further channel for additional reform contemplated by Lithuania. The insurance dimension mentioned above is one of the possible avenues that allows permit reformers to leverage the power of the market to achieve change efficiently. A further dimension that can be exploited relates to the inspection regime. Leveraging the interface between public and private actors responsible for enforcement control bears considerable potential. In the case of the liability and insurance, the triggering logic is provided by the fact that "bad" contractors have difficulty to insure themselves, or end up doing so at a higher price, only – what may constitute a stronger incentive than the fear of fines or sanctions.

Reviews of systems based on frequent controls by State or public authorities suggest that they are not always effective (VROM, 2009; Van der Heijden, 2009; and Visscher and Meijer, 2005, pp. 644-655). Because the construction process and sites progress every day, it is impossible for inspectors to be always present everywhere. Recurring to private (certified) partners to enforce construction safety regulation often constitutes a superior solution to state-based inspections (Blanc, 2012). A number of countries have introduced mixed or fully private-based approaches to inspection and enforcement (Box 9.10).

Box 9.10. Delegating inspection functions to the private sector: experiences in Europe

The Czech republic provides an example of a transition economy that pivoted its construction permit reforms around the introduction of a new independent profession which did not exist before – the "authorised inspector". The new Czech building code adopted in 2007 allows developers to either rely on the public building office to handle the entire permitting process or to contract out specific tasks to a private inspector. That inspector goes through the project's documentation to assess if it accords with the territorial plan and the relevant building regulations. Cutting the lengthy back and forth between builders and building offices, the authorised inspector can help builders address discrepancies between the design plans and the required standards right away.

At the end of the process the authorised inspector issues a certificate that the designed structure can be built. Although the certificate and the relevant documentation still have to be sent to the public building office, the builder can start construction immediately. Authorised inspectors can also issue the basic approval document at the end of construction, allowing builders to put the building into use. Inspections during construction are still carried out by the building offices, but they follow a schedule established by the inspector during the initial assessment. The most important inspiration came from England (where private inspectors can replace public buildings proceedings) and Bavaria (where private inspections complement public building proceedings).

In Germany, local building control contracts out many checking and inspection activities to specialised and recognised engineering firms. The check engineers (*Prüfingenieure*) are independent, freelance, fully qualified, legal persons with proven knowledge of static and structural problems. They are specialised, recognised, have to comply with heavy demands to qualify and are liable for the quality of their certification.

The United Kingdom also established a classification of buildings based on risks. Unlike many other countries (such as New Zealand) where the enforcement of risk management relies

Box 9.10. Delegating inspection functions to the private sector: Experiences in Europe *(cont.)*

on the individual risk profile established by each building designer, the UK system requires the automatic application of certain provisions of the State building code if the project exceeds certain risk thresholds in terms of size and complexity, and the control authorities, whether public or private, keep the upper hand and carry out more traditional checks and inspections.

Norway and Sweden have a control system based on self-confirmation. The applicant is always responsible for the execution of the plan checks and site inspections. Local building control authority checks the control plan in which the applicant indicates how all the necessary inspections – during design and on-site – are provided for. The local authority decides whether the guarantees presented by the applicant are satisfactory or whether an independent inspection by a specialised inspection body is necessary. A complex, risk-based classification system guides the degree of self-enforcement granted to the applicant.

Far from deregulating, best-practice countries have all introduced a measure of private sector solutions at the different process stages regulatory control chain, with the goal of increasing efficiency and providing consistent, high-quality services and delivery.

Source: World Bank (2008), "Creating a new profession from scratch: Doing Business Case Study: Czech Republic", in *Celebrating Reform 2008*, The World Bank Group, Washington DC, pp. 28-33; Visscher, H.J. and F.M. Meijer (2005), "Enforcing building regulations: Private versus public responsibilities", in the *Proceedings of W099 4th Triennial International Conference: Rethinking and Revitalizing Construction Safety, Health, Environment and Quality*, 17-20 May, Port Elizabeth (South Africa), pp. 644-655.

Streamlining permit disputes through swifter administrative and judicial appeal procedures or alternative settlement mechanisms is a further reform area under discussion. There is no evidence so far that the simplification measures introduced to date are going to significantly impact on the current redress system. Statistics referring to 2014 indicate that regional administrative courts received 333 cases regarding zoning, planning and construction and the average term to solve a case was 5.18 months. The Supreme Administrative court was seized 37 times in 2014 in relation to zoning, planning and construction and the average term to solve a case was 7.57 months (if it is normal appeal) and 2.42 months (if it is a separate request).[24] In broad terms, the whole litigation process for construction permits usually takes up to 8-12 months, while it can be longer (take up to 2 years) for cases related to zoning and planning disputes.

Such performance is generally not considered as particularly problematic, but the salience of disputed cases remains an open issue because of interpretation challenges. The stakeholders met by the OECD review team acknowledged that, while speedier procedures are always welcomed, the governance of litigation does not appear to be a strong priority for reform in the construction sector. A decreased number of complaints about procedural delays or appeals to technical permit decisions is on the other hand considered by the government as a significant indicator of the progressive optimisation of the process.[25] The issue of disputed cases remains nonetheless topical because of the allegedly frequent difficulties faced by even specialists in municipalities and other affected institutions in interpreting legal provisions.

The Construction Law already provides forms of alternative dispute settlements, but their effectiveness is questioned by a number of stakeholders. Should one or more certifying authorities disagree with issuing a permit authorisation, the municipality summons a meeting with the applicant, all the affected administrations and the head of the administration(s) in disagreement, with a view to explain the respective stances on the basis of technical design. This does not preclude any right by all parties to appeal to courts.

The STPCI also plays a role in arbitrating disagreements as it may be seized to screen the decision made by a municipality. However, not only is the opinion of the STPCI not binding on the municipality, but the STPCI is not obliged to issue such an opinion. This appears to trigger irregular interventions by the STPCI as a mediating instance, thereby also undermining the relevance of the right granted to the STPCI to bring the disputed case in front of the relevant court. Chapter 7 provides further details on the role of the STPCI and the questions it raises.

Besides addressing the complaints it receives, the STPCI has the faculty to proceed to randomised screenings of municipalities decisions. The Inspectorates reviews about 500 of such decisions each year, on the basis of a risk management system that considers the track record of municipalities, architects, building companies and other actors intervening in the chain. Evidence from such reviews over the past years indicates that some 30% of all construction permit decisions by municipalities present one or more problems, among which the most common are delays in meeting procedural deadlines and inconsistencies with territorial planning documents.[26]

Considering that one case review can take between two and three days to be processed and that the STPCI is staffed with five,[27] the resulting 250-300 days / year that each inspector must devote to this specific task raises the question of its actual efficiency. The decision to proceed to 500 randomised reviews in one year is also debatable if in Vilnius alone some 60 applications for construction works are filed every week, and considering that more than 18 800 construction permits were issued in Lithuania in 2014.

Reform achievements to date

The measures introduced over the past two years have produced immediate impacts on the construction permit legal framework. Positive results have for instance been recorded by the related Doing Business index, both in absolute and relative terms. In the Doing Business 2015 report, the simplification measures introduced in the construction permit framework contributed to improving the related index ranking by ten positions – bringing Lithuania to occupy the 15th rank (out of 189 economies) compared to the 25th rank in 2014.

Also relative performance has improved. Compared to the same 13 neighbouring countries considered above, Lithuania has stepped up three positions within two years and in 2015 comfortably featured third behind Denmark and Germany. The performance is particularly noteworthy if considered in relative terms, as Lithuania has gained 3.44 DTF points compared to only 0.15 DTF points by Germany and even a -1.75 DTF points regression by Denmark over the same period. As a result, the distance from the regional leader has been shorted from 9.6 to 4.6 DTF points (Table 9.5).

Also specific digitalisation targets have been met. In 2014, both the Lithuanian municipalities and the STPCI received a cumulated 75 139 applications related to a construction process – 46 931 of which (about 62.5%) were submitted through Infostatyba.[28] The applications to permits specifically pertaining to construction works were 45 424, of which 31 667 (69.7%) through Infostatyba. Both largely overcome the target of 47% for the same year set by the government.[29]

Table 9.5. **Doing Business construction permit index 2015**

Economy name	Rank	DTF	Procedures (number)	Time (days)	Cost (% of warehouse value)
Denmark	5	89.84	7	64	2.3
Germany	8	87.42	8	96	1.1
Lithuania	**15**	**85.27**	**11**	**91**	**0.3**
Sweden	18	84.73	7	116	2.4
Estonia	20	84.18	11	103	0.3
Finland	33	81.61	15	64	0.8
Latvia	47	78.38	12	149	0.3
Belarus	51	78.20	14	114	0.8
Ukraine	70	75.29	8	64	10.2
Hungary	103	69.37	23	91	0.2
Slovak Republic	110	68.19	10	286	0.1
Poland	137	62.97	19	212	0.3
Czech Republic	139	62.91	24	143	0.3
Russian Federation	156	56.70	19.8	238.4	1.9

Source: Doing Business data, www.doingbusiness.org/ (consulted 23 March 2015).

Such achievements have been broadly welcomed by the Lithuanian business community at large, although possible initial implementation bottlenecks might delay the concrete realisation of simplification benefits. The simplification efforts were valued also because the government signalled the intention to proceed to a progressive yet comprehensive revision of the overall legal framework affecting territorial development related investments (see below the section on putting the reform in context and reaping the full benefit potentials.

Figure 9.4. **Frequency of obstacles to daily operations**

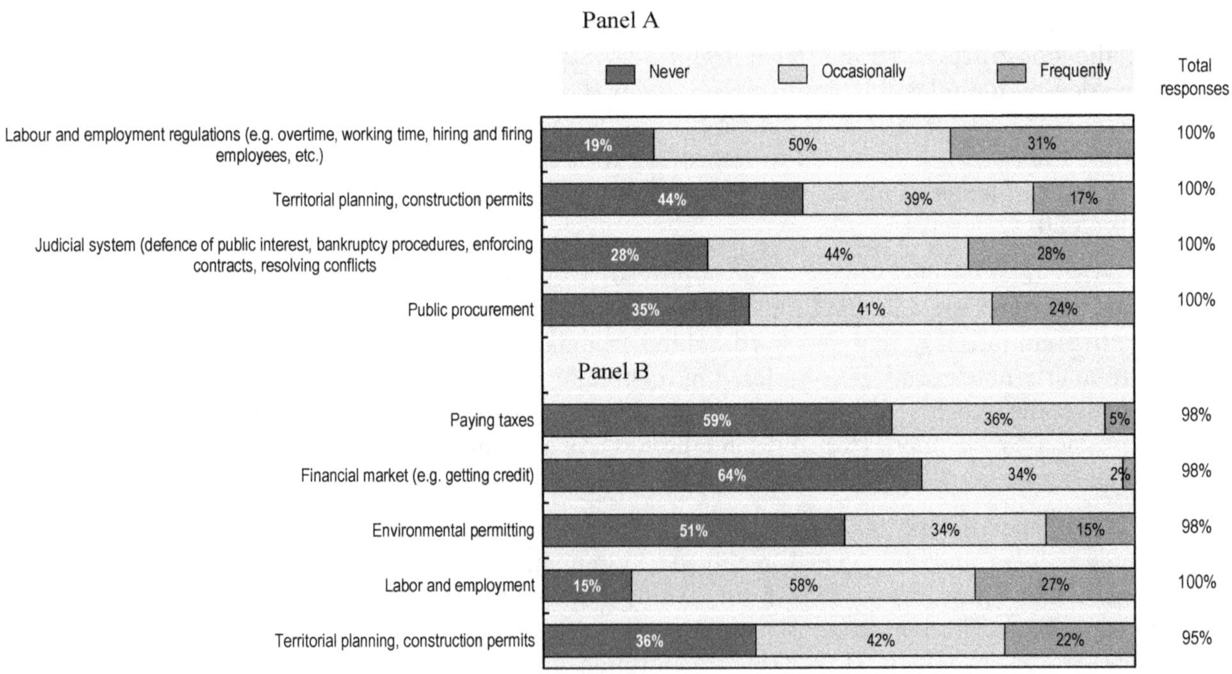

Source: Investors' Forum (2014a), *Investor Confidence Index for Lithuania 2014,* Q2 (Issue 1), Vilnius, p. 9; and Investors' Forum (2014b), *Investor Confidence Index for Lithuania 2014,* Q4 (Issue 2), Vilnius, Table 12, p. 5.

Findings from the Investors' Forum's *Investor Confidence Index 2014* nonetheless suggest a more unhurried reaction by entrepreneurs.[30] Asked twice during the year to identify how frequently they perceive to encounter problems in various day-to-day activities, the surveyed managers indicate little improvement in the field of territorial planning and construction permits. This ranks as the second largest troubling area also several months after the implementation of the changes. Twenty two per cent of companies participating in the survey report to face obstacles frequently against some 42% occasional challenges. Six months before, these figures were less negative (Figure 9.4).

Effective gains and saving are still to materialise. While the Forum's *Confidence Index* does not define in details the nature and scale of the challenges mentioned by the surveyed companies, it imaginable that difficulties and possible delays have emerged in the initial transition and implementation phases of the simplified procedures. This may well still affect the perception of investors.

A further possible reason for the sober results may lie with the fact that no structured measurement of the actual administrative burdens imposed by the permit procedures was carried out (Box 9.11). The Ministry of Environment carried out the simplification exercise without relying on this cost assessment methodology. Because of the lacking evidence, it is possible that developers and operators in the construction sector incur in equivalent levels of administrative burdens despite the reduced number of days formally allowed to issue a permit.

Box 9.11. Simplifying through measuring construction permits administrative burdens: Italy

In Italy, the construction sector is an area of shared competences between the State, the regions and local authorities. Because of its strategic importance and its economic significant, it has been selected by the government as one of the priority simplification areas to be subject to administrative burden measurement, as a part of the "Simplify Italy" government decree.[1]

The measurement exercise was carried out in 9 of the 21 Italian regions, covering almost 600 municipalities, upon an intensive programme of computer-assisted telephone interviewing with more than 2 700 professionals (mainly architects and surveyors). Subsequent national and regional focus groups with representatives of affected business associations were organised to validate the findings and consider the experience with one-stop shops. Six related procedures were screened, related to: the permit application; the certified notifications of construction start (so-called "SCIA" and "super-DIA"); the communication of the works' start and termination; and the issuance of the certificate of use and occupancy.

According to the measurement related to the years 2011 and 2012, the estimated annual total burdens generated by administrative procedures pertaining to the construction sector in Italy amounts to EUR 4.4 bn. The findings notably indicate that the correct use of the one-stop shop can potentially reduce the procedure's cost by up to 19% and the time by almost 26% for non-residential building permits. Such findings allowed for priority and targeted simplification measures, such as the upgrade of the competence of the one-stop shop (transforming it from an information-collecting to a decisional platform).

1. www.funzionepubblica.gov.it/lazione-del-ministro/tagli-alla-burocrazia/presentazione.aspx.

Source: Ministero della Funzione Pubblica (n.a.), "I risultati della misurazione nel settore edilizia", www.funzionepubblica.gov.it/media/1066310/edilizia_dossiermoa.pdf (consulted 23 March 2015).

Putting the reform in context: Reaping the spill-over potentials

Public sector reforms are likely to be most effective if they are designed and implemented as a function of broader and concomitant structural reforms. They are a tool to achieve further priority policy objectives of governments. Reforms of construction permits and the construction law in general do not make an exception. The often technical simplification changes brought about by the simplification packages need to be fine-tuned to further regulatory policy initiatives and with a revision of the way the (urban) territory is organised and managed, if economic growth and development are to be achieved.

Against this backdrop, this section contextualise the construction permit reform in Lithuania by considering measures taken by the government notably in relation to its territorial planning reform and the infrastructure law. In both cases, streamlined construction permit procedures help achieving spill-over and multiplying effects.

The reform of territorial planning in Lithuania

The contribution of zoning and territorial planning to development and life quality

Quality of life and economic growth largely depend on territorial planning policies. In an urban context, zoning is an essential administrative tool to stimulate development. Getting zoning right is a key element yielding to effective framework conditions for economic and social activities (Box 9.12).

Box 9.12. Correct zoning contributes to territorial development

Zoning is about mapping the territory into different areas based on the types of the desired purposes. Possible zone uses may range from residential or commercial, to industrial, public buildings, or parks and green purposes. As a norm, more or less detailed plans define the main characteristics of each zone and the rules governing activities and development there. Specific ordinances are usually issued to determine such factors as building size, height, shape and colour; building location; and urban densities.

Zoning is not only concerned with defining each individual area; it is also used to avoid the mixing of incompatible land uses and maximise economies of scale. This triggers economic, social and environmental benefits:

- economically, well-designed zoning mitigates or fully avoids the negative external effects associated with the proximity of incompatible land uses, thereby incentivising greater overall economic efficiency than would occur in the absence of regulation;
- social benefits are triggered when zoning helps ensure an adequate supply of safe clean water and the suitable disposal of waste; when it promotes gentrification, facilitates access to schools or hospitals; or when it reduces social ghettoisation; and
- from an environmental perspective, a good zoning plan can help reduce greenhouse gas emissions – for instance by reducing (private) vehicle travel through higher-density cluster development and concentration of residential settlements near job-intensive centres. A further means through which zoning can contribute to green policies is by rationalising and streamlining public transport networks.

Figure 9.5. **Enhancing the synergies between construction permit procedures and zoning**

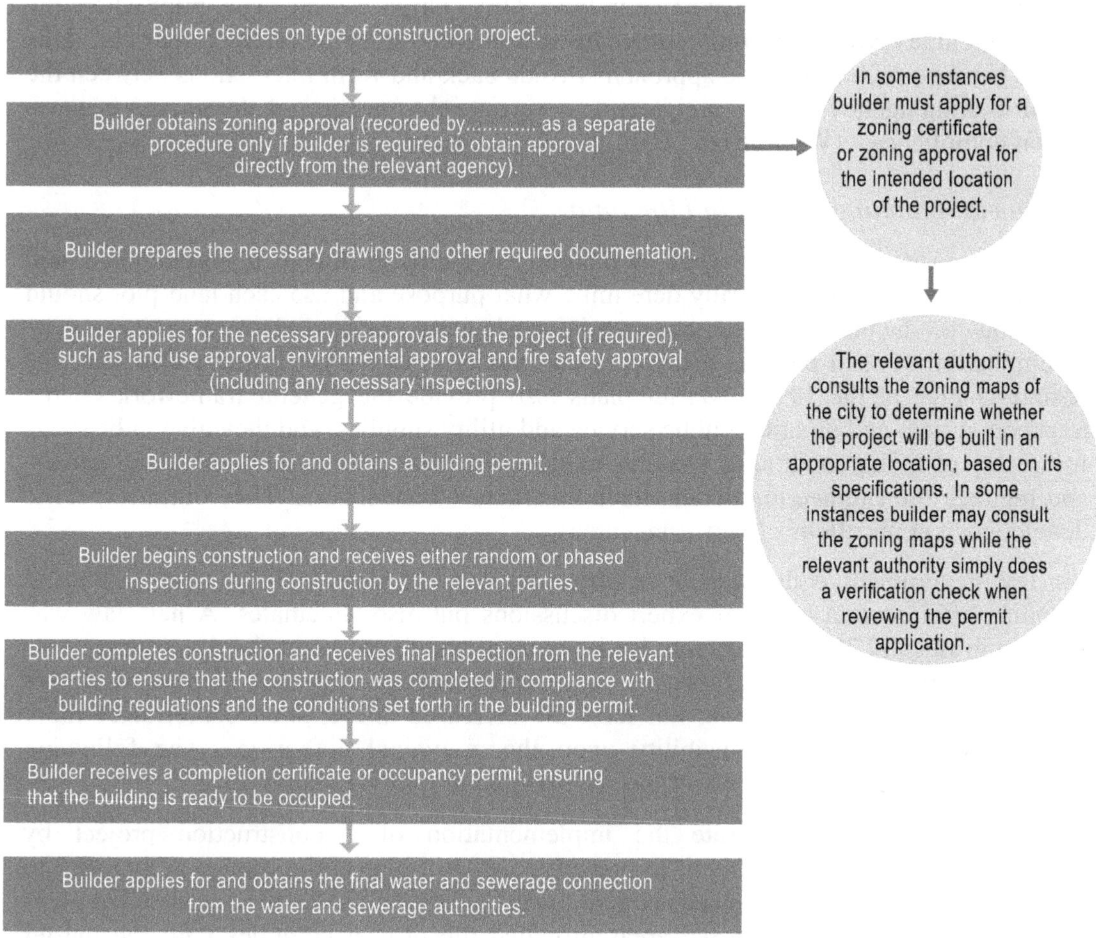

Source: World Bank (2015), *Doing Business 2015: Going Beyond Efficiency*, The World Bank Group, Washington, D.C., p. 54, Figure 6.1.

Disproportionately complex or restrictive zoning design, by contrast, rapidly produces negative impacts on the supply of residential and non-residential building as well as on their prices. In Sweden, for instance, designing or modifying a detailed development plan is required for more than half of all construction projects – a process that lasts 18 months on average, according to estimates from the municipality of Stockholm, and in 20% of cases it can take up to four years. Studies show that administrative barriers to new construction are one of the two main factors that have led to a housing shortage in Sweden over the past decade – the other being rent control policies (World Bank, 2015, p. 55).

Zoning and construction permit procedures mutually reinforce each other. Such a synergy enhances transparency, inter-agency co-ordination, predictability and efficiency. If well designed, zoning regulations specify the most appropriate location for individual projects, granting certainty about the framework within investors and developers may apply for their construction permits. Similarly, local authorities and municipalities can better structure and justify their decisions about approving or rejecting construction proposals thanks to clearly defined and transparent zoning regulations. This contributes to strengthening transparency and predictability (Figure 9.5).

Doing Business measurements show that the process for obtaining a construction permit takes 19 fewer days on average in those OECD high-income economies where the process includes synergetic zoning procedures, compared to those where it does not. This occurs because such synergetic approach "avoids back-and-forth interactions between the permit-issuing agency and the architect or even outright rejection of the project because of non-compliance." (World Bank, 2015, p. 56)

Territorial planning reform in Lithuania

Lithuania uses two main types of planning documents: so-called master plans and detailed plans. The first generally determine what purpose and use each land plot should be attributed – be that industrial, commercial, agriculture, residential, open space etc. The determination of such plans is mandatory and has been rather prescriptive also after the regime change in the 1990s. Master plans also provide the general framework on the transport system and on other public service and utility supplies; and they give indications for quality of living conditions. Detailed plans by contrast refer to individual land parcels and regulate the engineering details for infrastructure connections. They outline specific development applications of new estate areas.

The government embarked on a major revision of the 1995 Law on Territorial Planning after several years of expert discussions but also stalemates. A new law was adopted in January 2014[31] to incentivise investment and foster territorial development. As such, it was welcomed by both private sector and academic circles. A number of factors triggered such positive reaction, not least the increased and explicit conferral of more political and technical responsibility upon the municipal authorities. The following changes brought about by the new Law are believed to (among other):

- facilitate and accelerate the implementation of a construction project by abolishing the requirement to prepare a detailed plan if the project is intended to be carried out in urbanised areas or areas being urbanised where no detailed plans exist, or in non-urbanised areas provided the project complies with the master plan;
- provide more options for land holding projects without the need to present a detailed plan, if these correspond to the master plan, while at the same time defining the planning document scales more clearly in terms of the planning levels. In particular, the master plans cover a wider territory and allow for combined uses so as to achieve better targeted and more suitable activity mixes;
- allow for newly introduced graphic drawings requirements;
- allow to implement master plan solutions through the issuance of a construction permit, even if detailed plans or land holding projects are not processed; and
- clarify dispute settlement procedures.

Two further amendments introduced by the new Law on Territorial Development met with stakeholders demands. They both relate to accountability and transparency, and have positive implications also on the overall efficiency of the process. The first innovative element refers to the implementation of a digital supervisory information system processing territorial planning and zoning documents (TPDRIS),[32] which contributes to reduce time and costs because of easier technical adjustments. TPDRIS is accessible only by public administrations. At the same time, the Law simplified the procedures for the publication of specialised planning documents. A dedicated website for already prepared zoning documents is operational.[33] While these systems are reported to be operated below their actual potential, stakeholders believe current bottlenecks are likely to smooth over time and the systems constitute a solid step forward towards fully digitalising and publicising the construction permit administration.

The second innovative element introduced by the new Law on Territorial Planning refers to the attribution of the right of final decision to the Director of the municipal administration – theoretically an administrative and technical and not political office. The Law obliges all municipalities to adopt a master plan and, subsequently, prepare the implementing strategies and action plans. These determine the sequence and pace of implementation of the framework guidelines provided for in the master plan. To a large extent, drawing up such implementation action plans and above all ensuring their correct application are technical and not political tasks. The regime introduced by the 2014 Law allocates full responsibility for such tasks to the head of the municipal administration, while previous Council's boards are now excluded. Such change seeks to minimise the interface with political considerations in executing the plans; avoid blame-shifting and horse-trading; and increase transparency.[34]

The debate on the new Law on Infrastructure

The macro-economic impacts of good infrastructure

Providing and efficiently maintaining adequate infrastructure is a core task of economic and social governance. Infrastructure elements – communication and transportation axes (roads, railways, airports and harbours), water supply, sewers, energy grids and pipelines (electricity, gas, oil), and telecommunications – functionally facilitate the production of goods and services and allow markets and society to function. Infrastructure yields indirect benefits through the supply chain, land values, private sector (small business) development, consumer sales, access to opportunity and ultimately societal welfare. As such, infrastructure features among the twelve pillars of competitiveness – the latter being defined as "the set of institutions, policies, and factors that determine the level of productivity of a country." (World Economic Forum, 2009, p. 4)

The impact of infrastructure on territorial development and economic growth is significant and should trigger strategic public-private co-ordination. Recent studies point out that reducing supply chain barriers can increase global GDP up to 6 times more than removing all import tariffs (World Economic Forum, 2013).[35] Poor infrastructure features alongside other critical barriers to trade and growth (Table 9.6). Infrastructure investment and management is thus part of the strategic assets of an economy and most OECD countries have developed governance frameworks to foster economic growth and prosperity.

In the EU, stimulus efforts to incentivise infrastructure improvements are considered a fundamental means for economic recovery after the crisis. The European Commission indicates that besides investing in research, innovation and ICT, Europe should upgrade its energy and transport infrastructure to consolidate the integration, performance and competitiveness of the EU internal market. An assessment of the recent infrastructure-related investment patterns in the EU confirms the positive relationship between transport and electricity infrastructures and growth in the long term, although the empirical findings are disputed in the literature. The assessment also highlights the persisting general gap in infrastructure provision between the so-called "new" Member States and the EU15 group (European Commission, 2014) (Box 9.13).

Table 9.6. **Illustrative direct consequences of barriers on costs, delays, volume and risk**

	Costs		Delay		Volume	Risk
	Increased operational costs	Increased investment / working capital	Increased average delay	Increased variable delay (unpredictability)	Decreased volume	Increased (political) risk (unpredictability)
Domestic and foreign market access	●	-	●			
Efficiency of customs administration	-		●	●		
Efficiency of import-export procedures	-		●	●		
Transparency of border administration	-		●	●	-	●
Availability and quality of transport infrastructure	●	●	●	-		
Availability and quality of transport services	●	●	-	-		
Availability and use of ICTs	-	●	-	-		
Regulatory environment	●	●	●	-	-	●
Physical security	●	-				
Potential implications ● most likely - potentially			• Increased buffer stock • Increased stock transit • High depreciation/scrap rate • Customer satisfaction/opportunity costs/ lawsuits • Increased FX risk • Increased theft/breakage			• Incurred risk or insurance costs (i.e. hedging or spreading risk) • Higher return on investment required

Source: World Economic Forum (2013), *Enabling Trade: Valuing Growth Opportunities*, in collaboration with Bain & Company and the World Bank, Geneva, p. 12, http://www3.weforum.org/docs/wef_sct_enablingtrade_report_2013.pdf.

Box 9.13. **Pursuing infrastructure investment in the EU**

Growth is hampered by both lack of investment and over-investment. Reviewing recent investment patterns in the EU Member States is hence critical to appraise the capacity to recover from the economic crisis.

While EU aggregate data indicates that compared to other sectors, investments in energy and transport have slightly decreased after the crisis, disparities exist across Member States. In road infrastructure, for instance, there are indications of underinvestment in the Euro Area during the post-crisis period. This is likely to reflect an adjustment following the construction-focused investment boom in the pre-crisis years. By contrast, the other two Member States groups (New Member States and Rest of non-EA), display investment above the predicted rate during the post crisis period, following underinvestment in the preceding period. This pattern is most pronounced in the New Member States group, where it is linked to the sustained increase in the investment rate throughout the period under consideration. This reflects a catch-up effect in combination with increasing EU funding, which has been provided in the context of the cohesion policy. The assessment also suggests that overinvesting in new infrastructure is associated with underspending on maintenance, and vice versa.

As to the energy sector infrastructure, the analysis does not indicate underinvestment in the post-crisis period. The infrastructure investment rate in energy has generally increased since the turn of the century in all Member State groups, in part reflecting increasing investments in renewable energy infrastructure.

Current macro-economic conditions combined with the EU policy agenda provide opportunities to increase investment in infrastructure. However, this should be done in an appropriate way, taking account of the individual situation of economies in terms of infrastructure stock, transport and electricity demand as well as other parameters such as fiscal space and cost-benefit analysis of projects.

Source: European Commission (2014), "Infrastructure in the EU: Developments and Impact on Growth", *Occasional Papers 203*, December.

Towards a revised infrastructure law framework in Lithuania

Lithuania is currently working on revisiting the framework governance of infrastructure development and a new dedicate law is expected to be adopted in the course of 2015. This is considered a parallel policy dossier that is nonetheless closely linked to both the reform of construction permits and territorial planning and development in general. The new law is expected to regulate the development of infrastructure management and the related regulatory framework; as well as the rights, duties and responsibilities of all the persons involved in it.

One of the main challenges that the law should solve relates to the redefinition of the burden to be borne for connecting to the common infrastructure and network. At present, budgetary constraints prevent municipalities from providing common infrastructure to all the zones under development across their territory, notably peripheral zones where the return of investment is potentially higher. Municipalities are also reported to face difficulties in strategically designing and mapping their infrastructure strategies and priorities, failing to achieve economies of scale and effectively providing public services. As a result, the costs of connecting new constructions to the common infrastructure are both disproportionally high and allegedly misallocated.

It shall be noted that the municipalities of Vilnius and Klaipėda raise an informal levy[36] upon developers and builders (including private citizens) to feed an infrastructure fund that is supposed to finance infrastructure work. This practice is contested not only because of the burden placed on the developers. It is also ineffective because the levy's revenues are not earmarked. The money paid by a developer is not necessarily invested in providing the required infrastructure connecting the project to the existing network. A second dysfunctional feature of the current system refers to the disproportionate and inequitable allocation of the burden. The levy is paid by the "first" developer in need for infrastructural connection, where any subsequent neighbouring developers are exempted from it because the connection is in place. A further source of concern about the current infrastructure legal framework relates to the allocation of the costs of maintaining the connecting infrastructure, which are currently variously split between the network operator and the private users. Despite contributing to such costs, the latter are not exercising any right or control over the infrastructure. The future new Law on Infrastructure is expected to address these failures so as to avoid free riding and grant equal rights to and among developers; promote public strategic planning and stimulate investment.

Putting reforms in the context of progressive infrastructure development is therefore key. An example of the synergies that should be leverage in Lithuania is provided by the electricity sector. While the government has focused on shortening and simplifying construction permit procedures, the country's performance in other public service delivery indicators is more mixed. Doing Business data indicates that connecting to the electricity network takes on average 137 days and involves five different procedures for business customers. This generate a costs equalling 45.5% of income per capita, placing 105th in the ranking of 189 economies on the ease of getting electricity. In relative terms, Lithuania lags some 27 "distance to frontier" (DTF) points from the regional leader (Germany). Evidence from previous Doing Business reports suggests that Lithuania made getting electricity more difficult in 2012 by abolishing the one-stop shop for obtaining technical conditions for utility services (World Bank, 2015).

A further avenue to reap spill-over potential refers to the energy efficiency policy promoted by the government and enshrined in the Law on Construction. It is required that from 31 December 2020 onwards all new constructions built in Lithuania shall allow limited consumption of energy, as outlined through the energy classes and the deadlines established by the law.[37] Developing "green construction permits" is widely considered as one of the means to achieve energy saving efficiency besides financial incentives such subsidies and fiscal facilitations (Box 9.14). At the same time, the message that energy efficiency is good for business is gaining momentum across the real estate and construction sectors. A recent survey indicates that more quickly delivered construction permits for energy efficient buildings were the third most common form of incentive used by companies after tax rebates and direct grants. The same preferences were expressed in terms of the most influential form of incentive that companies consider when deciding on a new building investment (Economist Intelligence Unit, 2012, pp. 24; 25).

The government is actively promoting green building. Over the period 2014-20, LTL 1.3 billion are foreseen to be invested in the support of owners of multifamily buildings for the implementation of energy efficiency measures.

Box 9.14. Green building and renovating through regulatory instruments

Green building is defined as building activities complying "with several sustainability criteria over the life-cycle of a building: energy efficiency, water efficiency, good indoor air quality, use of environmentally sustainable materials, and use of the building lot or site in a sustainable manner" (World Bank, 2010, p. XVI). It reflects the rising interest in the potential of applying technical and technological innovation in building design and construction.

In Canada, the City of Vancouver is working to reduce the amount of energy consumed by the city's new homes 33% by 2020, with the goal of making all new buildings "carbon neutral" by 2030. It also committed to reduce greenhouse gas emissions from existing buildings by 20% over 2007 levels. The City is implementing a wide range of green building programs and policies to help reach this ambitious target, including the Green Homes programme. One of the measure consisted of amending all relevant regulation implementing the building code by introducing requirements directed at reducing the environmental impacts of new dwellings.

In the EU, a series of legal acts address energy efficiency in the building sector. They include among others the Energy Performance of Buildings Directive (EPBD); the Renewable Energy Directive (RED); the Energy Efficiency Directive (EED), as well as standards for Ecodesign and Ecolabelling. With regard to the construction sector, the aim is to reach the "near zero energy" standard for all new public buildings by 2018 and all new residential and commercial buildings by 2020.

Sources: World Bank (2010), Mainstreaming Building Energy Efficiency Codes in Developing Countries. Global Experiences and Lessons from Early Adopters, Working Paper 204, Washington DC, City of Vancouver, "Building and renovating", http://vancouver.ca/home-property-development/building-and-renovating.aspx (consulted on 25 February 2015).

Notes

1. Zoning is one element of construction, infrastructure and territorial development regulation. It regulates the location and use of certain types of buildings within a city or a given territory.
2. See www.oecd.org/gov/regional-policy/recommendation-effective-public-investment-across-levels-of-government.htm.
3. Statistics reported below were provided by the government of Lithuania (Ministry of Environment) in January 2015.
4. See http://en.delfi.lt/lithuania/economy/volume-of-construction-work-in-lithuania-up-168-percent.d?id=65563448.
5. See http://osp.stat.gov.lt/en/informaciniai-pranesimai?eventId=28161.
6. See http://osp.stat.gov.lt/en/informaciniai-pranesimai?eventId=28161.
7. Seismas of the Republic of Lithuania, Resolution No. XII-51 on the Programme of the Sixteenth Government of the Republic of Lithuania (2012-2016), Vilnius, 13 December 2012.
8. Ibid. p. 16.
9. Ibid. p. 16.
10. These sources of concern were reported to the OECD review team both in the official questionnaire answered by the Government and in the conversations held during the fact-finding mission to Vilnius.
11. See www.investorsforum.lt/.
12. See www.investlithuania.com/.
13. The distance to frontier score benchmarks economies with respect to regulatory practice, showing the absolute distance to the best performance in each *Doing Business* indicator. An economy's distance to frontier score is indicated on a scale from 0 to 100, where 0 represents the worst performance and 100 the frontier.
14. See Chapter 2 for an exhaustive list.
15. Government Resolution No. 4 of 11 January 2012 on "Regarding Adoption of Methodology for Identifying Administrative Burden for Businesses", https://www.e-tar.lt/portal/lt/legalact/tar.134272d720df.
16. Lithuanian Republic Law (XI-2386) of 8 November 2012 on "Administrative Burden Reduction", https://www.e-tar.lt/portal/lt/legalact/tar.de127819ae22.
17. Government Resolution No. 228 of 13 March 2013 on "Adoption of priority measures for the implementation of the Government of the Republic of Lithuania Programme for the years 2012-1016", accessible at https://www.e-tar.lt/portal/lt/legalact/tar.26da62d7e9f4.
18. Government Resolution No. 931 of 9 October 2013 on "Government's 2014 annual priorities" accessible at", https://www.e-tar.lt/portal/lt/legalact/tar.0f673b2d9bed.
19. Government Resolution No. 964 of 23 October 2013 on "Amendment of the 18 July 2012 Government Resolution No. 937 on adopting a description of the licensing framework", accessible at https://www.e-tar.lt/portal/lt/legalact/tar.62b1abb28b06.

20. The law can be accessed at http://www3.lrs.lt/pls/inter3/dokpaieska.showdoc_l?p_id=454053.

21. Law on Construction (Article 23.20), http://www3.lrs.lt/pls/inter3/dokpaieska.showdoc_l?p_id=454053.

22. See www.planuojustatyti.lt. Further to Government Resolution No. 1468 of 25 November 2003 on "Approving the Concept of e-government implementation measures", http://www3.lrs.lt/pls/inter3/dokpaieska.showdoc_l?p_id=273447.

23. See https://planuojustatyti.lt/infostatyba_isorine/apskaita-ir-statistika.htm.

24. Data retrieved from http://liteko.teismai.lt/.

25. Lithuanian government, answers to the OECD Questionnaire, January 2015.

26. Information from the State Territorial Planning and Construction Inspectorate during the OECD fact-finding mission, January 2015.

27. Information from the State Territorial Planning and Construction Inspectorate during the OECD fact-finding mission, January 2015.

28. Data from the State Territorial Planning and Construction Inspectorate, January 2015.

29. Government Resolution No. 931 of 9 October 2013 on "Government's 2014 annual priorities" accessible at https://www.e-tar.lt/portal/lt/legalAct/TAR.0F673B2D9BED.

30. The *Investor Confidence Index* reflects the Investor Forum's commitment to improving the business environment and investment climate in Lithuania. It reports a series of surveys carried out among top executives and senior officers of the country's largest foreign capital firms. The purpose of this index is to provide an alternative tool with which to assess the business conditions and investment climate in Lithuania, as well as to indicate the expectations of market participants for the short-term future. See www.investorsforum.lt/en/publications.

31. See www.infolex.lt/ta/Default.aspx?Id=7&item=doc&SubMenu=3&aktoid=77961.

32. See www.tpdris.lt/en_US/web/infoplanavimas-en/home, and https://map.tpdris.lt/tpdris-gis/index.jsp?action=tpdrisPortal.

33. See www.tpdr.lt/en_US/web/tpd-registras-en/home; and https://map.tpdr.lt/tpdr-gis/index.jsp?action=tpdrPortal.

34. See the Law on Territorial Planning (Chapter 27, Article 4).

35. Specifically, "if every country improved just two key supply chain barriers – border administration and transport and communications infrastructure and related services – even halfway to the world's best practices, global GDP could increase by USD 2.6 trillion (4.7%) and exports by USD 1.6 trillion (14.5%). For comparison, completely eliminating tariffs could increase global GDP by USD 0.4 trillion (0.7%) and exports by USD 1.1 trillion (10.1%)." World Economic Forum (2013), *Enabling Trade: Valuing Growth Opportunities*, in collaboration with Bain & Company and the World Bank, Geneva – here quoted here at p. 13.

36. In the case of the Vilnius municipality, such a levy may amount to up to 4 EUR/sq.

37. See Law on Construction, Art. 43-1, Chapter 5; as well as STR 2.01.09:2012, "Utility of Energy of Buildings – Certification of the Utility of Energy".

Bibliography

Blanc, F. (2012), "Inspection Reforms: Why, How, With What Results?", OECD, Paris.

Clark, G. (2014), "Business-Friendly and Investment-Ready Cities: City Government and the Local Business Growth and Investment Climate", Urban Land Institute, London.

International Finance Corporation (IFC) (2009), "Reforming Building Permits: Why Is It Important And What Can IFC Really Do?", The World Bank Group, Washington DC.

Investors' Forum (2014a), "Investor Confidence Index for Lithuania 2014", Q2 (Issue 1), Vilnius.

Investors' Forum (2014b), "Investor Confidence Index for Lithuania 2014", Q4 (Issue 2), Vilnius.

Investors' Forum (2013), "A Better Way To Grow", Vilnius.

OECD (2014), "Recommendation on Effective Public Investment across Levels of Government", www.oecd.org/gov/regional-policy/recommendation-effective-public-investment-across-levels-of-government.htm.

OECD (2013a), "Delivering Local Development: New Growth and Investment Strategies", OECD, Paris, www.oecd.org/cfe/leed/NGIS_final2.pdf.

OECD (2013b), *Investing Together: Working Effectively across Levels of Government*, OECD Publishing, Paris, http://dx.doi.org/10.1787/9789264197022-en.

OECD (2010), "Construction Industry", *OECD Journal: Competition Law and Policy*, Vol. 10/1, OECD Publishing, Paris, http://dx.doi.org/10.1787/clp-10-5kmhbhp87tbv, pp.156–57.

OECD (2007), *Competitive Cities: A New Entrepreneurial Paradigm in Spatial Development*, OECD Publishing, Paris, http://dx.doi.org/10.1787/9789264022591-en.

OECD (2006), *Competitive Cities in the Global Economy*, OECD Publishing, Paris, http://dx.doi.org/10.1787/9789264027091-en.

PriceWaterhouseCoopers (2005), "The Economic Impact of Accelerating Permit Processes on Local Development and Government Revenues", Study prepared for the American Institute of Architects, December.

The Economist Intelligence Unit (2012), "Energy efficiency and energy savings: A view from the building sector", London.

Van der Heijden, J. (2009), *Building Regulatory Enforcement Regimes. Comparative Analysis of Private Sector Involvement in the Enforcement of Public Building Regulations*, Delft University Press.

Visscher, H.J. and F.M. Meijer (2005), "Enforcing building regulations: Private versus public responsibilities", in the Proceedings of W099 4th Triennial International Conference, "Rethinking and Revitalizing Construction Safety, Health, Environment and Quality", 17-20 May, Port Elizabeth, South Africa.

VROM (2009), "Castle or House of Cards? Strengthening the Structural Safety Chain", Dutch VROM-Inspectorate of Housing, Spatial Planning and the Environment, The Hague.

World Bank (2015), *Doing Business 2015: Going Beyond Efficiency*, The World Bank Group, Washington, D.C.

World Bank (2014), "What role should risk-based inspections play in construction?", in *Doing Business 2014*, The World Bank Group, Washington D.C.

World Bank (2013), "Good Practices for Construction Regulation and Enforcement Reform: Guidelines for Reformers", Investment Climate / The World Bank Group, Washington D.C.

World Bank (2010), "Mainstreaming Building Energy Efficiency Codes in Developing Countries – Global Experiences and Lessons from Early Adopters", *Working Paper 204*, Washington DC.

World Bank (2009), *Doing Business 2010: Reforming through Difficult Times*, World Bank Group, Washington, D.C.

World Bank (2008), "Creating a new profession from scratch: Doing Business Case Study: Czech Republic", in *Celebrating Reform 2008*, The World Bank Group, Washington D.C.

World Economic Forum (2009), "The Global Competitiveness Report 2009-2010", Geneva.

World Economic Forum (2013), "Enabling Trade: Valuing Growth Opportunities, in collaboration with Bain and Company and the World Bank", Geneva.

Annex A

The importance of inspections and compliance

Relevance of inspections and enforcement issues

Designing and adopting sound regulations is of little use if they are not complied with – and, to promote such compliance, appropriate systems and measures need to be in place, including effective and efficient regulatory inspections and enforcement. International experience and research have shown that this is unfortunately often far from being the case, and that inspection and enforcement regimes are often simultaneously burdensome and ineffective (see e.g. Hampton 2005; World Bank Group, 2011; OECD, 2012, 2014).

Such a combination of ineffectiveness at achieving the stated goals of regulation (safety, health, or any other type of public benefit and welfare), and of considerable economic burden (loss of time, turnover and resources for active businesses – and decreased investment because of regulatory uncertainty), is particularly sharply in evidence in "transition" economies, notably those of countries that used to be part of the former Soviet Union. The reasons for this are many, and include several traits that have been "carried over" from the previous command-economy system:

Regulatory regimes that are highly prescriptive and cover far more aspects of economic activity than accepted good practice – resulting in more fields and types of regulatory control

A large number of institutions in charge of regulatory control and enforcement, with relatively high staffing levels – which mechanically drive a larger number of inspections, a high degree of fragmentation, as well as an important "constituency" that tends to resist changes towards a different (somewhat "lighter touch") system.

Crucially, an approach to regulatory enforcement and a vision of regulatory drivers that are founded on an "adversarial" approach to duty holders (businesses, and also citizens) – this approach emphasises deterrence rather than trust, and reflects a "presumed guilty" view.

In addition, in a number of countries, these aspects are compounded by an overall weak rule of law, insufficient compensation for inspectors, and deep ethical issues in public administration, and result in inspections being primarily an instrument of corruption.[1] This, of course, results in inspections that also completely cease to fulfil their stated function – ensuring that the goals of regulations are achieved.

1. See for instance, successive survey reports published by the IFC in Ukraine, Tajikistan etc., for e.g., : www.ifc.org/wps/wcm/connect/RegProjects_Ext_Content/IFC_External_Corporate_Site/TJBEE_Home/Overview/Survey/ and www.ifc.org/wps/wcm/connect/RegProjects_Ext_Content/IFC_External_Corporate_Site/USPP_Home/ProjectMaterials/PMSurveys/.

Improving regulatory inspections and enforcement regimes is thus a priority that corresponds to a set of objectives for governments: reducing the economic burden and thus facilitating investment and growth and maximising the regulatory effectiveness in terms of social welfare with constant or decreasing state resources (particularly important in times of economic crisis. In "transition" economies, reducing corruption (that contributes to both objectives) is also often specifically articulated as a priority. More deeply, inspection regimes that are more effective, efficient and transparent (and, of course, not corrupt) strongly contribute to reinforcing the legitimacy of public action and authorities, and this in turn drives improved compliance.

Drivers of compliance: striking the right balance

A common view underpinning "heavy handed" inspection and enforcement approaches is that people comply with rules only if they are under supervision and there is a realistic threat of punishment for violations. This "dissuasion-based" view results in efforts to inspect each and every establishment as often as possible. It is found in every country around the world, but is particularly strong in post-Soviet regulatory regimes, fueled by a history of hostility towards and suspicion of private initiative. Business operators are held to be pure rational calculators, only likely to comply if the costs of non-compliance are high, and punishment close to certain.

In fact, decades of research and international examples show decisively that this view is mistaken, and that such an approach results in disappointing compliance levels. Across a number of countries and fields, it has been found that compliance is fostered by at least three types of drivers: moral values, legitimacy of authorities, and rational calculations (dissuasion) – but that dissuasion appears to be the weakest of the three. In addition, even though inspections and enforcement can promote compliance through dissuasion, when they are perceived as excessive, heavy-handed, unethical or otherwise not transparent, they produce negative effects in terms of compliance that tend to outweigh whatever benefits dissuasion may have produced (see e.g. Tyler, 2003; Kirchler 2007; Blanc et al., 2015).

Moral values are one of the strongest drivers of compliance. Though primarily formed during childhood, they can be influenced through public policy and regulatory interventions – but on the long term (e.g. through school education). For this reason, and because moral values are not always easily connected to regulations, it is not possible to design interventions to promote regulatory compliance that would rely exclusively on moral values.

Dissuasion is, clearly, a driver of compliance that is more "straightforward" to use in regulatory interventions – but it has important limitations. First, even to the extent that probability of detection and fear of punishment do play a role, their effects are mediated by the values of the regulated subjects (see Kirchler, 2007) – meaning that those whose moral values already tend to support compliance will experience a stronger dissuasion effect, but those whose moral values do not will be far less influenced (whereas these are precisely those that *need* to be influenced). Second, really strong dissuasion tends to have considerable costs – both in terms of finances and freedom (personal and economic). In practice, strong deterrence is impossible to achieve in most cases: the resources required would be far too high (in a world of limited resources, society cannot commit enough resources to deterring violations in each and every regulatory field), and the intrusion on privacy and limitations of individual freedoms would be far too high (see Tyler, 2003). Finally, when efforts at dissuasion are felt to be excessively intrusive or even abusive (indiscriminate visits and checks, as well as sanctions imposed regardless of the risk level, disrespectful and/or unethical behaviour by inspectors, requirements that hinder initiative too strongly etc.), they tend to negatively affect procedural justice, which in turn weakens what is probably the strongest of compliance drivers. This phenomenon is particularly well in evidence in post-Soviet states, where extensive regulations and heavy enforcement are not accompanied by high compliance, but rather by a general disrespect of rules, which tend to be seen as being tools of oppression or graft, and not as instruments of safety and social welfare.

Indeed, the degree to which regulated subjects (citizens, business operators…) find authorities and rules legitimate has consistently been found to be one of the strongest drivers of compliance (possibly the strongest one). Most importantly, it is also the one that is most easily influenced (strengthened, or weakened) by the actions of public authorities. In turn, the strongest element influencing legitimacy has been found to be procedural justice – the extent to which actions of public authorities are perceived by those whom they affect as *fair*, not in terms of their results, but of the process which they follow. Key elements of procedural justice are fairness of interpersonal treatment, behaviour by authorities that fosters motive-based trust, giving duty holders a real voice in the process. It entails respectful treatment of duty holders, ethical behaviour and self-imposed limits on discretionary power (non-biased and consistent decision making), and demonstrating that regulated subjects are listened to and their arguments, issues, requests etc. carefully considered. When procedural justice is high, the legitimacy of authorities increases, and with it the legitimacy of the rules they edict and the decisions they take – and with increased legitimacy comes increased compliance (see Tyler, 2003). In addition procedural justice, and the legitimacy it fosters, are long-term drivers of compliance, and largely self-sustaining. They do not require an increase in resources – but a change in behaviours and approaches, in how authority is exercised, which may be very significant.

It is essential to design an approach to regulatory inspections and enforcement that finds the right balance between achieving the needed level of dissuasion, and fostering procedural justice. Repeated inspection visits, even handled in the most respectful and fair way possible, will still produce a feeling of accumulated burden which will reduce the feeling of procedural justice (one tends to feel unfairly treated when control is too frequent). This negative effect on compliance gets far worse when enforcement methods are not optimal in terms of behaviour, but feature abusive discretion, lack of transparency, disrespectful treatment, refusal to hear the duty holder's views or take them into account etc. Unfortunately, "oppressive enforcement and harassment" are quite frequent in regulatory inspection and enforcement practices, and this is a major factor in the failure of regulations to produce their desired effects, because of resistance by regulated subjects leading to low compliance. An optimal system should strike the right balance to fit all the different categories of regulated subjects – the majority which tend to comply voluntarily if the preconditions for compliance exist (legitimacy in particular, as well as knowledge, and regulations that are realistically within their means in terms of complexity and costs, investment etc.), as well as a minority which tend to be "rational calculators" (see Voermans, 2014; Elffers, 1997). For them, an element of dissuasion is essential to make them the "right" choice – and this dissuasion will also ensure the majority of "voluntary compliers" that there is a "level playing field" – but this dissuasion should not become so burdensome that it alienates the majority.

Best practice principles and fundamental elements for reform

Inspections and enforcement apply across a variety of regulatory fields: technical safety inspections (themselves quite diverse: food hygiene, environment, OSH, etc.), revenue inspections (taxes and customs), and often a number of other regulatory compliance checks (on employment law, state language, gambling, currency regulations etc.). Institutions conducting inspections range from small specialised outfits with a few staff, to major structures with dozens of thousands of employees (in particular tax inspectorates). Institutions, their status, governance etc. are likewise diverse. On the other hand, there is a considerable level of agreement on what good practices for inspections are, and on how to conduct reforms to improve existing regimes.

Box A.1. The OECD Best Practice Principles for Regulatory Enforcement and Inspections

1. **Evidence-based enforcement**. Regulatory enforcement and inspections should be evidence-based and measurement-based: deciding what to inspect and how should be grounded on data and evidence, and results should be evaluated regularly.
2. **Selectivity**. Promoting compliance and enforcing rules should be left to market forces, private sector and civil society actions wherever possible: inspections and enforcement cannot be everywhere and address everything, and there are many other ways to achieve regulations' objectives.
3. **Risk focus and proportionality**. Enforcement needs to be risk-based and proportionate: the frequency of inspections and the resources employed should be proportional to the level of risk and enforcement actions should be aiming at reducing the actual risk posed by infractions.
4. **Responsive regulation**. Enforcement should be based on "responsive regulation" principles: inspection enforcement actions should be modulated depending on the profile and behaviour of specific businesses.
5. **Long term vision**. Governments should adopt policies on regulatory enforcement and inspections: clear objectives should be set and institutional mechanisms set up with clear objectives and a long-term road-map.
6. **Co-ordination and consolidation**. Inspection functions should be co-ordinated and, where needed, consolidated: less duplication and overlaps will ensure better use of public resources, minimise burden on regulated subjects, and maximise effectiveness.
7. **Transparent governance**. Governance structures and human resources policies for regulatory enforcement should support transparency, professionalism, and results-oriented management. Execution of regulatory enforcement should be independent from political influence, and compliance promotion efforts should be rewarded.
8. **Information integration**. Information and communication technologies should be used to maximise risk-focus, co-ordination and information-sharing – as well as optimal use of resources.
9. **Clear and fair process**. Governments should ensure clarity of rules and process for enforcement and inspections: coherent legislation to organise inspections and enforcement needs to be adopted and published, and clearly articulate rights and obligations of officials and of businesses.
10. **Compliance promotion**. Transparency and compliance should be promoted through the use of appropriate instruments such as guidance, toolkits and checklists.
11. **Professionalism**. Inspectors should be trained and managed to ensure professionalism, integrity, consistency and transparency: this requires substantial training focusing not only on technical but also on generic inspection skills, and official guidelines for inspectors to help ensure consistency and fairness.

The OECD has compiled, based on international experience, a list of eleven good-practice principles for inspections and enforcement: evidence-based enforcement, selectivity, risk focus and proportionality, responsive regulation, long term vision, co-ordination and consolidation, transparent governance, information integration, clear and fair process, compliance promotion, Professionalism (Box A.1).

To implement these, the fundamental approaches on which reform should be based include:

- Risk focus and risk proportionality: inspection resources and targeting should be based on the level of risk presented by activities/establishments – and enforcement responses should be proportional to the risks identified during inspection visits.
- Co-ordination and consolidation: avoid duplication and overlaps in inspection mandates and missions – share information between different inspection fields
- Better inspection methods: tools (like checklists), training, guidelines, etc. should all contribute to more transparency and predictability in enforcement decisions, as well as more risk proportionality and more attention to compliance promotion.
- Compliance focus: all the work of inspectorates should be geared at improving compliance and public welfare outcomes – this means a major focus on information, outreach, guidance etc. – and a change in how inspectors interact with businesses.
- Governance and performance management: institutional design and structures, management, internal processes and procedures, compensation, performance management etc. should all be aligned with reform objectives, compliance promotion goal, and contribute to transparency, effectiveness, efficiency etc.

Shared information systems for inspections: characteristics and benefits

Risk-based planning cannot be done without each agency having data on all objects under supervision, which is costly and difficult to update – while, at the same time, because many of the risk dimensions are correlated, and because a non-compliant business tends to be thus in several areas, inspectorate would be able to improve their risk analysis if they also had data from other inspectorates. In addition, many inspectorates (even in OECD countries) have been found not to have proper information systems in the sense of systems allowing them to plan their activities based on risk, and to record the inspections results – setting up a system for each of these separately, and "populating" each separately with data on all objects, is far more costly than setting up a joint system. All these points speak strongly for setting up as much as possible joint information systems shared by most or all inspectorates.

The information system should be built on a database that includes the following data:

- List of all business entities and of all establishments (not only all companies/businesses, but also all separate premises) in the country.
- For each establishment, have data on a set of relevant parameters corresponding to different risk factors, some "general" risk parameters generally relevant to all or most types of inspections (e.g. size, volumes handled, type of technology or

process, etc.), and other more specific ones grouped by risk dimensions (e.g. food safety, workplace safety etc.).

- List all inspections and their results.
- Automatically generate risk ratings for each business and establishment.
- Automatically generate inspections selection and schedule.
- Filter and analyse data reporting.

More advanced systems can also incorporate functions to plan activities inside the inspectorate and manage processes, have online checklists, etc. (Blanc, 2012).

Best practice today dictates that various inspectorates should ideally co-ordinate their activities to ensure that all relevant risks are properly addressed during a joint inspection process. However, experience shows that inspections tend to be uncoordinated, unplanned and carried out in silos, regardless of industry or jurisdiction. Typically inspecting organisations do not share much information or regularly communicate Information technology has a key role in improving efficiency, transparency, and accountability in business inspections. A select number of jurisdictions have made efforts to implement inspection management solutions that are shared across multiple inspectorates, albeit with various levels of success. Online research and a series of in-depth interviews with government officials who participated in this study showed that a successful SIMS implementation yields:

- Improved targeting through a better identification and follow up of risks.
- Decreased administrative burden for businesses and entrepreneurs to comply with regulation.
- Increased quality and effectiveness of inspections leading to improved regulatory compliance.
- Improved internal efficiency and reduced administrative costs for governments.
- Increased transparency of inspection operations for businesses and citizens leading to a decrease in corruption.

These benefits usually result from:

- Gathering and consolidating more consistent and comprehensive information on enterprises subject to inspection.
- Streamlining the inspection process to increase inspector efficiency.
- Formalising policy and procedures to ensure consistency.
- Automating and supporting decision-making to reduce subjectivity in operations and maximise the use of resources.
- Sharing information across inspectorates to co-ordinate inspection scope, improve preparation and outcomes, as well as reduce the inspection burden of individual inspectorates.
- Providing public access to relevant information leading to increased transparency and accountability.

- Basic solutions incorporate information about businesses and entrepreneurs, their characteristics (e.g. locations, size, industry, etc.) and previous inspection results to allow for simple planning of future inspection activities. These systems typically provide a full inspection history by business and location and use a checklist to obtain consistency across inspections however, there is typically very limited automation.
- Intermediate solutions have functionality to trigger follow-up activities based on the outcome of an inspection and allow for automated integration of inspection practices across inspectorates. They are ideally integrated with government business registries or other sources of enterprise information.
- Advanced solutions include a variety of other features and functions including:

- Risk-based inspection planning allows for the scheduling and planning of inspections based on a risk assessment of the business that includes key information such as size of the business, previous inspection results, industry, geography, and data from other inspectorates or government information sources.
- Automated or real-time integration with other information sources, which generally fall under two broad categories: *i)* registry information (e.g., business/ company registration information, licences and permits); and *ii)* risk information (e.g., business/company risk based on its activities and profile, results of inspections or reports from other inspectorates).
- Comprehensive mobile inspection capabilities include tools and technologies that give inspectors the ability to view schedules and inspection records as well as record inspection results while onsite.
- Performance management capabilities enabled through business analytics is aligned with risk-based planning and provides capabilities for inspectorates to monitor the efficiency and output of their inspection programme and individual inspectors.
- Public portal capabilities involves providing access to businesses and the general public to view inspection requirements and results, submit complaints, and appeal an inspection (Wille and Blanc, 2013).

Bibliography

Ayres, I. and J. Braithwaite (1992), *Responsive regulation: transcending the Deregulation debate*, Oxford University Press, Oxford.

Blanc, F. (2012), "Reforming Inspections: Why, How and to What Effect?", OECD, Paris.

Braithwaite, J. (2011), "The essence of responsive regulation", *UBC Law Review* 44(3), pp. 475-520.

Gunningham, N. (2010), "Enforcement and Compliance Strategies", in *The Oxford Handbook of Regulation,* Baldwin, R., Cave, M. and Lodge, M. (ed.), pp. 120-145, Oxford University Press, Oxford.

Hampton, P. (2005), "Reducing administrative burdens: effective inspection and enforcement", HM Treasury, London, http://webarchive.nationalarchives.gov.uk/20090609003228/http://www.berr.gov.uk/files/file22988.pdf.

Hawkins, K. (ed.) (1992), *The Uses of Discretion*, Clarendon Press, Oxford.

Kirchler, E. (2007), *The Economic Psychology of Tax Behaviour,* Cambridge University Press.

Löfstedt, R.E. (2011), "Reclaiming health and safety for all: An independent review of health and safety legislation", Presented to the UK Parliament in 2011.

Macrory, R. (2006), "Regulatory Justice: Making Sanctions Effective", final Report, Better Regulation Executive, Department for Business, Innovation and Skills of the United Kingdom, London, November, http://webarchive.nationalarchives.gov.uk/20121212135622/http://www.bis.gov.uk/files/file44593.pdf.

OECD (2014), *Regulatory Enforcement and Inspections*, OECD Best Practice Principles for Regulatory Policy, OECD Publishing, Paris, http://dx.doi.org/10.1787/9789264208117-en.

Ogus, A. (1994), *Regulation: legal form and economic theory,* Clarendon Press, Oxford.

Scholz, J.T. (1994), "Managing Regulatory Enforcement in the United States", in *Handbook of Regulation and Administrative Law*, Rosenbloom, D.H. and Schwartz, R.D. (ed.), pp. 423-466, Marcel Dekker, New York.

Sparrow, M. (2008), *The character of harms: operational challenges in control,* Cambridge University Press, Cambridge.

Tyler, T.R. (2003), "Procedural Justice, Legitimacy, and the Effective Rule of Law", *Crime and Justice*, Vol. 30, pp. 283-357.

Tyler, T.R. (1990), *Why People Obey the Law*, Yale University, New Haven, Conn.

Voermans W. (2014), "Motive-Based Enforcement", in Mader, L., Kabyshev, S. (ed.), *Regulatory Reforms; Implementation and Compliance,* Proceedings of the Tenth Congress of the International Association of Legislation (IAL) in Veliky Novgorod, 28-29 June 2012, Nomos, Baden-Baden, pp. 41-61.

Wille, J. and F. Blanc (2013), "Implementing a shared inspection management system: insights from recent international experience", *Technical Guidance for Reform Implementation*, Nuts & bolts, Washington, D.C, World Bank Group. http://documents.worldbank.org/curated/en/2013/04/20217202/implementing-shared-inspection-management-system-insights-recent-international-experience.

Annex B

Organisations met during the fact-finding missions

The team interviewed representatives of the following organisations:

- Association of Local Authorities
- Environmental Protection Agency
- Free Market Institute
- Government Office
- Investors Forum
- Ministry of Agriculture
- Ministry of Economy
- Ministry of Energy
- Ministry of Environment
- Ministry of Finance
- Ministry of Foreign Affairs
- Ministry of Health
- Ministry of Interior
- Ministry of Justice
- Ministry of Social Security and Labour
- Ministry of Transport and Communications
- National Audit Office
- Parliament of the Republic of Lithuania (*Seimas*)
- Public Policy and Management Institute
- Lithuanian Builders Association
- Lithuanian Business Employers' Confederation
- Lithuanian Confederation of Industrialists
- Lithuanian Real Estate Development Association
- Lithuanian Small and Medium Business Council
- Lithuanian Trade Union Confederation

- State Food and Veterinary Service
- State Health Accreditation Agency
- State Labour Inspectorate
- State Medicines Control Agency
- State Non Food Products Inspectorate
- State Tax Inspectorate
- State Territorial Planning and Construction Inspectorate
- UAB "Sweco Lietuva"
- Vilnius Gediminas Technical University
- Vilnius Municipality
- Vilnius Regional Environmental Protection Department

ORGANISATION FOR ECONOMIC CO-OPERATION AND DEVELOPMENT

The OECD is a unique forum where governments work together to address the economic, social and environmental challenges of globalisation. The OECD is also at the forefront of efforts to understand and to help governments respond to new developments and concerns, such as corporate governance, the information economy and the challenges of an ageing population. The Organisation provides a setting where governments can compare policy experiences, seek answers to common problems, identify good practice and work to co-ordinate domestic and international policies.

The OECD member countries are: Australia, Austria, Belgium, Canada, Chile, the Czech Republic, Denmark, Estonia, Finland, France, Germany, Greece, Hungary, Iceland, Ireland, Israel, Italy, Japan, Korea, Luxembourg, Mexico, the Netherlands, New Zealand, Norway, Poland, Portugal, the Slovak Republic, Slovenia, Spain, Sweden, Switzerland, Turkey, the United Kingdom and the United States. The European Union takes part in the work of the OECD.

OECD Publishing disseminates widely the results of the Organisation's statistics gathering and research on economic, social and environmental issues, as well as the conventions, guidelines and standards agreed by its members.

OECD PUBLISHING, 2, rue André-Pascal, 75775 PARIS CEDEX 16
(42 2015 13 1 P) ISBN 978-92-64-23706-3 – 2015

www.ingramcontent.com/pod-product-compliance
Lightning Source LLC
Chambersburg PA
CBHW061211240926
51846CB00006B/1189